Gabby

Also by Carl Molesworth

Wing to Wing: Air Combat in China, 1943–45

Gabby

A FIGHTER PILOT'S LIFE

FRANCIS GABRESKI

AS TOLD TO

CARL MOLESWORTH

ORION BOOKS / NEW YORK

Published by Orion Books, a division of Crown Publishers, Inc., 201 East 50th Street, New York, New York 10022. Member of the Crown Publishing Group.

ORION and colophon are trademarks of Crown Publishers, Inc.

Manufactured in the United States of America

Library of Congress Cataloging-in-Publication Data
Gabreski, Francis.
    Gabby : a fighter pilot's life / by Francis Gabreski, as told to Carl Molesworth.
      p.   cm.
    1. Gabreski, Francis.   2. World War, 1939–1945—Aerial operations.
American.   3. World War, 1939–1945—Personal narratives, American.
4. Fighter pilots—United States—Biography.   5. United States.
Army Air Forces—Biography.   I. Molesworth, Carl.   II. Title.
D790.G23   1991
940.54′4973—dc20   91-2420
                                                                CIP

ISBN   0-517-57801-8

10   9   8   7   6   5   4   3   2   1

First Edition

To the fighter pilots of the 56th Fighter Group who made it possible for the bomber pilots—their "big friends"— to do the job and paid the supreme price

A C K N O W L E D G M E N T S

The authors wish to acknowledge the contributions of numerous people who answered our call for assistance in bringing this story together. Their advice, insight, and memorabilia have enriched this book beyond measure. They include Milton A. Anderson, Steve Blake, James R. Carter, Benjamin Cathers, Paul Conger, Virginia DiFranza, Jessie Hertel, Herbert R. Holtmeier, Gerald W. Johnson. Robert S. Johnson, George L. Jones, Frank W. Klibbe, Leo D. Lester, Walker M. Mahurin, Joel Popplewell, Ralph Safford, Felix Schacki, Christopher B. Scharping, Leslie C. Smith, John Thacker, Cleon C. Thomton, and Carl E. Westman. Special thanks go to our lovely wives, Kay Gabreski and Kris Molesworth, for their support and advice.

Pilots in the armed forces are an elite group. To become a superior pilot requires courage, skill, quick reflexes, a fast analytical mind, and perfect physical condition.

The bomber pilot is a team player. He carries the war home to the enemy. His accomplishments and sacrifices are well known and appreciated.

The fighter pilot is a rugged individualist. He is alone, up there, in his airplane, with just himself and his diety. He captures the imagination and enjoys the adulation of his associates and the public.

This book is about the life of a fighter pilot whose feats in two wars have become legendary. Francis S. Gabreski was recruited from the campus of Notre Dame University by the Army Air Corps in 1940. He became a top fighter ace in the European theater of operations with thirty-one German fighter planes to his credit. He was cool, fearless, aggressive, and determined to shoot down the enemy and not be shot down. Bob Johnson, the number-two American ace, frequently flew with Gabreski. In his biography, *Thunderbolt,* Bob said, "No better pilot ever flew." Bob, himself a superb pilot, was certainly in a position to analyze the situation and pass this accolade on to Gabreski.

As commander and leader of the 61st Squadron of the 56th Group of the 8th Air Force, he personally trained his squadron in the tactics and procedures that enabled it to become the top unit in kills during World War II.

The Korean War found him once again in mortal combat

with an enemy of our country. This was a jet war and although he had spent many hours practicing in jet fighters he soon found out that successful combat flying in jet fighters required new tactics. He promptly developed the required new tactics and became an ace for the second time. He ended his tour of duty with 6.5 MiGs destroyed in aerial combat.

Colonel Gabreski epitomizes the loyal type of American youth who answered the call to duty in his country's need; faced an experienced, war-hardened enemy; and by courage, skill, and determination defeated him.

I salute Colonel Gabreski and all those brave men who fought the enemy in the skies. No braver or finer group ever existed.

James H. Doolittle
Los Angeles, California

CHAPTER *One*

THE LATE summer sun was dropping toward the horizon as I left the airfield and started walking toward town. I was a young man with a big problem, and I was headed to the only place that offered me much chance of solving it—the Catholic church.

The problem was simple. I had one more chance to prove to the instructors at Park Air College that I could learn to fly. Otherwise, they were going to wash me out of army flight training, and my future as a military pilot would be over before it had a chance to begin. I'll have to admit that my first eighteen hours of instruction hadn't been very encouraging.

As I walked along Mississippi Avenue toward East St. Louis, I thought about how I'd gotten into this predicament. Why was it so important for me to become an army pilot?

Aviation sure hadn't been a lifelong dream. I wasn't one of those kids who read the pulp magazines like *Flying Aces* and built stick-and-paper models of airplanes to fly in the backyard on lazy summer days. We couldn't afford luxuries

1
—

like that in my family. We didn't even have a backyard at our house in Oil City, Pennsylvania.

My first memory of airplanes was the Cleveland Air Races of 1932. That was the year Jimmy Doolittle won the Thompson Trophy in the GeeBee, and he became my hero for life. I was thirteen that summer.

The National Air Races were a big deal back then, and when you lived in a small town, it was a thrill just to go to a great city like Cleveland. I didn't push Dad or anything. He just decided we would go. It was about 120 miles, so it took us about four hours to drive there. When the race was over we just got in the car and drove home. Who had money for a hotel? We were lucky to have wheels to get us there and the price of a ticket.

By that time my father was a grocer, owner of the Purity Market in Oil City. Stanley Gabryszewski wasn't prosperous by any means, but he'd come a long way from the day he stepped off the boat from Poland with little more than loose change in his pocket. Dad came over at the time when the situation in Poland was critical. In fact, at that time there really wasn't a Poland. It was partitioned between Russia and Germany. He was threatened with joining the Germany military forces, and knowing the history of Poland and that part of the world, he didn't want to do it. He knew about America—the land of opportunity and freedom—so he worked his way over here on a tramp steamer. He was sponsored by someone in Oil City, so he settled there.

My mother arrived about two years later. They both came to Oil City as casuals; that is, looking for work. Mother was looking for someone to take care of her. Dad was looking for someone to take care of him, too, so they came together. Their mutual interest was not only love but survival. They needed each other.

They lived in a Polish section of town, probably about three hundred families. It was a poor section, right next to the railroad tracks. It had its own Catholic church, the Assumption Church. The services were all in Polish and, of course, Latin. My mother never did learn to say more than "yes" and "no" in English. Dad eventually went to school to learn English so he could get into business.

Dad worked on the railroad as a young man. Oil City had been the hub of the Pennsylvania oil business since the 1860s, and there was a lot of work to do laying track and so forth. His earnings were feeble and he worked hard, but the worst part was that he had to walk four miles to work. There was no such thing as a bus. Later he went to work in a foundry that made equipment for the railroad. The pay was a little better and he didn't have to walk so far, but the work was just as hard.

Then Dad got sick. He had a thyroid problem that made him weak and caused him to lose weight. His eyes bulged. Eventually, it got so bad that he collapsed at work and had to have an operation. After it was over the doctor told him he was going to have to lighten his work load or he wasn't going to live very long.

The family was in a tough spot. By then there were five children. Ted was born in 1913, Lottie in 1915, me in 1919, Bernice in 1922, and Max in 1926. Dad had no skills, just a couple of rental houses he'd been able to buy over the past few years. They didn't provide nearly enough income to support seven of us, and the operation had wiped out most of his savings.

Dad did what came naturally: He went to our priest to ask for advice. Father Pulaski did better than that. He gave Dad a job as janitor for the church and rectory. It wasn't long before he collapsed again, however, so my mother took over the job in order to keep the money coming in.

3

My father was a proud man, and he probably had the strongest will of any person I ever met. There was no way he could sit home for long. Finally, he decided there was only one thing to do. He had to get into business someplace, but he would have to do it on his own. He heard about a man named Schiffer who owned a farm and a store in Oil City called the Purity Market. He would raise animals on the farm and sell their meat in the market, but the two operations were getting too much for him so he wanted to sell the market.

Somehow, Dad arranged to borrow enough money to buy the market, and he agreed to buy the meat that Mr. Schiffer would slaughter on his farm. The butcher who worked in the store stayed on with Dad, and that was a real break because Dad knew nothing about the business. He started from ground zero, and he stayed in the business and worked hard at it. It wasn't an eight-hour day. It was always twelve or fourteen hours for Dad. He had a truck and made deliveries all over town. He walked door to door drumming up customers. Mother left the janitorial job and began making Polish sausage to sell in the store. That went on for years. When Ted and Lottie were old enough they went to work in the store. The rest of us followed in turn. Lottie was a great asset. She became more or less the secretary and business manager. She stayed on until Dad retired, and then he turned the store over to her. Lottie worked there until she retired and sold the store.

We lived in half of a duplex house that Dad owned on Spruce Street. He rented out the other half. Across the street was the railroad yard, where trains would unload their cargoes of coal that fueled the big steam locomotives. A hill rose steeply behind the house. The house sure wasn't fancy, but it was typical of the homes in that section of Oil City.

Our neighborhood had its own elementary school, which

was paid for by the parishioners of Assumption Church. I started at Assumption School in the first grade and went all the way through the eighth grade. I must admit that I could speak better Polish than I could English in those days because Mother and Dad spoke Polish at home, and the people I associated with all were Poles. Even some of our school lessons were in Polish.

I wasn't much of a student. I just wasn't very interested in many of the classes. Still, there were lessons to be learned. Most of mine came from the firm hand of my father. We lived in a very serious time—the poverty, the competition. There wasn't much time to rejoice in anything. The major outlet was sports.

I spent quite a bit of time with the gang around the neighborhood. I was a little rough. We played a little basketball, a little football, and a lot of softball. We didn't have a yard, so we went down and played in the coal yard. It was right next to the railroad tracks across the street. There was just a little opening where you could find space to move around and throw the ball.

I was outdoors all the time. We played follow the arrow, usually in the evening. One team would go out about five minutes ahead of the next. Each one would draw an arrow with chalk on the pavement or whatever to guide the team behind. The object was to overtake the lead before they got home. I recall going all the way to Rossville, a distance of maybe eight to ten miles.

We were like any other kids. We liked to challenge authority, to do things on our own whenever we could get away with them. Sometimes we'd go too far, and that's when Dad would step in.

One time when I was about nine years old a couple of us decided we'd skip school. We took off during recess time and headed up to Hasson Park, which was about three miles away in the hills above Oil City. There were nice woods there and a pavilion with a smooth wooden floor where they held dances. No one was around, so we started sliding back and forth with stocking feet, each guy trying to slide farther than the others.

I got a good run and started sliding. Then I hit a rough spot and fell on my rear. My pants hooked on a sliver, and it dug deeply into my buttocks. It was too long for me to pull out, and it hurt like crazy. I had no choice but to go home and explain what happened.

Mother was the benevolent type. Dad was a disciplinarian. He believed if you did something wrong you had to be punished for it so you remember not to do it again. So even with this sliver, which had hurt my bottom already, I had a good licking coming for being disobedient and playing hooky. He had this stick with a rope on the end of it. Down we went to the basement, and he had me lie down across a bench. He gave me eight or nine whacks, and that took care of my bottom real good.

This wasn't the only occasion Dad had to take me down to the basement, but eventually I got his message: If you want to do something shady, you have to be willing to accept the consequences if you get caught. So before you do anything, you'd better think it through to decide whether or not it's worth the trouble.

Another time, I remember hitting a ball through someone's window and breaking the glass. The first thing that came to my mind was, "Oh my God, when Dad hears about this I'll be crucified." And I did get a licking. But Dad also went to the neighbor and paid for the window. He felt responsible to the neighbor for my actions. That was the environment I grew up in. There was a sense of responsibility, not just toward members of the family but toward the whole community.

The other strong moral influence on my life was the church. Going to a Catholic school, I was expected to be an altar boy and active in the church. Mother and Dad were staunch churchgoers, as I am to this day.

When I finished at Assumption School, I went into public school at a junior high. At that time I still spoke with a very pronounced Polish accent. It put me in a category at school as sort of a foreigner at first. I just had to work a little harder to overcome that. Still, I was not what anyone would call a scholar, even though education was very important to Mother and Dad. They were determined that all their children would complete their educations, and this included college for the three boys. They wanted their children to live prosperous and productive lives. It was their dream.

Throughout high school I continued on my happy-go-lucky way. I leaned on my friends for help with schoolwork. Algebra and calculus were difficult. Chemistry and biology were more enjoyable, and manual training was just great. That's what I enjoyed most—working with my hands. I was too small to be much of an athlete, but I did play on the junior varsity basketball team. Basketball was my forte. I was very quick and shifty, and I liked the sport tremendously. The coach, Mr. Collins, took an interest in me, and I responded well to that.

About that time I began to work in the market. It was a family affair. I was part of the delivery team on Saturdays. The driver would reach his destination in the truck, and I in turn would carry the groceries into the house. Other times I did different chores like stocking the shelves and cleaning up. There was no pay. We were expected to contribute to the household, and that's how we did it. I also had a paying job pumping gas and polishing cars at the local Pennzoil station.

My big brother Ted pretty well set the pace for the rest of us kids. He was a bright guy and a much better student than I. When he got to high school he decided he needed to change the spelling of our last name to make it easier to understand. Dad approved, and each of us followed Ted's lead when the time came. When Ted finished high school he wanted to be a doctor, so he chose to attend Notre Dame University. Again, that set the course for Max and me.

I graduated from high school in June 1938. That was the spring that Hitler's Nazis had annexed Austria, a prelude to the conflict that would soon engulf the whole world. But all that was far from my mind. I was looking forward to heading off to Notre Dame in the fall and following Ted into medical school. That summer we worked out all the details, including a National Youth Administration job for me washing glassware in a college laboratory for fifty cents an hour.

I think the best way to describe my first months at Notre Dame is to call it a tragic shock. At that time Notre Dame was riding high. I was impressed with everything: the dome, the stadium, the football team. As a matter of fact, the first three months I was there I thought there was nothing but Frank Leahy's powerhouse football team. Then the grades came out and I found myself on the failing list. My school career in Oil City hadn't prepared me for the level of education and maturity expected at Notre Dame. At the university the attitude was that you were working on your own. Take it or leave it; you paid for it.

I had to forget the niceties of Notre Dame and get down to work. I got in with a few fellows who were pretty good scholars, and they gave me a helping hand. I worked hard with them, and by the end of the semester I at least got up to the plus side.

That winter I got interested in airplanes again. I hadn't given flying much thought since that day I'd watched Doolittle race in the GeeBee, but at Notre Dame you could see airliners flying over the dome all the time. That was in their traffic lane, and I would look up and wonder what it would be like to be up there. On vacation back in Oil City a thought occurred to me: If I could get a few lessons, I could rent an airplane and fly home from South Bend, which was about four hundred miles away. Boy, that would really set you off in a category of your own! Never mind that Oil City didn't have an airport. That was just a minor detail.

When I returned to school, I hitchhiked out to Bendix Airfield near South Bend the first chance I got. There I found the office of Stockert Flying Service and its owner, Homer Stockert. Homer was a middle-aged man, balding and squat with an infectious smile. His office looked like something out of a Hollywood movie set with maps and manuals scattered here and there among the shabby furniture.

I told Homer what I had in mind and that I didn't have much money. He was as encouraging as I could have hoped, saying it would take me about eight hours of instruction to prepare for a solo flight. We started right away on that cold December afternoon in 1938.

Homer put me in the back seat of a small Taylorcraft monoplane and explained the controls to me. I noticed the plane's crude construction. There were gaps between the doors. There were panels that came down over the side. It was covered with cloth and painted a dark color like brown or black. I didn't care. I just wanted to learn how to fly it.

Once Homer had started the engine and taxied out to the

runway, we were ready to go. I loved the smell of the gas and oil, the staccato crackle of the engine's unmuffled exhaust pipes. The takeoff was exhilarating for me. I felt the plane bump along the ground, slowly at first. Then the tail lifted and I could see over the nose. Finally the bumping stopped as we cleared the ground. I was just flabbergasted to be able to take off in something that was not under my control, but was a part of me. It was cold, but I didn't feel it once we got off the ground. It was so exciting, and everything was white with snow down below. That was something I had never seen.

This was for me! I forgot about the cold, I forgot about the snow. I was determined to learn how to fly. First, Homer just showed me the controls—what happened when you used the stick, rudder, and throttle. He explained the coordination between the stick and the rudder, which was so important for maneuvering, and how you used the throttle to keep your speed up. Also very important: never lose your flying speed. I watched how the controls in front of me moved as Homer maneuvered the plane.

It looked real easy when Homer did it, but I quickly found out different when it was my turn to try. I clutched the stick tightly and dug my feet into the rudder pedals, then tried to control the plane myself.

Whoa, there! It seemed to have a mind of its own, dancing this way and that.

I just wanted the Taylorcraft to fly straight and level, but soon it started to nose down. When I pulled the stick back the nose came up too far and it mushed toward a stall. Turns were even worse as the little plane jerked here and there across the sky. This sure wasn't like driving a car. There was so much to do at once. The harder I tried to concentrate, the worse it got.

"Relax," Homer called over his shoulder, "relax!" But I couldn't.

After a while, Homer took the controls and brought the Taylorcraft in for a smooth landing. I was exhausted and a little disenchanted when I climbed out of the back seat, but Homer was encouraging.

"You'll learn to anticipate the airplane, and you'll learn to relax. But most of all," he urged me, "you have to fly the plane. You can't let it fly you."

I think I got about six hours of instruction from Homer in all. He really had a challenge on his hands. I just couldn't seem to get the hang of controlling the airplane. I sure wasn't ready to solo, much less make my triumphant flight back to Oil City, but it got me started. That was all I could afford during those lean student days before I ran out of money.

During my second year at Notre Dame an Army Air Corps recruiting team showed up on campus. By then, the war in Europe was well under way. I, of course, was more painfully aware of the fact that Poland had again been invaded and split up between Germany and Russia. If the United States was going to be involved, I knew I would have to fight, and I knew that I wanted my weapon to be the airplane.

The recruiting team gave us a little lecture on what the army could do for us if we became aviation cadets. They enticed us with the pay scale, the training, and everything that went along with it. The capper was that once we finished our second year of college, we wouldn't have to take a mental exam. All we had to do was pass the physical exam to be accepted as cadets.

I might have skipped the opportunity, except that a number of the fellows I knew went up afterward to ask questions. I figured I had nothing to lose, since my schoolwork still wasn't much to brag about, so I joined them and filled out an application. They told us they would contact us when we finished the school year, but I took that pretty lightly. I figured it would probably fizzle out. Nevertheless, I did fish out my copy of Assen Jordanoff's book *Flying and How to Do It* and started refreshing my memory of what I'd learned from Homer Stockert before I gave up his lessons.

When I came home from school after that second year I told Dad what I'd done. He was remorseful, but we both knew that I wasn't setting any academic records at Notre Dame, and we also knew that America was going to be drawn into the European war sooner or later. I was ashamed that I hadn't done better at the university, and I looked forward to this opportunity to make it up to my parents. I knew how much they had sacrificed for us. This was an opportunity to make them proud of me.

A couple of weeks later I got a letter from the War Department telling me I'd been selected for army pilot training. So that was how my military career began—entirely by chance. It wasn't like I calculated it. If that recruiting group hadn't shown up on campus, I don't know whether I would have taken the initiative to become an army pilot or not. My life was more or less groomed by the conditions and circumstances of the times.

The letter instructed me to report for induction and a physical exam to Pittsburgh. Assuming I passed the physical, I was to proceed to Parks Air College in East St. Louis, Illinois, for primary flight training.

It was July 1940. France had fallen to the Nazis the previous month. Now in the skies over southern England, Spitfire and Hurricane pilots of the Royal Air Force were fighting for the life of their nation against the powerful formations of Hitler's Luftwaffe.

I showed up in Pittsburgh on the proper day and went

through a cursory physical—eyes, ears, proper height, and little else. I passed everything just fine, so I was on my way. They gave me money to pay for my travel to Parks, but I decided to save the money and hitchhike there. That didn't last long. I ran into rain and had trouble picking up rides, so after a miserable day I gave up and bought a bus ticket for the rest of the trip.

The Parks setup was a pleasant surprise. The school looked like a normal college campus with nice trees and rustic buildings, except that it also contained an airfield. The school had been established back in 1927, not coincidentally during the same year that Lindbergh soloed across the Atlantic. By 1940 Parks had grown to have twenty-five buildings and a faculty of eighty-two. During the prewar military buildup, the government contracted with flying schools like Parks to train pilots for the armed services.

The first few weeks were spent in orientation and ground school. They fitted us with khaki uniforms and sent us off to classrooms to learn the rudiments of flying. This was pretty easy for me, thanks to Homer Stockert. We covered the theory of flight, aerodynamics, flight controls, meteorology, navigation, and more. All of it was familiar, and I was eager to get on with the flying. I could look out onto the field and see training planes parked here and there: PT-17 Stearman biplanes and sleek PT-19 Fairchild low-winged monoplanes. They glistened in the sun with their blue-and-yellow army paint jobs.

By the time we wrapped up the classroom work, all of us were itching to get into the air. We were introduced to our instructors, who were all civilian professionals, and I said hello to Mr. Myers. He was a stocky sort of a guy with a nice-looking face. I believe his first name was George, but I only knew him as Mr. Myers.

Up to this point, everything had been going fine, and I was feeling pretty confident. That ended abruptly as soon as Mr. Myers and I fired up the big radial engine on the front of one of the PT-17s and taxied out for our first flight. Suddenly all the tightness and apprehension I'd felt in the Taylorcraft flooded back into me. My arms and legs felt as if they were made of wood as soon as Mr. Myers handed the controls over to me.

There was a big difference now, however. Whereas Homer Stockert had been patient and encouraging, Mr. Myers was brittle and demanding. There was no problem with the PT-17. Its two wings gave the pilot plenty of control, and it was very responsive in turns. But Mr. Myers and I were like oil and water, even in a nice trainer like the PT-17. His instructions and my uneasiness just didn't mix. I couldn't seem to understand what he wanted and correlate it to the flight controls. And I was trying too hard, the typical fledgling's problem.

The PT-17 had two open cockpits, one behind the other. The student sat in front, and the instructor gave him orders through a flexible tube that ran between the cockpits. I can still hear Mr. Myers yelling at me through that tube, his frustration growing with every mistake I'd make.

I had about twelve hours of instruction behind me when Mr. Myers finally sent me off on my first solo flight. Most of the other guys had soloed by then, and I was running out of time. We landed at one of the auxiliary fields that we used nearby, and Mr. Myers hopped out, saying something encouraging like it was better for me to kill myself than to kill both of us.

I sat there in the plane alone for a moment, trying to get control of myself. I was nearly petrified. My instructions were to take off, make a couple of turns around the landing pattern, then shoot a couple of touch-and-go landings. The idea there was to come in like you were going to land, but when the wheels touch the runway you stabilize the airplane, add power, and take off again without stopping. Then I was to come back and land.

Taking off wasn't the problem. I taxied out and gave her the gun. In no time the tail lifted and I was off the ground— alone. There wasn't anyone in the back seat to bring me back down this time. I'm sure Mr. Myers could hear the sound of my heart pounding above the roar of the motor as he watched from below. I flew around the field a few times, and then I couldn't put it off any longer. I had to try a touch-and-go.

I tried to relax as I flew the downwind leg of the pattern and turned onto the base leg. I was in reasonably good position when I turned onto final approach. But when I brought the airplane down and tried to land it on the sod, I didn't pull the throttle all the way back. I hit the ground hard and bounced. As I was bouncing I concentrated on the bounce and tried to stabilize the airplane; I forgot about the throttle, which was still partly open. Before I knew it, I was running out of field. I had to make a decision quickly, so I shoved the throttle forward to pick up enough flying speed to get out of there. I just barely cleared the trees at the end of the field and returned to the landing pattern for another try.

By this time I was really shook. My stomach was queasy and my face burned. I would have paid somebody a million dollars at that moment to bring the airplane down for me. But I said to myself there's nobody here to help me, so I'll have to pull my wits together and give it another try. The second time I came down I had the throttle cut all the way back, and I made a bouncy landing, but it was sort of normal. I put the tail wheel down and decelerated to a stop before I taxied over to where Mr. Myers was standing.

He just shook his head. Then he got back in the plane and we flew back to Parks. At least I had soloed.

From then on I continued to be shaky whenever Mr. Myers and I would fly. It was a miserable period of time. I knew I wasn't progressing as fast as most of the other students. But I just couldn't fail again, not after I had disappointed Mother and Dad at Notre Dame.

One of the maneuvers he tried to teach me was the lazy eight. It's actually two loops side by side, connected in the middle. If a pilot does it right, the maneuver looks like an eight lying on its side. The purpose is to teach you to get the feel of the airplane. You dive the plane and pull it back over the top of the loop, roll it out and do another loop going the other direction. You're changing the speed and altitude of the airplane, getting the feel of the rudder, the throttle, and the stick.

When you're doing a lazy eight, you're referencing your flight pattern over a point on the ground, and the crossing of the eight has to be over that point. My lazy eights looked more like amoebas than numbers, with the PT-17 wobbling all over the sky. I was having a heck of a time picking it up, and Mr. Myers was beginning to doubt whether I ever would.

It wasn't long before Mr. Myers ran out of patience. I can't blame him. The army needed pilots, and it needed them in a hurry. There wasn't time to waste on slow learners, much less guys who might never learn to fly well. When I reached about eighteen hours of instruction and still wasn't satisfying Mr. Myers, he told me he just didn't think I had what it took. He said he was afraid if I continued flight training I would kill myself and maybe even take someone with me. So he put me up for an elimination flight.

The civilian instructors at Parks couldn't wash out the army cadets. That was the job of Capt. Ray Wassel, an army pilot who was stationed there to oversee the training. When cadets were put up for elimination, he would take them up for a final ride and decide whether to wash them out or not. Very few cadets survived an elimination ride to complete their training. Of course, we all knew this.

When Mr. Myers told me he was going to send me up for elimination, that just about devastated me because my heart and soul were in flying. I wasn't a kid anymore, just doing the minimum amount to get by. I was really trying to learn. I didn't want to do anything in this world but fly airplanes.

So on a September evening in 1940 I set out to find help in the Catholic church. The next day I would be facing the end of my dream, and I didn't intend to wash out without having tried everything I could to avoid it. No one was in the church, so I just knelt there and talked to the good Lord for about half an hour. I told Him I wasn't about to get out. I had to fly. This wasn't just for me. It was for my family, and perhaps even my nation.

I had been praying my whole life, but never had I prayed so long for such a specific request. As I knelt there a feeling of confidence came over me. I got the feeling that all I had to do the next day was go out and do my best. I left the church feeling much better, and I slept well that night.

The next morning when I met Captain Wassel for my check ride, I was no longer frustrated. I was actually rather collected. He explained to me the significance of the flight: This is your last chance, so give me the best you have.

We fired up the PT-17 and took off. I did lazy eights, chandelles. I did a couple of loops and slow rolls. I felt real secure, and I went through all the maneuvers in reasonable style. I didn't burn up the course, but I did pretty well. So far, Captain Wassel had been quiet in the back seat. No yelling, no complaining. The longer he stayed quiet, the better I felt.

Finally, Captain Wassel gave me a forced landing in the auxiliary field. With no warning, he cut the throttle and ordered me to bring the plane down without power. I managed to get the plane down without hitting the trees or messing up the landing. Then we took off again and returned to the home field for a chat about my future.

Captain Wassel had a little office in one of the hangars at Parks. We went in there and sat down. He took long moments in silence to look over my records. About the time I was ready to burst, he began to speak.

"Well, I'm not so sure about you," he said. "You know, you aren't real strong. However, I think you just need a little bit more time to catch up with the other students. I'll recommend they change your instructor, and we'll give you some more time. Maybe you and Mr. Myers just don't quite hit it off together."

That was the end of my flying problems, right there. I walked out of the office with my feet barely touching the ground. I always believed I had the ability to fly. Now someone agreed with me.

I had about three or four more hours with my new instructor, Mr. Peterson, whose style was a lot more like Homer Stockert's. At the end of my little probationary period he told Captain Wassel that I was going to make the grade, and I did. I think it was my love of flying and my determination to stay in the program that saved the day. They could see my intent, interest, and desire to become a pilot. There was a bit of my father's spirit starting to come out in me, after all. And a little help from up above didn't hurt either.

I finished at Parks in November and was sent straight to Gunther Army Airbase, just outside of Montgomery, Alabama, for basic training. Now I was really in the military.

CHAPTER Two

I GOT my first real taste of army life at Gunther Field. This was a permanent military base, not a converted college. No longer did I stand out in my khaki shirt and pants, like the cadets had at Parks. Now everyone was in khaki. Gunther was spit-and-polish, saluting, the whole bit.

I arrived in November 1940, just as the weather had been starting to get nasty up in Illinois. But down south in Alabama we could fly all winter, and that's exactly why the army wanted us there.

I was disappointed to be sent to Gunther. We all thought of Kelly and Randolph fields in Texas as the elite training centers, and I thought our training in Alabama might be substandard. I needn't have worried. The Air Corps was in the middle of a tremendous expansion effort, far greater than we could imagine. It went from twenty-five thousand men to millions in no time, and we were lucky to be training at all. In fact, there was nothing substandard about my training.

At Gunther, we flew in Vultee BT-13s. These were low-winged basic trainers with a radial engine mounted up front. The two cockpits were mounted in tandem, like the PT-17, but in this airplane the pilots were enclosed by a single canopy, which was nice, especially in bad weather.

With the BT-13, we were getting into a heavier, more powerful airplane. It wasn't as forgiving as the biplanes I was accustomed to. The instructors used to tell us there were three things to remember when you're flying this airplane: airspeed, airspeed, and airspeed. You had to keep the airspeed up or you were dead. It was just that simple.

But I think the thing I remember most about the BT-13 was the noise. Man, that was a loud airplane to ride in! It had a resonance or vibration built into it. We called it the Vultee Vibrator.

My training progressed normally at Gunther—no more traumas. I was never one of the hot rocks, but I was steady. I worked hard, and I listened closely to the instruction we were getting. I think this probably served me better in the long run than if I'd been one of the top students. Then I'd have gotten cocky and wouldn't have paid such close attention.

Most of our flying was between 2,000 and 4,000 feet altitude, so you didn't have much room to recover if you got in trouble. We learned the whole list of aerobatic maneuvers, and we practiced a lot of takeoffs and landings. The whole point was to get us comfortable with the bigger, heavier aircraft.

We also got our first taste of instrument flying in the BT-13s. The idea here was to teach us how to fly the plane when we couldn't see out, like when we were in the middle of a cloud. The instruments would tell us everything we needed to know, but we had to learn to trust them.

The BT-13 had a hood that would cover the student's cockpit under the canopy. The instructor would sit in back and tell us what to do, and we were supposed to fly where he ordered us based on what the instruments said. Fly two minutes at such-and-such a heading; turn 120 degrees to the left and fly another two minutes while losing 200 feet of altitude; then turn 120 degrees again and fly another two minutes while gaining 200 feet; the wind is from the west at five knots. If you did it right, you'd wind up in the same place where you started. Not many guys succeeded on the first try.

It's a funny feeling. After a while, you'd swear the instruments were lying. It felt like the plane was in a dive, a spin, or anything else your imagination could conjure up. But if you reacted to your instincts and disregarded the instruments, sure enough you were going to get in that spin or dive you were trying to avoid. If you've ever tried to walk across an empty parking lot with your eyes closed, you know the feeling, only this was a lot worse.

Normally, we would fly with an instructor long enough for him to show us what the next lesson was what we needed to learn. They went by the book. Maybe one day you'd go out and do slow rolls. First he'd go over the elements one by one. Then the two of us would put them together into the maneuver. The student would practice the maneuver solo. In basic training, unlike at Parks, we weren't assigned a particular instructor. We just flew with whoever was on duty at the time.

We also had ground school at Gunther. A lot of this had to do with navigation. That was tough for me. Aerial maps have a whole language all their own, and it took a lot of study to master the colors, symbols, and terms. It sure wasn't like plotting my course in Dad's old Buick down Highway 8 from Oil City through Franklin and Butler on the way to Pittsburgh.

The other part of ground school that was new to me was the Link trainer. This wonderful device gave trainees the chance to develop their instrument flying skills without the risk of busting their butts. It was a complete airplane cockpit with stick, throttle, rudder pedals, and instruments that was installed in a classroom. You flew it just like an airplane, and it responded somewhat realistically. It wasn't quite like the real thing—flying the Link trainer was just eye, ear, and stick—but it helped. We spent quite a few hours in the Link.

It was a good thing we were getting the instrument training, because weather began to be a factor in basic training. In primary, if it was a bad day you didn't fly. We were flying higher and more often now. The weather could be closed in at a certain point, and you'd have to come down through it. They tried to keep that to a minimum, though, because we weren't real proficient yet.

When you handled an airplane like the BT-13, if you got yourself in trouble in the clouds you had a serious problem because you might not be able to pull out of a dive or spin in time to save yourself and the airplane. That happened several times, and guys had to bail out.

One incident I remember clearly involved a guy named Black. He was doing aerobatics when he got himself into a spin and couldn't get out. The plane started coming down like a falling leaf. Blackie had enough wits to realize he needed to bail out, but as he jumped free of the plane it swung around, and the prop chopped his legs off. The chute opened and he floated to the ground, but by that time he'd already bled to death.

We all ran out to where Blackie landed. The plane had hit nearby and exploded, but the sight of Blackie himself was the big shock. He was the first fatality I'd seen. It was sobering to realize that those things happen, and they could happen to anybody. The shock was penetrating, and we all felt the same. But there wasn't time to dwell on it. We had to keep flying because we were working against time. The entire training program only took you up to about two hundred hours, and it was a short two hundred actually.

After hours we had some free time, but there was a bedtime check in the barracks so we didn't go out. As a matter of fact, on your flying days you didn't want to go anywhere. You were tuckered. There wasn't anywhere to go around Gunther anyway. It was sort of isolated, so you would have to go all the way into Montgomery to get away. We spent most of our time talking among ourselves about the one thing we had in common: flying. We all had our strong points and weak points. We tried to learn from each other.

I made a few friends at Gunther who stayed with me through the next two years. Maxwell Hearn would be my roommate when we got to Hawaii, and Fred Schifflet was another one who went to Hawaii with me. They both fought in the Pacific, and both were killed.

We all made the move over to Maxwell Field for advanced training once we finished the basic course at Gunther. The two bases were close enough to each other that the Maxwell flight pattern kind of went in and around the Gunther pattern.

Maxwell was the Southeastern Training Center, and this is where we got our officer training, in addition to the advanced flight training. They really gave us the business at Maxwell. We were class 41-B, the second class to finish training there.

The base could handle two classes at a time, and class 41-A had arrived a couple of weeks ahead of us. We lived in long World War I–style barracks, three or four men to a room.

The airplanes we flew at Maxwell were really a step up. The AT-6 Texan looked sort of like a BT-13, but it was bigger and had a more powerful engine. It was graceful in the air, and a lot quieter than the Vibrators.

The thing that really set the AT-6 apart for us was its retractable landing gear. It was sort of the Cadillac of training planes—almost like flying a fighter. We were real careful to remember about the landing gear, and I don't recall anyone ever forgetting to drop the wheels before landing during our course there. Of course, it helped that the plane had a horn that would go off whenever the airspeed dropped to a certain level with the wheels up. But it can happen, especially if you're really concentrating on a tough landing. You might not even hear the horn. That happened to me one time years later while I was flying an operational plane. The snow was coming down, so I couldn't see the runway very well, and I was low on fuel. I was so intent on picking up the runway and getting the plane on the ground that I forgot all about the wheels. I was set up on final when I saw this red flare go up in front of me, warning me of danger. I gave it the gun, and only then did I hear the horn going off in my ear. If it hadn't been for that flare, I would have landed with the wheels up.

Advanced flight training taught us how to use the airplanes, now that we knew how to control them. We practiced formation flying, which I liked, and radio procedures. The AT-6 was the first airplane I flew that had a radio in it so you could talk to other airplanes or communicate with the ground. It also was the first airplane I flew that carried guns.

We did a little bit of gunnery training at Maxwell, but not

enough for me to get very good at it. We did air-to-ground firing out in the boondocks, and we practiced air-to-air shooting at a target sleeve towed by an airplane over the Gulf of Mexico. Some guys seemed to have a natural talent for shooting from a moving airplane, but I wasn't one of them. Still, it was exciting to line the plane up on a target and fire the machine gun. You could feel a rumble all the way through the airframe and sense the power of the weapon.

The officer training was far less enjoyable than flying. Captain Luper, a West Pointer, was in charge, and he was the hardest-nosed guy I ever ran into when it came to spit and polish. Besides him, we had the upperclassmen of 41-A to contend with. They gave us a lot of hazing, especially the officers of the class; made us hup-two and all those things. And boy, if you didn't do what they wanted they'd brace you at attention, and you just had to stand there and take it until they were finished.

We had a strict routine for the day. As I recall it, we got up at 5 A.M., and had to fall out in formation on the parade ground by 5:20 for inspection and roll check. That didn't give us very much time to get dressed, brush our teeth, and so forth. Then it was off to breakfast in this big mess hall. After breakfast the day began with whatever was on the schedule. Some days it was flying, other times classwork or drill practice. Every Saturday morning we fell out for parades, when we would march in unison by graduating class. After that we were on our own until Monday morning, and we often would go into Montgomery to blow off steam.

My flying was progressing well by this time. Nothing fancy, but I was gaining confidence. Still, I had one more brush with elimination coming. It started one night toward the end of our training when Max Hearn convinced me that we ought to go into Montgomery and celebrate our impending graduation. Max, the prototypical southern gentleman, was quite a bit more worldly than I was. He thought it would be a good idea to go to the Drum Room in the Jefferson Davis Hotel and let our hair down with a couple of sloe gin fizzes. I reluctantly agreed, though I wasn't much of a drinker.

The sloe gin was sweet, which made it easy for a guy like me to get ahead of himself. The pink stuff tasted like sugar, and I probably had a couple of more drinks than I should have. We stayed out late, but we got back to the barracks okay.

The next morning five o'clock came awfully early. I knew I had to get out of bed at the sound of the bugle, but I wasn't what you'd call bright-eyed and bushy-tailed. I lagged a few minutes, and pretty soon I was running out of time to make it outside for inspection. I yanked on my pants and shirt, pulled the comb through my hair, and raced out the door toward the parade ground.

I ran for all I was worth and reached my spot in the formation. We were supposed to be braced at rigid attention, but I was in no condition to do that for very long without starting to waver. In a few moments I began to feel woozy, and then I passed out momentarily and fell down.

At that time (and perhaps even today) it was the kiss of death for a flying cadet to pass out. So they picked me up and carted me off to the flight surgeon to find out what was the matter with me. Of course, I already knew what was wrong, but I wasn't going to tell anyone because I didn't want to get Max in trouble. The doctor gave me a physical right there on the spot: checked my history, pulse, blood pressure, etc. He couldn't find anything the matter, and I wasn't talking, so he told me to come back for the next few days so he could check my blood pressure some more.

Now I could see I was in a tight spot. When I went back

the next day the doctor found my blood pressure was up. It wasn't critical, but it also wasn't where it should be, the doctor told me. Come back again tomorrow. I had to do something, so I went to a civilian doctor in town and told him my problem. He gave me some medicine that would lower my blood pressure, but when I went back to the flight surgeon for the third time, he still wasn't satisfied with it. He sent a report to Captain Luper, and it wasn't long before Captain Luper called me into his office.

Luper told me that unless there was some extenuating circumstance, passing out meant an automatic washout for any cadet. If I didn't have a good reason, he would have to order a medical discharge for me. Still, I stuck to my story that I didn't know what happened, but I was really shook. How could I come all this way in flight training only to fail on such a stupid mistake?

I returned to the barracks and talked over my problem with several of the guys. They eventually convinced me that I should go back to Captain Luper and tell the truth.

"Why didn't you tell us that in the first place?" he fumed when I spilled the beans. "Those are extenuating circumstances in my book."

So I was reinstated in the flight program, but not without a price to pay. It was just like back in the old days, with Dad's whip. Captain Luper ordered me to stand guard duty, walking the ramp, for an hour. I accepted that gladly, and on the prescribed day I went down there, got my rifle, and did my duty. That was the end of my problems in advanced.

Just before we were ready to graduate from flight training, they gave us a form to fill out to tell the army where we wanted to go from here. Did we want to be a bomber pilot, reconnaissance pilot, or a fighter pilot? Of course, all of us wanted to be fighter pilots. Then it asked where we would like to be stationed. We all figured it was more of a dream sheet than anything else, because we knew the army was going to assign our duties according to the instructors' recommendations and send us where it needed us. If the instructor had said I'd make a good recon pilot, and they needed recon pilots in Alaska, that's where I would have been sent.

I wanted to go somewhere exotic, so I put down Hawaii first, the Philippines second, and the Zone of Interior third. I could see it all in my mind's eye: dashing fighter pilot Frank Gabreski breezes his sleek P-40 fighter in for a landing on a palm tree–lined runway as hula girls watch appreciatively from the beach, ready to greet me with a necklace of flowers as soon as I pulled to a stop. Sure, it was too much to hope for, but what the heck? They asked.

The big day came on March 14, 1941: graduation. Mother and Dad came all the way down to Alabama from Oil City with some friends from the neighborhood for the commissioning ceremony. Also, big brother Ted, who was newly married and just starting his medical practice, made the trip as part of his honeymoon. I was one proud new second lieutenant. After all the trips to the basement as a boy, the disappointment of Notre Dame, and the close shaves during flight training, I had finally succeeded at something. If anything, Dad was even more pleased than I.

During that weekend, I had a chance to take Ted up for a ride in an AT-6. I'm sure Ted had no idea what was in store for him, but I did. It wouldn't do just to take him up for a sightseeing trip; I wanted to show him what I could do with an airplane. So he got the full treatment—rolls, loops, stalls, spins. Sometime in the middle of my performance it got too wild for Ted's stomach, and he threw up all over the inside of the airplane.

When we landed he was white as a sheet and quite embarrassed about the mess he'd made. He might have been angry at me as well, but he didn't show it. Anyway, that incident was the source of jokes in our family about Ted's soft constitution for years to come. He always took them with good nature.

Even more exciting that weekend than Ted's flight was the posting of our assignments. I could hardly believe it when I saw where I was going: Hawaii! And even better than that, I was assigned to a fighter outfit. The frosting on the cake was that several of my friends, including Max Hearn and Fred Schifflet, were going with me.

There was no time for leave before we embarked. By this time the war in Europe had settled into a temporary stalemate while Luftwaffe bombers blitzed London night after night. In North Africa, British forces were expecting an attack by Rommel any day. Our own government could see its dealings with Japan growing increasingly tense. The American military buildup was under way, and there was no time to spare.

Those of us assigned to Hawaii and the Philippines were ordered to Charleston, South Carolina, where the SS *Washington* was waiting to take us there. It was a new ocean liner that had been converted to a troop ship, and vestiges of its former luxury, such as the fancy decor in the officers' dining room, were still visible.

The ship went south to Panama and through the canal. We stopped for a night in Panama City, but it wasn't too pleasant. A few of us went to a nightclub, but we got the distinct feeling from the people there that we weren't particularly welcome, especially by the local men. I can't say I blame them really, since we just breezed in for the night, figuring we could dance with their girls, have a little fun, and then go on our way.

On board ship, each officer was responsible for a certain

number of the enlisted men, about two hundred apiece. About all it amounted to was coordinating meal times and calling roll. It didn't take any of us long to figure out that the noncoms really ran the show. We just gave the sergeants a free hand to do what was needed to keep the men under control.

The next port was San Francisco, where we stopped for two days to pick up supplies. What a difference from Panama City! People there just couldn't do enough for us. A man in uniform couldn't buy a drink for himself; someone always wanted to pick up the tab.

The Pacific crossing to Honolulu took about four days. I recall the first view of Diamond Head was breathtaking. A band was playing as the ship docked in Pearl Harbor, and lovely Hawaiian girls were there to place leis around our necks as we disembarked. About twenty of us new second lieutenants were assigned to the fighter base at Wheeler Field. A representative from the base had cars lined up to take us on the twenty-five-minute trip into the Waianae Mountains to our new home.

Wheeler Field was a vision in green for a young pilot eager to show his stuff. The whole field was sod except for the concrete ramp in front of the hangars, and the wooded hills nearby added to the impression. The runways were sod for a good reason: It was easier to land airplanes on grass, and their tires didn't wear out as quickly as they would on a paved surface. It made a perfect setup for fighter aircraft, and there were plenty of them to see: sleek new Curtiss P-40s, radial-engined P-36s; even a few old Boeing P-26 Peashooters with their humped-up fuselages and spatted landing gears. I could hardly wait to get my hands on them.

Two fighter groups, with about seventy-five planes apiece, were stationed at Wheeler. Max Hearn and I were assigned to the 45th Fighter Squadron of the 15th Fighter Group. Fred Schifflet went to the 46th Squadron, but it didn't make much difference since the single officers in the group lived in the barracks together anyway. My squadron commander was Capt. Aaron Tyer, a southerner and a West Point graduate. We didn't have much to do with him, because in those days the squadron commander didn't fly much. His job was more administrative than anything else. Flying was in the hands of the operations officer and the flight leaders.

When it came to flight leaders, I had a dandy: 1st Lt. Woody Wilmot. I would say Woody had more to do with me becoming a successful fighter pilot than anyone. He had come out of flight school about a year ahead of me, and he could really handle a fighter plane. More important, Woody also was a good teacher, since his job was to pass his skills along to the pilots in his flight to form an effective combat team. He thought like a fighter pilot, he worked like a fighter pilot, he flew like a fighter pilot, and he expected everyone in his flight to do the same. He was one of the best instructors that anyone could hope to have. He demanded a lot, and that's the way we learned.

I was only at Wheeler a few days before I got back into flying, but this time there was a difference. The 45th was an operational fighter squadron, so all its aircraft were single-seat fighters. Up to this time I'd never flown anything more challenging than an AT-6, which had a 600-horsepower engine and a maximum speed of about 200 mph. Now I was stepping up to the P-36 and P-40, which both had engines of over 1,000 horsepower and top speeds of 300 mph or better. Furthermore, there was no back seat for an instructor in a fighter plane!

I was eager to resume flying, but nervous as well. After all, I'd been off flying for a couple of months, and besides that I was stepping into a fighter for the first time. I got through it okay, though I'm still not sure how.

I remember clearly my first flight in a P-40. Now there was an aggravating airplane. The models we had were early ones. They looked like someone had sliced the radial engine off the nose of a P-36 and just grafted on a long snout to cover its Allison in-line engine. When the plane was sitting on the ground, that big nose stuck right out in front of the pilot, completely blocking his forward vision. Once the plane started to move, you could feel the tremendous torque from the engine trying to pull the nose left. If the pilot didn't compensate with plenty of rudder, he'd wind up in a ditch long before he gained enough speed to get airborne.

Woody had me read the P-40 manual thoroughly before he let me try to fly the plane. We went through an extensive cockpit drill until he was satisfied I knew where all the controls and instruments were, and then he talked at length about the P-40's idiosyncrasies including its sluggish climb and its breathtaking dive. But he never really did stress the difference in torque between the P-40 and the radial-engined airplanes I was used to.

Then it was time to fly the P-40. I weaved back and forth as I taxied out so I could see around the nose. Otherwise, I would have no way to be sure I wasn't about to run into something in front of me. When I got to the end of the sod, I turned in the direction of takeoff and checked all the instruments to make sure everything was normal. Once the tower cleared me for takeoff I got off the brakes and began to roll forward, picking up speed rapidly. When the tail came up I decided to give it full throttle, all the way to the firewall. That extra boost caught me by surprise as the torque pulled the nose over to the left. I wasn't quick enough on the right rudder pedal, and the P-40 started veering left. I was running out of time and room, but the aircraft was moving pretty fast by now, so I decided the best thing to do was to yank it off the runway and then try to straighten it out in the air. Lucky for me, I had enough speed, because it would have been a disastrous mistake if I hadn't.

Once I was off the ground, I got myself and the P-40 under control. Then I turned away from the field and climbed up to do a little air work. Man, that airplane was a dog in a climb! I took the airplane and stalled it. Just at the verge of stalling the airplane would start burbling and I let the nose go down. That was the other side of the roller coaster: She picked up speed in a hurry. I did some full-power climbs and practiced turning the plane. Anything to get the feel of the airplane and its engine torque.

I approached every maneuver with trepidation. The P-40 was not a plane I could take to immediately and say, "Gee, this feels comfortable. I love it." It was not at all comfortable. After I had been airborne about fifty minutes it was time to come back and land. Of course, the landing was not very smooth because I still wasn't that proficient with the P-40. I made a little bounce but I got it under control. Thank God there was sod to the left and right, so I could land on any portion of the field, even turn a little bit on the landing, and not hit anything.

That was an experience I'll never forget. It was not scary, but it made me realize that every airplane design has a little different personality of its own, and a pilot had to get in touch with that personality.

The other plane I flew a lot in Hawaii was the P-36. It, like the P-40, was built by Curtiss, so the two had a lot of similarities. But the P-36 was about 1,500 pounds lighter than the P-40, which made it a joy to fly. It had a short nose with a radial engine that pumped out enough power to give you full control during all the aerobatic maneuvers, and it was responsive to the flight controls.

We also had some P-26s, which were little Boeing monoplanes with an open cockpit and wings braced with wire. The P-26 was so small that when you sat in the cockpit you felt as if you could reach out and touch the wingtips. We mostly just played around with these, since they were obsolete and no longer considered operational fighters. But they were sure fun to fly.

The 45th Fighter Squadron was equipped with a mixed complement of P-36s and P-40s, so we flew whatever type was available on any given day. Normally we didn't fly mixed formations of the two types, however, for safety reasons. Their flight characteristics were too different.

We probably flew about thirty hours a month, and most of that time, after the initial familiarity flights, was spent practicing combat maneuvers. We still did all the lazy eights, loops, rolls, and so forth, but now we were learning to fly the plane by feel without looking at the instruments. The flying was done at about 5,000 feet. It was very rare to get up much beyond 10,000, and when we went up there we had to suck oxygen through a tube because we didn't have any masks—just a leather helmet with earphones, goggles, and a parachute.

Much of our flight time was spent practicing combat one-on-one. The idea for the new pilots was to stay behind the leader through all his maneuvers and gyrations. You had to fly with your head out of the cockpit and depend on your eyesight. After a while I didn't really think about controlling the airplane anymore. My eyes showed me where I was going, and my hands and feet took care of the controls automatically. At that point I finally was beginning to become a fighter pilot.

There were certain guys who were better at this type of

flying than others, and you would really find out when you went up and started doing a little combat with them. Some were very tenacious and had full control of the airplane. They were the ones who came out on top, whether it was against me or the next guy. Then there were certain individuals who were good pilots but not real good combat fighter pilots. They were too busy flying the plane to get maximum performance out of it. It's a combination: You have to have feel, you have to have sight, you have to have perception, and you have to have training. They're all combined into one. You have to have them all working for you.

I would say there's no such thing as a natural-born pilot. Everyone has to be given proper training and a proper introduction into their combat assignment, be it fighters, bombers, or whatever. The training brings about experience, and once you get the experience, you have that final edge—professionalism. I pushed myself to the maximum every time I took an airplane off the ground. I wanted to make that airplane become a part of me.

This was hard work. We did most of our flying in the mornings, often getting in two flights before 1 P.M. Even though the flying time was only about an hour per flight, after two hours we were tired and drenched with sweat. It takes a lot out of your system when you're pulling heavy G's during tight turns and pullouts from dives. The gravitational force just pulls the blood out of your head down into the lower extremities of your body. I tried to pull as many G's as I could stand, just short of blacking out.

After the day's flying ended, our usual routine was to go catch a quick shower and then head over to the officers' club. The club was really the center of life at Wheeler Field. We did most of our eating and drinking there. It was a low, Spanish-style building that enclosed a courtyard. The bar opened onto the courtyard, as did rooms where the senior bachelor officers lived. Often they would set up an open-air bar under the palm trees in the courtyard and hold dances there on the weekends. It was an ideal arrangement.

Mostly we talked about flying. We would discuss the problems we had encountered that day and critique each other's performances. I tried to learn all I could, especially from Woody, because it was getting pretty clear to me that we were going to be flying real combat real soon.

The bachelor junior officers palled around together, and after hours our ranks didn't mean much. Johnny Thacker was a first lieutenant and a flight leader in the 46th Squadron. But more important, he was a great guy and he had a car. We spent a lot of time together. Another guy I got a big kick out of was George Welch, who was in one of the squadrons of the 18th Fighter Group. He was a rich kid, heir to the grape juice family, and we couldn't figure out why he was there since he probably could have avoided military service altogether if he wanted to. George was a real hell-raiser, but he also was an excellent fighter pilot, as we would soon find out.

Sometimes on the weekends we'd go into Honolulu and have dinner at the Royal Hawaiian or somewhere like that. Maybe we'd watch the hula dancers for a while, then head back to Wheeler. We weren't that interested in the city, with all its tourists.

Most of the time we had our fun at the beach. The army had an officers-only beach at Haleiwa, which was about a twenty-minute drive from base on the northwest coast of Oahu. It was beautiful at Haleiwa, with a long, white beach and an outdoor bar. We swam, fished, and surfed there. Surfing was the most popular sport in Hawaii then, just like today. I never got to be very good at it, but years later when

I was stationed in Hawaii my son made surfing his main pastime.

The other attraction at the beach was the girls. We might have been intensely interested in flying, but that wasn't our only topic of discussion. Pretty girls were every bit as fascinating as a high-speed dive or the latest rumor about a new model of the P-40. Most of the girls we got to know were army brats, daughters of career military officers, and their friends.

One Sunday morning I got up late and missed mass at the Wheeler Field chapel, so I headed over to catch the service at Schofield Barracks, the big army base that adjoined Wheeler. There in the congregation I caught sight of two attractive girls sitting with an army colonel. I decided a twenty-one-year-old guy like me ought to meet these girls, who appeared to be about sixteen or seventeen. I didn't pursue the matter immediately, but I did keep an eye on where I might get to see them again. Eventually I learned they were Mary Bush, daughter of the colonel, and her cousin, Kay Cochran, who lived with the Bush family.

One day when I was on the beach at Haleiwa I saw Kay sitting nearby on a blanket. At that time I thought I was more interested in her cousin, but I decided to go introduce myself. I walked over, plunked myself down on the blanket next to her, and said, "Hi, Kay. I'm Gabby."

Things just seemed to progress from there. I got to know both girls, and as time went by I changed my mind about them and put my focus completely on Kay. She was young, just sixteen, with dark hair and a pretty smile that flashed often. Mrs. Bush was her mother's sister. Kay had been living with them since her father abandoned the Cochran family during the Depression.

Because of her age, the Bushes controlled Kay closely. Our

dates ended promptly at eleven o'clock, which was frustrating for both of us—especially me. But the more time we spent together, the more I liked her. We would go to the movies, to a dance at the club, to the beach. When September came she went back to school at Sacred Heart in Honolulu, but we continued to spend as much time together as we could.

On the night of December 6, 1941, Kay and I had a date to go to the Saturday night dance at the officers' club. We were doubling with Johnny Thacker and his girlfriend, who by chance was another Kay. Kay Ledingham was the daughter of a plantation owner out near Haleiwa. Johnny and I had wanted to take the girls into Honolulu for the evening, but they didn't want to go. His Kay thought it would take too much driving to get there, and my Kay was afraid we wouldn't get home in time for her curfew.

So we stayed at the club, and things went downhill from there. Johnny and I were pretty peeved about the turn of events, and pretty soon we adjourned to the bar to drink while the girls waited for us at a table. A little before eleven, Kay announced it was time for her to go.

I borrowed Johnny's car and drove Kay home in silence. We barely spoke when I dropped her off, but I did tell her I'd see her the next day. When I returned to the club Johnny and his Kay were sitting together again. I gave him his car keys and walked back to the barracks, wondering what tomorrow would bring.

Three

I WAS lying in my bed, staring up at the ceiling. I had a problem. Kay and I had had our first falling-out the night before, and I had to figure out how to handle it. Should I go to mass at the Wheeler chapel this sunny Sunday morning and seek some divine guidance on how to handle it? Or should I go straight over to Schofield, where I knew she would be attending services, and try to work things out right away? It was December 7, 1941, a little before eight o'clock in the morning.

I got up and went into the bathroom in our barracks to clean up and shave. At first I didn't pay much attention to the roar of low-flying aircraft passing by outside. After all, this was an airbase here at Wheeler. But when I heard the rumble of explosions and the rattle of machine-gun fire I went to the window to see what the hell was going on.

Just then a gray monoplane roared past the barracks. I could see its fixed landing gear and the red circles it carried for insignia. And the gunner sitting behind the pilot was firing away for all he was worth. I stood there in shock for a second until the truth hit me. That was a Japanese aircraft. We were under attack!

In fact, a Japanese task force of six aircraft carriers had launched an air strike of 189 planes at six o'clock that morning. Their primary target was the U.S. Pacific Fleet, most of which was anchored peacefully at Pearl Harbor when the attack commenced at 7:50 A.M. They also hit our airfields at Hickam, Ford Island, Kaneohe, Ewa, and of course, Wheeler.

Once I figured out what was happening, I started running up and down the hallway, yelling at the pilots to get out of bed because we were under attack by the Japs. As the guys gathered in the hallway, I tried to make some sense of what I'd just seen. We could hear explosions going off in the distance, so everyone crowded to the windows to see what we could see.

The front of our building faced the airfield from higher ground. We could see smoke billowing from the airplanes burning on the flight line. There was black smoke coming from the hangars as well, but they weren't engulfed in flames. It also looked as if the airmen's mess hall had been hit. We pilots all pulled on our flying clothes as quickly as we could and headed out the door.

The flight line was about 500 yards from the barracks, and a road ran between the two. To the left of the road, you could see the hangar line, up on a slight rise. Everything was going up in flames. We got out the front door, and just as we were ready to get into our cars and head over there, another Japanese plane headed right for us and started shooting. All of us hit the dirt; some of the guys ducked under the barracks for cover. Others hopped under the cars. Fortunately, no one was hit. As near as I can figure it, this must have been one of the bombers from the first wave that attacked Pearl Harbor, returning to his aircraft carrier.

I decided to make my way to the flight line on foot, but I hadn't gone far before a car full of pilots pulled up and I joined them for the short ride. No one seemed to be in charge at the hangars, so we just pitched in where it looked like we could be most useful.

The first thing was to try to separate the undamaged fighters from the ones that were on fire. For some reason I've never figured out, the planes were parked in straight lines and quite close together, which made them sitting ducks for strafing Japanese aircraft. I plunged into the work with the other guys. The heat and smoke were terrible. We would pull the chocks out from a fighter's wheels and then push for all we were worth until it looked as if the plane was a safe distance out of the way. Then we'd start on another one. We didn't have time to think about how dangerous the work was. Most of the fighters we saved were P-36s, because the P-40s had been parked together in the most exposed position.

All this time the fires continued to burn in the hangars. At one point, someone noticed that all the refueling trucks were parked in there and in growing danger of exploding. But when we tried to start the trucks so we could drive them out, we found they were locked. What was worse, no one seemed to know where the keys were.

Then the ammunition that was stored in the hangars began to cook off. Bullets were exploding in the fire and shooting every which way. It was chaos. We just had to leave the fuel trucks where they were.

After about an hour we had salvaged everything we could. Things that were on fire, like tires, we just left to burn themselves out. The only good thing about the situation was that the planes on the ramp contained no ammunition and very little fuel. That made it a bit easier to save the planes, though it also made them useless for the time being.

Finally we caught up with Captain Tyer in the squadron operations office, which was in an undamaged area of one of the hangars. He didn't have any more idea of what was going on than the rest of us, but he did know that we wouldn't be any use to anybody if we didn't get our fighters fueled and armed. He told the ground crews to get it done; he didn't know or care how they did it. Somehow, they managed.

Captain Tyer still hadn't received any orders, much less any intelligence about where the Japanese carriers might be. But as soon as we got some airplanes ready he decided we should get airborne and see what we could do. Then if some orders came through, they could be relayed to the planes by radio. It would give us a jump.

Only about ten or eleven planes were ready, so Captain Tyer and the flight leaders looked over who was available to fly them and came up with a flight roster. Woody Wilmot must have read in my eyes that I was eager to go, so he assigned me to fly number four in his flight.

This was it. War was on, and I was going up to do my part. I took it for granted that we probably would be getting into combat. Maybe I would shoot down an enemy plane. Maybe I would get shot down myself. I didn't expect to be killed, but I'll have to admit the thought crossed my mind. It didn't matter. The main thing was to attack the enemy.

We had a mixed group of P-40s and P-36s; I got a P-36. I tried to keep myself calm as we climbed out together, heading south. In a few minutes we were over Pearl Harbor. Boy, what a sight. Black, billowing smoke rose high into the heavens. I could see ships over on their sides, burning. It was a horrible mess.

We flew over at about 4,000 feet, but by now everybody

down there on the ground was so jittery that they fired on any airplanes they could see—including ours. We were high enough that small-arms fire couldn't reach us, but they blasted away nevertheless. We could see tracers arc up toward us, and occasionally a smoky burst of flak would explode nearby.

Crazy Fred Schifflet, who was flying a P-40, decided he'd go down lower so the people on the ground could identify us as friendly aircraft and stop shooting at us. I guess everyone makes foolish mistakes at one time or another. Anyway, he rolled out of the formation and zoomed down across Hickam Field, waggling his wings so everyone could see the U.S. insignias on them. The only trouble was the insignias in those days consisted of a blue disc with a white star on it and a red circle in the middle of the star. Forget the disc. Forget the star. All those people at Hickam saw was that red circle. They opened up with everything they had on old Fred: pistols, rifles, machine guns, probably even a few rocks and beer bottles.

Almost immediately Fred yelled over the radio that he had been hit. A little peevishly, Captain Tyer told him to head back to Wheeler. The rest of us steered clear of Pearl Harbor and continued to search the skies for another forty-five minutes, but the Japanese were long gone. We never did receive any orders from the ground, so when our fuel started to get low Captain Tyer led us back to Wheeler.

I was pretty discouraged as I taxied to our hangar area. Pearl Harbor was a shambles. The other airfields had been damaged as badly or worse than ours. We had accomplished nothing. Then I caught sight of Fred's airplane. It was so pathetic it was almost funny. The P-40 was full of small holes where it had been punctured by small-arms fire. You could see where bullets had hit in the cockpit area, but luckily none of them struck Fred. The plane was junk, good only for salvaging parts to fix other P-40s.

Fred was already in the operations office when we arrived, and he was complaining loud and long about the rude greeting he had received from the Hickam gunners. He didn't get much sympathy from us. What did he expect them to do under the circumstances, after the pounding they had taken all morning?

We spent a tense afternoon awaiting further instructions. The questions mounted. Had anyone located the Japanese carriers yet? Would they attack again? Worse yet, would they invade the island? No one knew anything except what we had seen.

We stayed at the operations office until evening. A curfew was established that night. We were instructed to stay close to the phone and return the next morning with our sidearms, which were .45-caliber pistols.

Once we began to disperse and the married fellows headed off to rejoin their families, I started to think about Kay. In all the excitement of the day I had hardly given her a thought, but now I was worried about her. I tried to call her at Colonel Bush's house, but I couldn't get through. It wouldn't have done any good anyway, since all the civilians had been moved from Schofield into Honolulu during the day. She finally reached me by phone about three days later.

It was a tense night for everyone because we had no idea that the Japanese task force had already turned around and was on its way back across the Pacific. We were worried about saboteurs or even a full-scale invasion, but in fact the Japanese had done all the damage they intended to do. A final tally established later showed 18 warships sunk, capsized, or damaged; 164 aircraft destroyed; 2,403 American

servicemen and civilians killed. On the other side of the ledger, the Japanese lost just 29 aircraft, 1 large submarine, and
5 midget subs.

One bright spot emerged for us fighter pilots because two
of our boys had themselves quite a day. George Welch and
Ken Taylor of the 47th Squadron had shot down seven Japanese planes between them. Their P-40Bs had been parked on
our auxiliary strip near Haleiwa for gunnery training. They
had raced out from Wheeler in George's car and gotten airborne by 8:30 A.M. They got four kills on their first flight and
then landed at Wheeler to refuel just before the second Japanese wave arrived. Off they went again, scoring three more
kills.

George came out tops among the twelve army fighter pilots
who were able to engage the attackers during the day. He
was credited with four confirmed kills, and he told us all
about them at the officers' club that evening. We laughed
and joked along with him, letting off steam. But the atmo-
sphere was different, more grim. I tried to make sense out of
the situation and evaluate my own actions of the day. Had I
done enough? Had I been aggressive enough? George hadn't
waited for orders, and he shot down four Japs. I waited and
got nothing. On the other hand, I was proud of the work I
had done during the day. Mostly, I decided, I wanted another
crack at the enemy.

Monday morning President Roosevelt declared war. It was
the beginning of a chaotic few days. We dispersed the aircraft
around Wheeler, dug slit trenches, cleared debris, and flew
countless patrols. The 18th Group moved over to Schofield
and flew off the golf course there.

Kay finally got through to me on the phone about Wednes-
day, and we made arrangements to get together. It didn't take
long for me to see that the coming war had changed our

relationship, as much as it had changed everything else in my life. She meant a lot to me, and I could see that the feeling was mutual. Dare I call it love? It's pretty clear now, after nearly fifty years with Kay, that I made the right call.

That was the turning point. Here I was twenty-one years old. I hadn't really done anything yet, and the normal pattern was to get married and start a family. I was afraid the war was going to destroy my opportunity to do that. Kay and I discussed the risks. It could be a long war, and there was always the chance I might not survive.

Pretty soon the decision came down that my squadron, the 45th, was to move out to an airstrip near Kaena Point. Our men lived at Castle and Cook's plantation, and the 46th stayed at Dillingham Ranch. We shared the airstrip.

That duty turned out to be a far cry from Wheeler. Someone got the bright idea that we ought to start flying standing patrols so we would have airplanes aloft during all daylight hours. Three problems quickly came to light: Standing patrols not only used up a lot of fuel but they also wore down the stamina of the pilots and wore out the airplanes. When we started to run out of planes, the orders were changed. Now we were to keep several planes on ground alert, ready to go up at a moment's notice to investigate in case something happened. Nothing did. And, of course, our combat training continued. I was getting good enough by now to stay with most everyone in the outfit except Woody and Emmett "Cyclone" Davis, who was almost in a league by himself when it came to dogfighting.

At about the end of the year we began to get some new P-40Es to fly. This was an advanced version of the P-40s we were used to, with the main differences being a bigger canopy for better visibility and the installation of six .50-caliber guns in the wings. It was a pretty good airplane, but it was heavier than the early P-40s with no increase in power, so it was a dog in performance. That was neither here nor there. It was an airplane with a lot of firepower, and that's what we were interested in at the time.

Then the next fighters we saw were P-39 Airacobras. At first we thought they were going to be a great addition to the defensive forces in Hawaii, but they didn't turn out to be much of anything. It was a slick-looking plane. Sitting on the ground it looked like it wanted to fly, but once it got into the air it wasn't much improvement over anything we had. Even worse, the P-39 had a tendency to tumble instead of spin because it had the engine mounted amidships. If you got into a stalling condition, it took forever to get out. So we lost a few guys before they learned how to fly the airplane.

During these periods of dispersal to Kaena Point and else-where, Kay and I were able to see each other off and on. Finally we decided to talk to Colonel Bush, Kay's uncle, about getting married.

The colonel was a very practical guy, and he told me he didn't think it would be fair to either one of us to get married immediately because there was no telling what the future might hold. He suggested we get engaged. Then when the war ended we could evaluate our situation and decide whether we wanted to go ahead with our lives together. Kay and I agreed 100 percent.

In short order I had a miniature air force ring made for Kay, and I presented it to her at an engagement party with Colonel and Mrs. Bush and their kids. We continued to spend as much time together as possible until March of 1942, when all military dependents were evacuated to the mainland. She went with Mrs. Bush and the rest of the family to Grand Rapids, Michigan, where Kay's mother lived.

My life got pretty dull after Kay left, considering I was a

fighter pilot in the middle of what was rapidly becoming the biggest war in world history. For the moment at least, the war was a long way off. The Flying Tigers were fighting in Burma and China, the Eagle squadrons were flying with England's Royal Air Force, and our own air force was being pushed back from the Philippines and Java on down to New Guinea and Australia.

The only change of pace I got was a temporary deployment to Barking Sands on the island of Kauai, where we did some gunnery training. We roughed it at Barking Sands, living in tents next to the bare airstrip and testing the ability of a squadron to live on field rations under those conditions. About the only fun we had was shaking up the natives with our flying. We practiced gunnery by flying in pairs close to the water. The plane in back would fire into the water and try to hit the shadow of the lead ship. Then we'd trade places and the other guy would get a chance to shoot. The bullets kicked up quite a spray.

During the summer of 1942 I met several of the pilots who made names for themselves in the early days of the war. Navy Comdr. Butch O'Hare, who won the Medal of Honor for his exploits flying Grumman Wildcats off the USS *Lexington*, visited the squadron when he stopped in Hawaii on his way back to the mainland. The same was true of Lt. Col. Buzz Wagner, the army's first ace of the war. He had commanded a squadron during the defense of the Philippines.

Wagner gave us a rundown on the conditions in the South Pacific, and it really opened my eyes. Some of our guys had already left for reassignment to Australia and New Guinea, but Wagner told us that he already could see how the European theater was getting the priority from our government. The Pacific was left pretty much in the hands of the navy, he told us, and the Army Air Force was number two on the priority list.

That set me to thinking. I wanted to go to war in the main event where I could possibly be of a lot more use to the war effort. Besides, coming from a family of recent immigrants my orientation was more toward Europe. I felt strongly about what the Nazis had done to Poland.

I had read about the Battle of Britain, and especially about the great job done by the Polish flyers of 303 Squadron. By now they were seasoned veterans with a lot of experience that would be useful to the American fighter pilots who would soon begin arriving in England. The idea jelled: I was a fighter pilot and I could speak Polish. Why not see if I could get myself assigned to Europe so I could learn from the Poles and pass the information along to my own people?

It was a long shot, but I figured the worst they could do was say no. I went to pitch the idea to Captain Tyer, who was still my squadron commander. To my surprise he liked my plan and agreed to pass it up the line to our group commander, Lt. Col. William Steele. The next thing I knew, Lieutenant Colonel Steele called me into his office to discuss my idea. Again it passed muster, as he agreed to submit my name to the War Department for transfer to England.

Months went by before I heard anything, and by then I'd pretty well given up hope of getting reassigned to Europe. Then lo and behold a wire arrived from the War Department directing me to report to the 8th Air Force headquarters in England for further processing to a Polish fighter squadron. In addition, I was directed to stop enroute at the Pentagon in Washington, D.C., for a debriefing on the events of December 7, 1941. I also was granted a week's leave at home.

As pleased as I was to be going to England, it was difficult to say good-bye to my squadronmates. There was no telling where any of us would wind up or how many of us would survive the war. Some, like Crazy Fred Schifflet, wouldn't make it. Others, like Johnny Thacker, would serve with me again in later years.

Apparently, someone in Washington, D.C., thought my Polish idea was pretty good. Rather than shipping me back to the mainland by boat, they arranged for me to fly to the West Coast on Pan American's famous China Clipper. On the appointed morning in September 1942 I reported to Honolulu and took my seat in the big Martin flying boat. In a matter of hours we were landing at Treasure Island, San Francisco.

From San Francisco I took another commerical flight, this time on a DC-3, across the country to Chicago. From there I took a train to Washington, D.C., where I had been instructed to report in at the Pentagon. I found a hotel room downtown, and the next morning I headed across the Potomac River to the new nerve center of America's military, the Pentagon.

I was feeling pretty good when I presented myself to the officer in the appropriate office that morning. My dress uniform was freshly pressed, and silver first lieutenant's bars shined proudly on my shoulders. I quickly learned, however, that the Pentagon was a lot more interested in where I had been than where I was going. Rather than briefing me on my assignment in England, the officer told me he wanted me to brief a panel of Pentagon bigwigs on what had happened at Pearl Harbor on December 7.

I was perfectly willing to give them my views, but I was a little disappointed that no one seemed terribly interested in my upcoming assignment with the Poles. In fact, no one even seemed to know very much about it. I asked about taking some leave before I left for England. After all, it had been more than two years since I had left for Parks Air College, and I hadn't been home at all during that time.

"Why don't we have you take your leave at home now, and I'll get this lined up for the week after that when you're ready to proceed on to England?" the officer suggested. That was fine by me. I called Kay in Michigan immediately and arranged for her to join me in Oil City so she could meet my family. I caught the next train to Pittsburgh, then traveled by bus to Oil City. Kay was already there when I arrived at the old house on Spruce Street.

We spent a pleasant, though somewhat tense, week together. Kay got along fine with my family, especially Pop. Mother still spoke very little English, so she and Kay couldn't communicate much, but I could tell Mother approved as well. I showed Kay around Oil City, and we caught each other up on our mutual friends. But we had a hard time talking about ourselves and the future. The war just created too many unknowns.

At the end of our week I put Kay back on the train to Grand Rapids, and then someone drove me down to Pittsburgh so I could catch the train back to Washington.

When I returned to the Pentagon my escort officer informed me that I would be speaking to several groups of people there. I nonchalantly explained to them what had happened to me on December 7, what I had seen from the air, and what had happened during the following days. I doubt that it helped them find the answer to the big question of the day, which was how our forces could have been caught napping to such devastating effect. As a junior officer and fighter pilot, I simply didn't have any knowledge of such matters.

While I was at the Pentagon, I was issued a civilian passport on which I was to travel to England. I never did understand the reason for doing this, but it didn't make any difference to me. I also was informed that I was being promoted to captain. This was a surprise, since I'd only been a first lieutenant for a few months. My guess was that someone thought the higher rank would give me better standing with the Poles when I arrived in England. However, that seemed to be about the only thought anyone at the Pentagon had put into my assignment.

Again, I was to travel by air to my next destination. I caught the Yankee Clipper, another Pan Am flying boat, in New York bound for Lisbon, Portugal, by way of Bermuda and the Azores.

I spent a couple of days in Lisbon waiting for transportation, and that was a nice experience. All the spies in the world were down in Portugal because it was a neutral country. I was put up in a very fancy hotel, with gambling casinos and everything going on. On the surface you'd never have known a war was going on. But it was all subterfuge. There were spies and counterspies moving all around the place.

Finally I got a ride on a British civilian plane to Shannon, Ireland (also neutral, technically), and from there I was flown to London. Everyone was in civilian dress on both flights, but I suspected most of the passengers were no more civilian than I was.

I rode by cab from the London airport downtown to 8th Air Force headquarters. It was quite a sight. Even though the Battle of Britain had taken place two years previously and the Luftwaffe's night blitz had subsided, London was still quite a shambles. Piles of rubble and burned-out buildings were everywhere.

Eighth Air Force headquarters was another shock for me. I'm not sure exactly what I expected, but what I found was about twenty people running around in what looked to me like complete confusion. It was October 1942, and the American buildup in England was in its embryonic stages. Its few combat outfits had flown only about a dozen missions, and they were now being transferred out to serve in the upcoming North African invasion.

I presented my orders to a friendly major who viewed them vaguely. Neither he nor anyone else seemed to know anything about me or my assignment to a Polish combat squadron. For the time being, he had me fill out some administrative paperwork and then sent me off to a hotel for quarters.

Again I was in for a shock. The hotel was missing an entire wall, which had been blown off by a German bomb. My room consisted of three walls with a tarpaulin covering the opening to the outside. I spent a horrible night in the cold, damp air. Having come from the warm climate of Hawaii so recently, it really had an impact on me.

Returning to headquarters the next day, I got down to the business of catching up with a Polish fighter outfit. Again, I was met with blank stares.

"Right now we don't have anybody in authority who could work this up for you," the major told me. "Since you're a pilot, why don't we send you up to Prestwick for some ferry work until we can put it together? We have a lot of airplanes that are passing into Prestwick and being distributed to our bases in England."

"Well, if it's a temporary measure, at least I'll be flying," I replied.

In short order I found myself in a transport plane flying north to Prestwick, which is on the west coast of Scotland not far from Glasgow. The airport there was used as an entry point for aircraft being ferried across the Atlantic, and some P-38s that had been sent by ship in crates were assembled there as well. I checked out in a P-38, which seemed to be a nice flying ship. It had twin engines located in booms on either side of the cockpit pod, and the propellors turned in opposite directions so there was no engine torque to contend with on takeoff. The Lightning had quite a high rate of climb compared to the P-40s and P-39s I had flown in Hawaii. I also checked out in B-17 and B-24 bombers, but most of my flight time in them was spent as co-pilot.

Most of the ferry pilots were civilians, and I had a couple of scares flying in the right seat with them. My first flight to London in a B-24 was with an older pilot who had a lot of hours and was well seasoned, but as we approached land I could see he was flying the plane like a fighter. When we came in over the treetops and let down on the runway I could see we were never going to get the plane stopped in time. We were coming in too hot, and we didn't touch down until we were about halfway down the runway. The trees at the end of the runway were coming up fast, so I jumped on the brake pedals for all I was worth.

By the time we ran off the runway into the mud we had slowed down quite a bit. The big plane sank in and mushed to a stop. They didn't have the proper equipment on the field to hoist the B-24 out of the mud, so we had to jack the wheels up and put planks under them, then literally push the plane back onto the runway. It was about a three-hour job with practically everyone on the base pitching in. Once we got her back on solid macadam, we fired up an engine and taxied to her parking spot. This wasn't how I pictured myself contributing to the war effort, to say the least!

During this time 8th Fighter Command was formed, and it set up shop at Bushey Hall on the outskirts of London under the command of Brig. Gen. Frank O. D. "Monk" Hunter. I checked in periodically to see if any progress had been made on my assignment, but each time I got the same discouraging answer.

At the other end of the line, in Prestwick, between flights I would watch people getting off the transports that arrived from the States. One day in November I saw a face I recognized departing from a C-54. It was Col. Bob Landry, who had served in Hawaii at the same time I was there. I didn't know him personally, but I knew he was a pilot in every sense of the word.

Desperate by now to find someone who could help me get assigned to the Poles, I approached him in the terminal and explained my plight. He told me that he was being assigned to help organize 8th Fighter Command, which encouraged me to ask him to help me.

"I hardly even have my feet wet right now, and I don't even know where Eighth Fighter Command is yet," he replied. "I tell you what. Give me a week or ten days and by then I'll have a pretty good idea of what I can and can't do. We'll pick it up from there."

Landry wasn't able to be very specific, but it was the first word of encouragement I'd received.

I had some time off coming, so I went down to London for a few days. While I was there, one evening I went over to the Embassy Club, which was a big nightclub where lots of military types congregated. I was sitting at the bar nursing a beer and feeling a little sorry for myself when through the din I heard a familiar language. It was Polish!

I turned and saw a group of young men in blue Royal Air Force uniforms talking about flying as only fighter pilots do, their hands waving around as they illustrated one maneuver or another. Here was my chance. I walked over and introduced myself in Polish.

They looked up in surprise to hear a Polish greeting coming from this obviously American officer. Their looks turned to delight as they realized who I was: a Polish Yankee, and a pilot to boot.

I joined them at their table, and quite a discussion ensued. I was anxious to learn all I could about their operations, and they in turn were curious about the mood and future plans of the United States with respect to the war. Before long I had an invitation to join them at Northolt, the RAF base where their Polish wing was stationed.

During the course of the evening I learned a lot about how the Poles had come to be flying in the RAF. Most of them had been fighter pilots in the Polish Air Force when Germany attacked their country in 1939. They put up a spirited but short-lived defense before Poland was overrun, some of them even managing to shoot down German aircraft with their outdated PZL parasol fighters. They escaped by various means to England, some reaching France in time to fly combat again before that nation, too, was conquered in 1940.

The first all-Polish squadron was No. 303, which ran up a score of 117½ German aircraft destroyed during the Battle of Britain, tops in the RAF. Eventually, the number of Polish fighter squadrons grew to eight, and my new friends were assigned to one of them, No. 315. This squadron was formed at Northolt in January 1941 flying Hurricanes, but it had converted to Spitfires before commencing combat operations later that year. Just recently 315 Squadron had been assigned the latest model Spitfire, the Mark 9, which had equal or better performance than the newest versions of the Me-109 and FW-190 fighters in service with the Luftwaffe squadrons on the other side of the English Channel. At that time, the Spit 9 was considered the finest fighter plane in the business.

The Poles invited me to return to Northolt with them that

very evening, but I thought that might be pushing my luck. I told them I would come see them the following day. I left the Embassy Club that night feeling the best I'd felt since arriving in England.

The next afternoon I found my way out to Northolt and 315 Squadron. There I was introduced to Group Captain Mümler, who greeted me warmly. We had a long talk, and I wound up being invited to stay for dinner. When I explained my desire to fly with the Poles, he became even more enthusiastic.

"Sure, we would just love to have you," he told me. "As a matter of fact, anything I can do at the Air Ministry I would be happy to do."

I told him of my offer of help from Colonel Landry and suggested that if the assignment were being pushed from both sides, perhaps it would speed things along. I could tell I was getting ever closer to success.

By now it was time for me to return to Prestwick for more of the dreary ferry work. After about ten days I got a chance to run out to Bushey Hall during a stop in London, and I checked with Colonel Landry to see if he'd had a chance to pursue my assignment.

"Yeah, I did talk to the Air Ministry about you, and there's no problem whatsoever," he told me. "Whenever you're ready to go, they're ready to have you." He went on to emphasize that this was only to be a temporary assignment in order to give me some combat experience that I could apply in one of the new American fighter outfits that were due to arrive from the States soon. That was fine with me.

I went back to Prestwick just long enough to clear out, and then stopped back at 8th Air Force headquarters in London to pick up my orders assigning me to the Polish wing at Northolt. At last, I was going to see some action.

CHAPTER Four

IT WAS a blustery day in December 1942 when I presented myself to Group Captain Mümler at Northolt and told him I'd received my assignment to his wing. He was so delighted he didn't even bother to look at my orders.

It had now been a year since I'd flown that fruitless patrol over Pearl Harbor looking for the Japanese attackers, a year well spent honing my flying skills. I was confident I could fly with anyone, but I also knew there was more to combat than merely controlling your aircraft. You had to know how to fight, and that's what I had come to Northolt to learn. As it turned out, I couldn't have found a better place to do that.

I'm not sure I appreciated it at the time, but Northolt was the very base where 303 Squadron had distinguished itself during the Battle of Britain, thereby planting in my mind the idea that was about to blossom. Back then, in the fall of 1940, 303 had shared the base with just one other squadron. Now in December 1942, two full Polish wings (six squadrons) were stationed at Northolt.

The base itself was pretty nice for a wartime installation. Located just west of London, Northolt had a macadam runway and permanent buildings. The hangars were small but well placed, though much of the maintenance work on the Spitfires was done outdoors. Sleeping quarters were excellent.

Mümler assigned me to 315 Squadron, whose pilots I had met at the Embassy Club. My squadron commander would be Squadron Leader Thaddeus Sawicz, but I was placed in the special care of one of his flight commanders, Flight Lt. Tadensc Andersz. It was from these two men that I would learn my most valuable lessons about air combat.

From that very first day, I had a warm relationship with the men of 315 Squadron, especially Tadek Andersz. He was a slender, handsome man a few years older than I was, product of a well-to-do family whom he had been forced to leave behind when he fled Poland. I met all the pilots and ground crew members, and since I could speak their language they were all very cordial. We wasted no time getting me ready to fly with the squadron. The first chore was to introduce me to the Spitfire.

All the pilots were enthusiastic about their new Mark IX Spitfires. Compared to the Mark V models they had flown earlier, the new fighters were faster and had better high-altitude performance, but they hadn't lost any of the earlier model's high rate of climb or maneuverability. The Mark V had been able to hold its own against the Luftwaffe's Messerschmitt Bf-109Es, but the introduction of later models of the 109 and the Focke-Wulf FW-190 fighter had tipped the balance in favor of the Germans. The Spit IX was designed to return the performance edge to the boys on our side of the English Channel.

Tadek gave me an operational manual for the Spit IX, and then we walked out onto the flight line to take a look at one.

The basic configuration was similar to the P-40: Both were low-winged monoplanes with liquid-cooled engines and sat nose-high on two retractable main wheels and a small tail wheel. The Spit was a sleek design, with its Rolls Royce Merlin engine tightly cowled in a long, pointed nose. I also noticed how thin its rounded wings were; so thin, in fact, that they were bulged on the upper surface to make room for the 20-millimeter cannons mounted inside them. The thin wings were one of the keys to the Spitfire's speed. Another was its narrow fuselage, which needed a door hinging downward below the canopy to make room for the pilot to enter the cockpit.

The Spits of 315 Squadron carried standard RAF camouflage, which was dark green and dark gray on top and a lighter gray on the undersides. In addition, they carried the RAF bull's-eye roundels on the wings and rear fuselage, and red, white, and blue vertical stripes on the fin. A duck-egg green propeller spinner and band around the rear of the fuselage, plus yellow leading edges of the wings, completed the regulation paint job. To this 315 Squadron had added a few touches of its own. Each plane had the squadron's code letters, PK, painted ahead of the fuselage roundel, and an individual letter behind it. They also displayed a red-and-white Polish checkerboard insignia on the nose below the engine's exhaust stacks.

Andersz pointed out some of the Spitfire's unique features. Rather than the control stick with pistol-grip handle I was used to, the Spit had a circular handle at the top of the stick with the gun switches and air brake controls on it. Those air brakes were very sensitive, and you had to be careful with them while taxiing or else you could plop the plane over on its nose. Another difference was the Spit's power-to-weight ratio. The aircraft was roughly the same size as the P-40s I had flown, but it weighed about 500 pounds less,and its Merlin engine put out over 1,500 horsepower, at least 400 more than the P-40's Allison powerplant.

A key to the Spit's high-altitude performance was the Merlin's two-speed supercharger, which allowed the engine to produce power at over 30,000 feet, while the P-40's single-speed blower limited it to about 20,000 feet, and even that was pushing it. With such high-altitude capability, the Spitfire needed a sophisticated oxygen system you keep its pilot alive up where the air gets thin. On the rare occasions when we used oxygen in Hawaii, we had sucked it from a tube; in the Spitfire an oxygen mask with built-in radio microphone was provided.

In a few days I was ready to take a Spitfire up to get the feel of it. Andersz gave me a few final words of encouragement, and then off I went. The plane was everything I expected and more: light on the controls, fast climbing, and maneuverable. The only thing it wouldn't do very well was dive. The plane was just too light to come down very fast. I practiced some rolls, loops, and stalls. Then I found a cloud and shot some landing approaches: This Polish Yankee wasn't about to mess up his first Spitfire landing with the whole Polish air force watching.

By the time I landed at Northolt I understood why the Royal Air Force had decided not to use any of the P-40s we had sent them on lend-lease for combat over Europe. The Spitfire was in a whole different league, and so apparently were the Luftwaffe's fighters.

The other part of my indoctrination at Northolt was to learn about the tactics used by 315 Squadron. Andersz explained to me that most of the missions were dictated by the Spitfire's limited endurance. The plane carried only enough fuel to fly missions of about 1 hour and 20 minutes, so your combat time was very, very short.

At this point in the war, the Allies had taken the offensive in the air over northern Europe, but most of the actual damage was being done by the RAF heavy bombers at night. The Luftwaffe was heavily engaged in North Africa and against the Russians on the Eastern Front, so only two day-fighter wings could be spared for the defense of France and the Low Countries. The daylight bomber offensive of the U.S. 8th Air Force, which would become so important to my life in a few months, was in its infancy.

Most of the fighter missions were what the RAF called "rodeos," in which a formation of Spitfires would sweep across the Channel over to France or Belgium and see whether they could antagonize the Germans to come up and fight. When they did, the fight wouldn't last long; just a skirmish really. Sometimes the Germans jumped the Spitfires, and sometimes the Spitfires jumped them. The ones who saw the enemy formation first took the advantage and made a pass. Then they would break off and look for another opportunity. That's why it was important to keep your eyes open at all times, Andersz told me.

The other common mission was called a "circus." It had the same purpose as a rodeo—to entice the Luftwaffe to come up and fight. But on a circus mission a large number of Spitfires would escort a few light bombers and try to decoy the Germans into an interception.

Before I was ready to fly any actual combat, Andersz took me up with his flight on several practice missions so I could get used to the Poles' formations and procedures. They did it a little differently than we had in Hawaii. When the squadron flew at full strength, it consisted of three flights of four planes each, as opposed to the American sixteen-plane squadron. The Poles used a line-abreast battle formation with the four planes of a flight lined up as if you were looking down at the backs of the fingers of your right hand. The leader was the middle finger, and his wingman flew to the far left. The element leader ("Number Three" in RAF slang) flew on the other side of the flight leader, and his wingman was at the far right. This way, everyone could keep an eye on the tail of someone else. And during an attack, all planes in the flight could bring their guns to bear, though the wingmen's job was primarily to guard the tail of their leaders. The only shortcoming of this formation was that it was less maneuverable than the line-astern string formations then in use in the American air forces in England.

After these practice missions, I felt more confident than ever that I was ready for the real thing. The day finally came in early January 1943, when Squadron Leader Sawicz assigned me to fly Andersz's wing on a circus mission to Le Havre on the French coast.

I was awake before dawn that morning and pulled on my flying clothes. It would be cold in the cockpit of my Spitfire at altitude, so I wore long underwear and extra socks, along with a thick sweater, under my flight suit. My fleece-lined flight jacket and boots completed the wardrobe. On top of that I would be wearing an inflatable yellow Mae West life preserver and a parachute strapped to my rear. I took time for a short prayer, then headed to breakfast.

I couldn't help but notice the change in my fellow pilots at the mess. The jokes were a little coarser, the laughs a little louder. There was a fine edge of excitement in the faces of the men who were going on the mission, including mine, I suppose.

Andersz and I spoke quietly before it was time to man our

planes. He reminded me that the wingman's job was to guard his leader and keep his eyes open. He reassured me that he thought I was as ready as I'd ever be, and that meant a lot coming from him. Finally, we shook hands next to my Spitfire, and it was time to go.

I climbed up on back of the port side wing root of my Spit and then, facing forward, swung my right leg into the cockpit. Next I maneuvered the parachute strapped to my bottom into position and settled down on it in the bucket seat. I hooked up the radio and oxygen leads to my mask, turned the radio to the proper channel, and prepared to start the engine: brakes on; throttle open about a third; several pumps to prime the engine; thumbs up to the airman manning the battery cart; start engine.

The big Merlin rumbled to life, and I pulled the throttle back to idle. It was a chilly day, but I was sweating with excitement even though the Perspex canopy that covered the cockpit was still pulled back in the open position. I kept a close eye on Andersz's plane, and when he began to taxi I signaled my crewmen to pull the chocks away from my Spit's wheels. I followed him down the perimeter track to takeoff position and reviewed the takeoff checklist: brakes, trim, flaps, contacts, petrol pressures, undercarriage, and radiator. All the while I S-turned the aircraft, using a combination of the rudder pedals and brake lever. We reached the end of the runway, and as soon as it was clear we turned into the wind. One last check of the magnetos, and we were ready to go.

Andersz gave me a wave, and then we began our takeoff roll. As the engine note rose, I felt the Spit's nose characteristically trying to swing right as the engine torque asserted itself. A gentle press on the left rudder straightened her out, and then I pushed the stick forward to lift the tail when I felt the elevators beginning to bite. Soon the bumpy ride smoothed out as I cleared the runway and followed Andersz into the sky.

I reached down to pull the lever that retracted the wheels and adjusted the throttle and boost to climb setting, all the while keeping my eyes glued to Andersz's Spitfire. We were under strict radio silence, so the only sound was the bellow of the Merlin engine, it's twelve unmuffled exhaust stacks only a few feet in front of my face. Soon I began to hear a maddening buzz in my radio earphones. I was prepared for that, however, since Andersz had told me to expect the Germans to be jamming our radio frequency with interference. We climbed through a thin layer of mist as we headed south toward the Channel, and I had time to think about this amazing situation I had created for myself.

I knew I was as ready for combat as I could be, but I still felt the dread of the unknown. Strangely, I wasn't afraid of getting hurt. But what if I made a mistake? What if I'd missed some key piece of information? What if I panicked and let the Poles down? No, I wasn't going to do that, I assured myself. I'd come too far, and I wasn't going to disgrace myself, my family, or my country.

I imagined my father standing behind the counter in the Purity Market and how he'd smile if he knew what I was doing this very minute. He would appreciate the irony of my situation: I wasn't really qualified to get in a fight with an experienced enemy, but the only way to learn how was to go out and give it a try.

Before long we crossed the coast and headed out over the English Channel. I knew from Andersz's instructions that I needed to be on my toes from here on. It was a typical winter sky with clouds all around—plenty of places for a gaggle of 109s to pop out and make a mess of you. I swiveled my head this way and that, searching every corner of the sky and pausing every so often to make sure I kept my position in the formation.

After a while I realized we were not alone in the sky. Below us was a small formation of Bostons, a twin-engine light bomber built in the United States by Douglas as the A-20 and provided on lend-lease to the RAF. We followed them across the French coast near Le Havre at 20,000 feet. Now I was over enemy territory for the first time. It was an eerie feeling, knowing the only things between me and death or capture were this Spitfire and my ability to fly it. But the Merlin continued to run smoothly. We turned onto a new heading, then turned again a few minutes later. I never saw the Bostons drop any bombs, but I assume they did at some point in the mission.

By that time in the war, the Germans had developed a pretty good radar system to keep track of what was flying over their territory. It gave them instantaneous intelligence, so they had the flexibility of deciding whether it was in their best interests to attack an intruding formation or not. On this day, they must have figured out what we were up to and decided not to take the bait of our Bostons. We turned north back toward England without seeing a sign of the enemy— not a single Luftwaffe fighter, not even a burst of flak. Just that buzz of jamming in the radio.

I returned to Northolt with mixed feelings of relief and disappointment over the lack of action on our mission. But the way the Poles greeted me, you might have thought I'd just shot down half a dozen 109s. They had been friendly before, but now I was one of them in every sense of the word. In their eyes I was a combat pilot, though we all knew I still had a lot to learn.

This wasn't an honor I took lightly. Some of these guys had been in the war since the first day back in 1939 when I was still a kid marking time on the campus at Notre Dame. They had fought with dilapidated, obsolete fighters until the last moment, then escaped by various means as the Germans overran their territory. Most of them went to Rumania, Bulgaria, and so forth. They made it to England on their own initiative because that was the only place they could get the equipment they needed to fight again. The 315 Squadron didn't happen to have many high-scoring aces in it at the time I was at Northolt, but the pilots were all seasoned, tough, and aggressive. To a man, they were filled with determination to destroy the enemy.

The friendship and respect of guys like Andersz, Sawicz, and Stanislaw Blok filled me with confidence and made me eager to come to grips with the Luftwaffe. I wouldn't have to wait long for that.

I flew several more missions with 315 during January as weather and operational requirements permitted, but the only evidence of German opposition we saw were occasional bursts of flak. By the end of the month I was getting pretty familiar with the lay of the land in the small corner of France that we could cover in our Spits.

On February 3, 1943, the mission was a circus to St. Omer, a French town inland from Calais and south of Dunkirk. The familiar hum of radio jamming was with us as we crossed the Strait of Dover and made landfall just west of Calais. A few bursts of flak welcomed us to occupied France, but they were well off to the left and below us.

My eyes were scanning a bank of clouds in front of us over St. Omer when the electrifying call came over the radio in Polish: "One-nineties, coming out of the sun!" My mind went blank in excitement for a split second before I could swivel my head around for a look. By then they were right on top of us and beginning to open fire.

Stick with your leader! I remembered Andersz just in time to follow him as he whipped his Spitfire into a tight turn. The crafty Luftwaffe pilots had caught us in a tight spot. Since they were above and behind us, there was no point in trying to dive away. That wasn't the Poles' style anyway, so Andersz turned to fight.

The next few moments were a blur of motion. I stayed glued to Andersz as he dodged among the blunt-nosed German fighters, occasionally firing his guns. Then I heard his voice in my earphones:

"Boy, do you see them? They're right ahead of you. Shoot!"

"No. I don't see them," I called back. I was too excited and too scared to make any sense out of what I was seeing through the windscreen.

"They're right in front of you, right in front!" Andersz called again.

I concentrated harder and saw a group of dots way out in front of us. They must be the ones he's talking about, I thought.

"Shoot! Shoot!" Andersz called again, so I pointed my guns roughly in the direction of the dots and pressed on the trigger. Tracers danced out in front of me, but I couldn't see whether they were hitting anything.

Then in another heartbeat it was over. The planes in front of me rolled over and stuck their noses straight down, breaking off the engagement as they dove for home. Andersz turned sharply to the left and I followed him. I looked around the sky and saw nothing. Our Spitfires were alone.

My heart was still pounding as we headed westward back across the Channel. I was drenched with sweat and more than a little perplexed. I had been in a fight with the enemy, and yet I had hardly seen a thing. How long would it take before I really knew what I was doing? How long until I developed the Polish eagle eyes that Andersz had?

Back at Northolt, the pilots were in a state of excitement I hadn't seen before. Everyone wanted to talk at once, and I was very glad my command of Polish was good or I wouldn't have had the slightest idea what anyone was saying. Once everything had been sorted out, it was determined we had shot down three 190s without losing anyone—a pretty good showing considering we had been surprised from above. Andersz and Sawicz praised me for holding my position throughout the engagement, but I was still disturbed.

"Did you see that airplane underneath?" Andersz asked me.

"Not really, but I saw the ones directly in front of me, and they're the ones I shot at," I replied.

"No, there was one right under you that wouldn't go away," Andersz said. "You'll see it on your film."

That evening we sat down to view the gun camera films of the scrap. Each Spitfire was equipped with a small movie camera in the wing that would take pictures whenever the guns were fired. It also was possible to shoot film without shooting the guns. The films were used as an aid to the intelligence officers in confirming pilots' claims, and they provided a terrific training tool for critizing pilots' combat techniques. After the mission, the exposed film would be processed and pieced together into a movie. Pilots could learn a lot by seeing what worked and what didn't.

When we came to my film from the day I was in for a rude shock. There on the screen I could barely see the fleeing dots I had fired at, but in the lower corner of the screen, right under my nose, was a Focke-Wulf 190 that I hadn't seen. It was big as a barn door!

If I had seen him, all I'd have had to do was slip down a

little bit and press the trigger. That would have been the end of him. This was the target Andersz had been yelling about.

Now as we talked about combat tactics I had a better frame of reference, and it began to make sense. You had to settle down and be calm about the situation when you were over enemy territory. When the fight started you obviously got excited, but you couldn't let yourself stop looking around. Even if you got an enemy plane in your sights you couldn't fix your attention on it. You had to remain completely aware of what was going on around you, and fire only when it was expedient. Otherwise, there might be someone else on one side or the other coming in on your tail.

In the case of my 190, I had no problem with anybody closing in on me, because the German pilot obviously hadn't seen me either. Andersz advised me not to lose any sleep over it.

"Well, that's just natural," he said. "We were all like that at first—kind of frozen." Then he added something else that stuck with me throughout the war.

"You've got to always respect your enemy. The Germans have been at war for quite a while, and they have a lot of experience. So whatever encounter you may get into, always remember you have to respect their ability to shoot you down."

I learned a few more lessons from the February 3 mission, not the least of which was the need for strict discipline on the radio during a fight. The Poles knew that you had to keep the channels as clear as possible so they could warn each other of danger or help each other get in firing position. I never heard them exclaim over making a kill or anything like that. They saved all the chitchat for the bar after they got home. In the air they were all business.

Another important lesson from the mission had to do with

shooting. Like most novices, I was having trouble estimating the range of a target in front of me. Depth perception is very difficult at high altitudes because you have nothing to compare the target to. The Poles were well seasoned, and most of them knew to hold their fire until they came well into range, which was about 250 to 300 yards.

As it turned out, I took a long time to learn how to hold fire until I was completely in range. You had to take into consideration your overtaking speed, because if you were overhauling your target at a rapid rate it didn't leave you much time to fire before you overran him. As a matter of fact, you might go past him before you had a chance to destroy him, and then you were in trouble, because now *he* was behind *you*. But once I learned how to get in close before starting to shoot, I began to have some success as a fighter pilot.

The final lesson was one that every pilot has been told since the earliest air battles of World War I: Beware of the enemy attacking from out of the sun. The Poles of 315 Squadron all lived by this maxim and used the sun to their advantage every chance they got, yet on this day the 190s still had been able to surprise us by using the bright rays of the sun to shield their approach. It's one thing to be told something like that, but quite another to actually experience it on the receiving end. One moment I had looked back into an empty sky above me, and the next moment it had been full of 190s that seemed to have come out of nowhere. I was lucky to have survived the lesson; a lot of inexperienced pilots didn't.

I flew about two dozen more missions with the Poles, but we didn't get into any more scraps with the Luftwaffe while I was at Northolt. As February neared its end my confidence was growing with each day, each mission.

I learned how to search the sky by relaxing so I didn't stare into space intently, because that would rob you of your peripheral vision. Instead I would scan the sky looking for flickers of light. When an airplane is up in your sky, even if it's camouflaged with dull paint you can see it if the sun flashes on its cockpit canopy. The canopy is a good reflector, so if you scan the sky using your peripheral vision as well as your forward vision, you could pick up everything that is a dramatic change in the sky, even a flash far off to one side or the other.

Fighter pilots can develop their sky vision with training and experience, but there were some guys who just seemed to have an uncanny knack for seeing things before anyone else did. The first pilot I always think of in this regard is Bob Johnson, the great ace who flew with me in the 56th Fighter Group. His eyes were very keenly tuned to the sky. If he looked into a certain area and enemy aircraft were there, he saw them way ahead of the rest of us.

I found that flight goggles inhibited my peripheral vision, so I didn't wear them unless I was in trouble such as when the aircraft was damaged or if I had needed to bail out (which thank God I never did). I always flew with the goggles pushed up on top of my helmet so I could pull them on if I needed them, but that wasn't often. I did use sunglasses, however, especially at high altitudes where you got intense white reflection off the tops of the clouds.

Pretty soon I got word from Col. Bob Landry that it was time for me to leave the Poles and return to 8th Air Force Fighter Command. I went to see him at Bushey Hall, and we discussed my next move.

He explained that Fighter Command now consisted of three fighter groups, all equipped with brand new P-47 Thunderbolts. I had never seen a P-47 at that time, but I felt confident that my Spitfire experience would be useful, no matter what kind of fighter I was to fly.

Of the three fighter groups, two were untested in combat, the 56th and 78th. Both had arrived from the United States in the previous two months and were preparing to go on operations. The third group was the 4th. It had been formed from the American personnel of the RAF's three Eagle squadrons back in September 1942 and flew combat in Spitfires until sufficient numbers of P-47s arrived to reequip with the American-built fighters.

The 4th was full of pilots who had more experience than I had, so it made more sense to assign me to one of the green groups. For no particular reason that I can recall, Colonel Landry and I settled on the 56th. It turned out to be a very fortunate choice.

Within a few days I received orders transferring me to the 56th Fighter Group at Kings Cliffe airfield near Peterborough. It was difficult to say goodbye to all the great friends I'd made in 315 Squadron, especially Andersz. We spent a raucus evening at the bar, and then it was time for me to go.

"Remember, my friend," Andersz said. "Don't shoot until you're close enough to make a sure kill."

Neither of us knew it at the time, but we would fly together again.

CHAPTER *Five*

     I WAS still a kid back in Oil City when the decisions were made that would determine the course of my service in World War II—in fact, the course of my entire air force career.

Beginning in about 1930, advocates of pursuit (what we later called fighter) aviation fought a losing political battle within the U.S. Army Air Corps against officers who believed that strategic bombers would render pursuit obsolete. In those lean Depression years, when every dollar in the military budget was dear, decisions on aircraft procurement were even more critical than they are today. By 1933, the bomber advocates had convinced themselves and the War Department that a heavy bomber could be built that would be impervious to attack from intercepting pursuit aircraft. That bomber would take flight two years later as the Boeing B-17, optimistically nicknamed the "Flying Fortress."

Over the objections of a few dedicated fighter pilots like Claire Chennault, who would later gain fame as the commander of the "Flying Tigers" in China, the Air Corps went about developing plans for strategic bombing. The most zealous B-17 supporters believed that formations of their bombers could win a war alone by destroying an enemy nation's military and industrial installations. Without the capacity to wage war, they argued, an enemy nation would be forced to surrender.

As a result of this philosophy, most of the funds available to the Air Corps for developing and procuring aircraft during the late 1930s went into the bomber program. Pursuit aviation lagged, reaching its lowest point in 1937. In that year, the first line U.S. fighter and bomber aircraft were both Boeing products, the P-26 and the B-17. The P-26, as I described earlier, was an open-cockpit, wire-braced monoplane with a top speed around 230 mph and an operational ceiling of about 10,000 feet. The B-17, on the other hand, was some 75 mph faster and could operate at altitudes in excess of 25,000 feet. More modern fighters would follow slowly at the end of the decade as current design and technology were applied, but they continued to lack high-altitude capability.

The late summer of 1940 brought the Battle of Britain, which contained some valuable lessons for American military planners. The battle proved conclusively that with radar to locate incoming enemy bombers and with fighters that had sufficient performance to engage them, a nation could in fact defend itself from aerial attack. British Hurricanes and Spitfires not only caught up with German bombers but also shot them down in great numbers. This was especially true when the bombers were caught without the protection of escorting Me-109 fighters. Still, the German bombers did considerable damage, especially to the British airfields and radar stations, before Hitler called off the daylight assault and turned to night terror bombing of British cities.

Britain's Royal Air Force and the U.S. Army Air Force took

two distinctly different lessons from the Battle of Britain. British planners decided that their bombers, like the Luftwaffe's, would have to attack at night to survive in sufficient numbers to be effective. They were willing to trade bombing accuracy for the relative safety of darkness.

The American approach, on the other hand, was to add more defensive firepower to the B-17. Starting with the B-17E model, the American bomber carried ten or more .50-caliber machine guns, most in power turrets. If the bombers stayed close together and coordinated their defensive fire, enemy interceptors would be unable to penetrate their formations, the planners figured.

American military planners also learned from the Battle of Britain that the United States needed interceptor fighters that could fly faster and higher—and hit harder—than the P-40s that were just coming into service in 1940. The two most promising designs were the radical Lockheed P-38 Lightning, with its twin Allison engines, and the more conventional Republic P-47 Thunderbolt. Both aircraft were heavily armed and could fly at speeds over 400 mph while reaching altitudes well above 30,000 feet. Fortunately, neither aircraft ever had to fight in its intended role, defending the skies over the United States, but both were destined to see plenty of combat during the war.

Shortly after the Pearl Harbor attack, American President Franklin Roosevelt and British Prime Minister Winston Churchill met for the Arcadia Conference in Washington, D.C., to discuss how they intended to conduct the war against the Axis powers. It was there that the "Europe first" strategy emerged, and part of that strategy would be the employment of American strategic air power against targets on the European continent. The newly formed U.S. 8th Air Force was the unit assigned to the job.

The 8th Air Force set up shop in England in June 1942 under the command of Maj. Gen. Carl Spaatz. Its mission was to gain air superiority over Western Europe to make an invasion across the English Channel possible. As subsequent events would show, that was a pretty tall order.

It took several months to build up any significant combat forces. Initially assigned were three heavy bomb groups, one light bomb group and two fighter groups. The first B-17 missions were flown in August 1942, and by October it was beginning to look as if the American bomber advocates were right. The B-17s flew fifteen missions over France and the Low Countries in the first three months of operations, suffering only seven losses. For the most part, these missions were flown with the protection of American and RAF escort fighters, primarily Spitfires.

Operation Torch, the Allied invasion of North Africa, sapped some of the 8th's growing strength in the fall of 1942, as two heavy bomber groups and four fighter groups were transferred to the 12th Air Force. At the same time, the Luftwaffe fighter defense was gathering strength and developing more effective tactics for taking on the American bombers. And at 8th Air Force headquarters, the planners were looking beyond the present targets to their ultimate goal: striking Germany itself.

Experience had shown the need for escort fighters to help protect the bombers over enemy territory in daylight. But the Spitfires flown by the 8th's single remaining fighter group, the 4th, lacked sufficient range to stay with the bombers much beyond the French coast. A new American-made escort fighter was needed, and the only one available in sufficient numbers that had the potential for matching the performance of the Luftwaffe's Me-109s and Fw-190s was the Republic P-47 Thunderbolt. Plans were made to reequip the 4th and send two new fighter groups, the 56th and 78th, to England. All three groups were in the process of working up on their new P-47s at the time I left 315 Squadron.

I saw a P-47 in the flesh for the first time on February 27, 1943, the day I reported for duty with the 56th Fighter Group at Kings Cliffe airfield.

I had come up from London on the train that morning. An enlisted man met me at the station and drove me a short distance to the field. Kings Cliffe was a new base that still had a temporary, scratched-together look about it. A single large hangar dominated the base, and the headquarters of the 56th was located in an office at the base of the control tower.

First impressions are lasting ones, and the two things that struck me most about the 56th Fighter Group that first day were the immensity of its P-47 fighters and the obvious military bearing of the outfit. Several P-47s were parked near the tower when I got out of the car to report in at group headquarters. I walked over to take a look, and was struck immediately by their size. They looked big enough from a distance, but up close they were downright immense.

It's not much wonder I was so surprised. The Spitfires I'd been flying were the product of an entirely different design philosophy than the one that shaped the P-47. Where the Spit was built small and light to give it agility and a fast climb, the P-47 was built around the most powerful airplane engine available at the time, the Pratt & Whitney R-2800 radial, which boasted 2,000 horsepower. In addition to its large engine, the P-47 was designed to carry tremendous firepower, with eight .50-caliber machine guns mounted in its wings.

As a result, Republic Aviation made the P-47 big, with a wingspan over 40 feet and takeoff weight approaching 15,000 pounds. I had a hard time imagining how these bulbous, dark green airplanes were going to acquit themselves against the swift 109s and 190s I had encountered over France. But, of course, I hadn't flown a P-47 yet.

If I was less than impressed with the P-47, the same couldn't be said for my new outfit. From the moment I set foot inside the headquarters office, I could see that the 56th was something special. Shoes were shined, pants were pressed, and the men I met were friendly, yet correct. In the course of time I would learn that this was no accident, but rather a result of the firm leadership of one man: Col. Hubert Zemke.

The 56th was new to England, having arrived about the same time I started flying with the Poles, but it was not a new organization. The group had been formed in January 1941 at Savannah, Georgia, borrowing men from the 27th Bomb Group. Its three squadrons, the 61st, 62nd, and 63rd, were equipped with a handful of P-39s and aging P-40s.

The army's Carolina maneuvers of October 1941 brought ten new P-39s to the group, and soon thereafter the 56th moved to Myrtle Beach for aerial gunnery training. This work proved extremely valuable, since the skills learned on the gunnery range would eventually be applied with devastating effect on the Luftwaffe.

Training was intensified following the Pearl Harbor attack of December 7, 1941, and a month later the group was transferred to 1st Fighter Command, which was assigned to provide air defense for the northeastern United States. Group headquarters moved to Teaneck, New Jersey, with the squadrons at airports in New Jersey, Connecticut, and Long Island.

In June 1942, the 56th became the first group to be equipped with Republic's new P-47s, which were just starting to come off the production lines at Farmingdale, New York, on Long Island. Now, in addition to providing air defense, the 56th was given the task of working the bugs out of this new airplane. In the coming months, pilots of the 56th would put the P-47 through every conceivable test as the Thunderbolts were evaluated and modified in preparation for sending them into combat. Again, this experience would pay off for the 56th when the group commenced combat operations.

Hub Zemke, then a major, was appointed commanding officer of the 56th in September 1942. He had won his army wings back in 1937 and served in the 56th after being sent to Russia in 1941 to teach Red air force pilots how to fly lend-lease P-40s.

The 56th Fighter Group was alerted for overseas duty on Thanksgiving Day 1942, its debugging work on the P-47 complete. The group sailed from New York aboard the converted ocean liner *Queen Mary* on January 6, 1943, destination England and the 8th Air Force Fighter Command. A week later the ship arrived in Scotland, and the group made its way to King's Cliffe to begin final preparations prior to opening combat operations. The 56th was about half-finished with this training when I showed up.

I met Zemke at the officers' club shortly after I had checked in at group headquarters. He wasn't a drinker, nor much of a socializer, so how he happened to be at the club that afternoon I don't know. I walked over to introduce myself and was met with a steady gaze as he looked me over. He had a round, pleasant face, but his eyes were cool and intense. I wouldn't say he was unfriendly, but neither did I get the feeling that I was being warmly welcomed into the 56th. Acceptance was something I would have to earn in Hub Zemke's fighter group.

We had a short discussion about my experience and the capabilities of the P-47, then he told me I would begin flying tomorrow with the 61st Fighter Squadron. That was it.

I got some dinner and went to my quarters to try to get a good night's sleep. But sleep didn't come easily. After my happy experience with the Poles, this was starting out altogether differently. I thought about those big, green fighters waiting for me on the hardstand and realized I was going to have to prove myself all over again.

Early the next morning I made my way to the operations office of the 61st Fighter Squadron, there to meet my new squadron commander. Maj. Loren G. "Mac" McCollom. He was of average height, with a thin face and receding hairline. Just then he was recovering from a bout with pneumonia, so he was pretty pale.

McCollom welcomed me and said he was glad to have someone with combat experience, but he had a personnel problem. All the slots for men with the rank of captain were full, and in fact I was more senior than several of the captains he already had. One of them, Merle Eby, was the squadron operations officer. Bob Wetherbee and Don Renwick commanded A and C flights, respectively. A senior first lieutenant, Dick Allison, commanded B Flight.

It didn't take me long to see that these guys were very tight. They had served together in the squadron for a year or more and were very comfortable with each other. Now there was a new guy in their midst, and something would have to give. McCollom put off the problem for the time being by naming me assistant operations officer, though that was hardly a job at all. This arrangement would work for now, however, because the most pressing matter was getting me proficient with the P-47.

Mac told me to fly as much as I needed, and I set out immediately to do just that. I spent the best part of the morning with one of the experienced pilots—I think it was Eby— learning all I could about the P-47. He told me it was a pretty straightforward airplane, with no nasty habits, and he spent a lot of time explaining the operation of its turbosupercharger, which was new to me.

The turbo was the key to the P-47's high-altitude performance. It used the flow of the engine's exhaust to turn an impellor that compressed the air going into the engine through an intercooler, just like the turbos mounted on many high-performance cars today. The pilot had controls for the intercooler doors, and a boost control for the turbo itself on the throttle quadrant. A light on the instrument panel warned the pilot if the turbo impeller overrevved, which was important to avoid. The light came on when the engine started, and flickered as long as the turbo was operating within limits. If it began to glow steadily, the pilot knew he had to reduce rpms. This all sounded pretty complicated to me, but in fact it took only a few flights to get used to the turbo operation.

My first flight was uneventful, which came as no surprise because I was a competent, confident fighter by this time. Again I was struck by how big the plane was. I'm a normal-sized guy, but even so it was a big first step up onto the left wing root from the back of the wing. From there, hand and foot holds were provided to help the pilot make his way up into the cockpit. The cockpit had more room than any fighter I had flown, and it gave me quite a sense of power to look out and see the big, four-bladed prop in front and the four .50-caliber machine gun barrels sticking out of the front of each wing.

Taxiing the P-47 required S-turns for safety because the pilot couldn't see over the big nose that poked out in front. When the takeoff roll began, I could appreciate the wide stance of the landing gear, because torque swing was much less pronounced than on the P-40 or the Spitfire. The smooth roar of the big radial engine brought back memories of flying P-36s in Hawaii. The engine was loud, to be sure, but it didn't have the staccato bark of an in-line Allison or Rolls Royce.

Once airborne, I found the handling characteristics of the P-47 to be, well . . . nice. I immediately forgot about how big the plane was, and I noticed that it required smooth coordination of stick and rudder to keep the ball centered. The Thunderbolts assigned to the 56th at this time were P-47C models and a few early Ds, neither of which had much climb performance. They turned pretty well for their size, and they would roll with anything in the sky. But the P-47 really shined when it was headed downhill. The dive performance was truly spectacular.

I was bothered by the design of the canopy and windshield, which hampered the pilot's vision quite a bit more than the clear bubbles fitted on Spitfires. On the other hand, I really liked the cockpit heating system, which kept the pilot reasonably comfortable even at 30,000 feet, where the temperature was minus 60 degrees. The heating system also did a good job of keeping the windshield clear of frost. In a Spitfire, if you made a long dive the windshield would frost over at about 15,000 feet, leaving the pilot blind until it cleared. That didn't happen in the P-47.

My mind was full of questions when I landed the plane. The P-47 felt sluggish compared to the Spit 9, and I couldn't imagine what it was going to be like to fly combat against the agile 190s and 109s. On the plus side, I could hardly wait to get the plane out on a firing range and see what those eight .50-caliber guns could do.

Over the next few days I made it a point to get to know as many of the pilots as I could. It wasn't easy at first, because they knew each other and looked at the 61st as a team. They'd been molded back in the States. They had flown together and lived together, and now they were looking forward to going into combat together. I didn't experience any animosity exactly, but I think they took exception to somebody coming in and breaking into their fraternity. Eby probably felt it most, since he and I both were captains, and he might have thought I was going to come in and steal his thunder. That wasn't my intention at all, and within a short time they all could see that.

The pilots I met were a capable bunch, and in time they would begin to run up some impressive records. Jerry Johnson in A Flight was the first to make friends with me. He pumped me for information about flying combat against the Germans, and I quizzed him closely about the capabilities of the P-47. We got along very well from the start, and still do today. Some of the other pilots who impressed me were Bob Johnson, Paul Conger, Les Smith, Jim Carter, Don Smith, and Joe Powers—all super pilots and future aces. Bob Johnson had phenomenal eyesight, and Conger was absolutely fearless. But as far as I'm concerned, Jerry Johnson was the greatest gunner of them all, myself included.

During this time I also began to get to know some of the leadership in the other units of the 56th. The most flamboyant of these men was Maj. Dave Schilling, commander of the 62nd Fighter Squadron. He was a tall, handsome guy a few years older than I. Schilling always was cooking up some new idea or scheme, and he wasn't shy about trying them out. He also turned out to be quite a fighter pilot, as aggressive in the air as he was on the ground. The commander of the 63rd, Maj. Phil Tukey, stood in sharp contrast to Schilling. He was a quiet guy, and his squadron reflected his demeanor.

McCollom stood somewhere in between these two. Mac was older, and probably wiser, than either of them; a real steady, dependable man.

Here is how Jerry Johnson described the squadron at that time, in a letter forty-plus years later:

> We were a pretty close-knit group. We had been together for 8–10 months before Gabby arrived. He was an outsider . . . and a captain. Needless to say, there was some concern about how he would fit in and what change in the pecking order might occur.
>
> Gabby might have been a bit arrogant, also. After all, he had been at Pearl Harbor when the Japanese attacked and had some combat experience with a Polish squadron. I liked Gabby from the start and felt he was not being treated fairly by most of the squadron. We spent a lot of time together and I learned a lot about the man: his Kay, his principles, his strong religious motivation, and his moral standards.

Les Smith adds his recollections of those days:

> Gabby was treated as an outsider when he first joined the group. That was unfortunate but I think not unexpected since he had not trained with us in the States, had not shipped with us, and had no personal friendships or even acquaintances within the group.
>
> There was another unfortunate factor over which he had no control which contributed to this problem—his rank as captain. This put him in direct competition with the old captains already assigned to our squadron, and in indirect competition with our older first lieutenants, who hoped to become captains. We new second lieutenants were not

I arrived at Wheeler Field, Hawaii, in 1941, as a second lieutenant fresh out of flying school. My squadron, the 45th, was on temporary deployment at Castle and Cook's plantation on the beach at Heleiwa when this picture was taken.

Kay Cochran and I met several months after I arrived in Hawaii. By November 1941, when this picture was taken at Haleiwa, we were dating steadily. Visible in the background are some of the P-36s of the 45th Fighter Squadron.

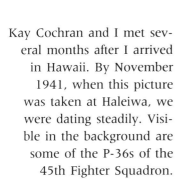

Smoke rises from the hangar area at Wheeler Field during the
Japanese attack on December 7, 1941, in this photo taken from a
Japanese plane. The grass runway lies behind the smoke, and our
quarters are on the hill beyond, where I got my first glimpse of
war. (U.S. Navy)

The best fighters we had available on Hawaii during the first months
of the war were early model P-40 Tomahawks. This P-40B was
assigned to my friend Johnny Thacker and was named for his girlfriend, Kay Ledingham. Many people who have seen pictures of
this plane over the years assumed it was assigned to me, for obvious
reasons.

After the Pearl Harbor attack, my squadron was deployed to an airstrip at Kaena Point. We lived right on the beach, and I found the area was excellent for spear fishing, even with my modest skills. Here I'm holding a small shark I speared.

Maj. Mac McCollom briefs the 61st Fighter Squadron as we pause in front of Lt. Milt Anderson's P-47C, the "Idaho Spud," shortly after I joined the squadron in March 1943. *Top row, from left,* Don Renwick, Bob Wetherbee (KIA), Norm Brooks, Dick Mudge, and Les Smith. *Bottom row,* Joe Powers, Kirby Tracy (KIA), me, Mac, and Joe Curtis. (Les Smith)

I made it a habit to pray before each mission, though I wasn't always able to go to the chapel as I did for this posed picture. Note the shine on those flying boots!

P-47s of the 61st Fighter Squadron sit on the field at Horsham St. Faith during the summer of 1943. Nearest to the camera is HV-X, which was "Poison Dick" Mudge's bird.

On duty, P-47s spew contrails as they patrol above a formation of B-17s. The spike in the center of the picture is the rudder of the B-17 from which the picture was shot. (Paul Conger)

I became an ace on November 26, 1943, when I destroyed two ME-110 twin-engine German fighters on a mission to Bremen, Germany. This might be one of them, considering that it has been hit from my favorite position, dead astern at close range. (Paul Conger)

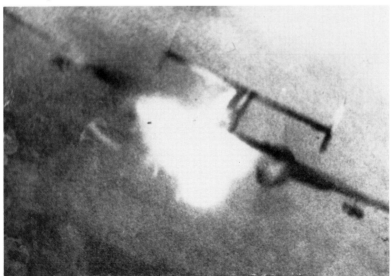

One of the many fine replacement pilots we got in the 61st was Lt. Frank Klibbe, shown here using the classic fighter pilot's hand language to describe the day's combat to me, Eugene Barnum, and Justus Foster.

I had a close call on December 1, 1943, when the rear gunner in an Me-110 hit my P-47. Luckily, the damage was minor and I was able to return to Halesworth. Here, I show our flight surgeon, Doc Hornig, a German slug the mechanics dug out from between the cylinders of my engine.

Pilots relax with coffee and sandwiches distributed by Doc Hornig after a tough mission in late 1943. *Sitting from left,* Paul Conger, me, Eugene Barnum, Bill Marangello (KIA), Dave Shilling, and Norm Brooks.

My ground crew poses with me in front of my last P-47, probably in July 1944, *From left,* Ralph Safford, crew chief; Felix Schacki, assistant crew chief; Joe DiFranza, armorer; and me. (Mrs. Joe DiFranza)

I flew this P-47 longer than any other, from December 1943 to May 1944, scoring 10 kills and three damaged. It was a D-11 model, serial 42-75510, with a red nose band and rudder. Note the highly polished finish. (Carl Westman)

This was my last and favorite P-47, the first bubbletop D-25 model assigned to our squadron, serial 42-26418. Its markings included 28 kill flags and black-and-white invasion stripes on the undersurfaces. I crash-landed this plane in Germany on my final mission of World War II. (Mrs. Joe DiFranza)

Col. Hub Zemke, *left,* welcomes the brass to Halesworth on March 14, 1944. Visitors included Lt. Gen. Carl Spaatz, *center,* and Maj. Gens. Jimmy Doolittle (behind Spaatz) and William Kepner (back to camera). Also visible behind Doolittle is Maj. Jimmy Stewart. (Paul Conger)

really involved in this rivalry, but we held the older pilots in great esteem and if they didn't like the new stranger, we weren't going to be too friendly either.

We eventually recognized Gabby's superior ability as a pilot and his very aggressive fighting spirit and we respected him for them.

In one way, the pilots of the 56th were just like fighter pilots everywhere. They loved to talk about flying more than anything, except possibly sex. A constant topic during those early days was combat formations. All of us had been trained out of the prewar combat manual, which stressed arranging flights in string, or line-astern. Most were aware, however, that the Luftwaffe, and later the RAF, were now flying line-abreast in flights of four, as I had done with the Poles. The argument came down to maneuverability on the string side versus firepower and mutual support on the other. My experience made me a firm believer in the latter, and I didn't hesitate to expound on my feelings. In time my arguments must have made an impression, because by the time we began combat operations, the 56th was using line-abreast, which became known as the finger-four formation, exclusively.

I flew as much as the weather would allow during our stay at Kings Cliffe, and on March 11 McCollom gave me a new job. I was assigned commander of B Flight, and Dick Allison moved down a notch to element leader. About that time, the squadron was sent to Llanbedr on the coast of Wales for gunnery practice. This was what I'd been waiting for, but it turned out to be a disappointment. The weather was miserable, and I was able to make only a few flights during our two weeks there. First it was foggy. Then it was just murky weather. We even had snow flurries periodically.

When we could get airborne, we practiced our marksmanship by firing at sleeves towed behind an RAF Lysander cooperation plane. I found out what I had expected: Those eight .50s would really tear up a target if you hit it.

Around the first of April we got the word that 8th Air Force Fighter Commander was satisfied that its three fighter groups—the 4th, the 78th, and us—were ready to take their P-47s into combat. The last order of business before that could happen was to move the 56th to an airfield closer to the coast. The reason was simple. The P-47 had marginally better range than the Spitfire, but it still couldn't go as far as a B-17. The less friendly territory we had to fly over to get at the enemy, the more time we would be able to spend with the bombers.

The new base was Horsham St. Faith at Norwich, 100 miles northeast of London. We flew our P-47s there on April 5 hands were pleasantly surprised by what we found there. It was a sod field, but it had permanent hangars and comfortable brick barracks. We settled in quickly and continued flying as much as possible.

My goal as flight commander was to build a team. Nine pilots made up the flight, and four of them would fly at a time on combat missions. I was fortunate to have Bob Johnson, Paul Conger, Jim Carter, and Joe Powers in B Flight, along with Dick Allison, Kirby Tracy, and Justus Foster, and Louis Barron.

All of our flying was done with teamwork in mind, and that wasn't just putting a leader up front and having him say, "I'll lead and you follow." The pilots had to have confidence in their leader, and the only way to build that confidence was by flying together. They had to see my abilities, and I had to see theirs.

Jim Carter recalls one of our more exciting training flights from about that time:

Shortly after Gabby took over B Flight, he took a four-ship flight up to see how well we could hold position. He insisted on a really close formation and that we maintain the same plane as his aircraft whether straight and level or in a vertical bank. Before Gabby joined us, we stayed in the same plane as the leader's longitudinal axis regardless of his degree of bank, which is considerably easier for wing-men to maintain position (i.e., in level turns the wingmen banked in position and stayed on the horizontal plane, not the plane of the leader's aircraft's wings).

On this particular day, Paul Conger was flying Number Two on Gabby's left wing and I was Number Three on his right with Bob Johnson Number Four on my right. We had been above the clouds, and on our descent at a steep angle of dive and left bank of a near vertical plane, we broke [from under the clouds] and headed directly into some barrage balloons. Gabby instantly reversed from the near vertical left bank to a near vertical right bank in order to avoid the balloons. My position changed instantly from high outside to low inside of the formation and from near full throttle to instant off. I was barely able to hold my position. My only thoughts were that it would be totally impossible for Bob to hold his even higher and then lower positions on my wing, and I fully expected to see him slice through me. I dared not look away from Gabby to see when it was coming and with the ground approaching rapidly I did not believe I had room to duck under Gabby.

It seemed like forever before we were clear of those balloons. Finally we straightened out and I could sneak a glance at Bob who, I was surprised to see, was right where he should have been. He later told me he had to fishtail and cross-control with all his might to keep from crashing into me and just managed to stay in position. I believe Bob's civilian flying experience in light aircraft, where he practiced side-slip landings, is what averted the collision. I think this incident also gave Gabby confidence in those he was leading.

On April 8, 1943, Zemke and Schilling went with two flight commanders from the 62nd on a practice mission with pilots form the 4th and 78th groups. They flew down to St. Omer, France, and came back. Mostly, they were just getting the lay of the land in preparation for the group's first actual mission. Everyone knew it was coming soon, and we all hoped we would be chosen to fly it.

The big day finally came on April 13, and I was disappointed but not surprised to see that my name wasn't on the board to fly. Each squadron of the 56th would send just one flight. McCollom and Eby, naturally enough, would go from the 61st. Their second element consisted of Don Renwick, A Flight commander, and Les Smith from his flight. Again, the three groups would fly together to St. Omer. They went into France over Le Tourquet at 31,000 feet, swept eastward to St. Omer, then continued north back across the Channel toward home. They saw no German fighters and just a little flak. Capt. Roger Dyer's engine died on the way out over Dunkirk, but they were still high enough that the 63rd Squadron pilot was able to glide across the Channel and make a forced landing in a field about five miles inland from the English coast.

Again, Les Smith recalls:

The first combat mission the 56th flew occurred on April 13, 1943. Each squadron put up four planes each to form one squadron of twelve ships. The four pilots on that first mission from the 61st were Major McCollom, Captains Eby and Renwick, and I was assigned to fly tail-end charlie. We were told to fly the traditional RAF javelin formation in which B Flight and C Flight each flew in rather close proximity to, and in on opposite sides of, A Flight, which was led by the squadron leader. Each flight of four ships flew in-trail and stepped down so that we formed a box-like formation, which was unmaneuverable and quite uncomfortable.

Even before we landed from that first uneventful sweep over the coast of continental Europe, we knew we didn't want to fly that formation again, regardless of what the RAF might recommend. We immediately went into a study session with all the pilots of the 61st to talk about alternative formations. I don't remember who suggested the spread, fingertip formation—it may very well have been Gabby—but I do know it wasn't given to us as a finished product. We diagramed many different ways to fly it and went into the air to try out the different suggestions. It took several weeks to arrive at a consensus as to how it should be flown, and even then the flights within the 61st each had a little different version.

A similar mission went to St. Omer on the fifteenth and again I wasn't assigned. Two days later I flew my first mission with the 56th, a rodeo to Knocke and Blankenberge on the Belgian coast. It went just like the others had, with no opposition except for a little flak. Nevertheless, the guys from my flight were pretty excited just to have gone. I was more matter-of-fact about it, though I'll have to admit I had butterflies in my stomach until we got over enemy territory. After all, we were going up against the best in the business, and some of those German pilots had been in combat since 1939. On top of that, we were taking a new plane against their 109s and 190s. I already knew how good they were, but I wasn't sure about the P-47 yet. Then once we crossed the coastline I was too busy searching the sky to have time to worry. That's the way it is on operations: Fear lasts only as long as the anticipation, and then your training takes over. You do what you have to do: Destroy him before he destroys you. It just happened that no one destroyed anyone else that day.

On the way back I had time to think about the mission. I knew our pilots, myself included, were very green, so I wasn't too disappointed that we hadn't met up with any German fighters. On the other hand, we would have to start fighting sometime, and the sooner we started the sooner we could get good at it. I did feel pleased that my flight had held together well and that our P-47s hadn't given us any trouble, since the engines were still having some teething problems at this time.

During the following week I got a couple of surprises. First, McCollom named me squadron operations officer and assigned Eby to take my place as B Flight commander. As operations officer, my job was to help run the squadron, mostly by preparing mission plans and overseeing training.

Then on the twenty-fourth I got word that the Poles had given me a medal for the flying I had done with them. Gen. Wladyslaw Sikorski, Polish prime minister in exile, presented me with the Polish Cross of Valor. It was a little embarrassing, because the Poles in 315 Squadron had cooked up an exaggerated description of our February 3 mission, and the award was based on that. Finally, at the end of the month, I got the first American combat award presented to a 56th Fighter Group pilot, an Air Medal "for the completion of operational sorties over enemy territory."

On April 29, the 56th got into its first fight with German fighters, and again I wasn't involved. Mac was leading the 61st as top cover for the 62nd and 63rd on another rodeo to Blankenbergè and the Hague when about twenty German fighters attacked the lower squadrons head-on. The Germans broke up and away, but Schilling's radio was out so he couldn't call the 61st down to help. Two pilots of the 62nd went down, and we learned later that both had been captured. It wasn't much of a fight, but at least the 56th could say that it had seen combat. Now we were ready to start our real job, escorting the B-17s of 8th Air Force Bomber Command.

The 56th flew its first ramrod mission on May 4, escorting fifty-four B-17s to Antwerp, where their target was a Ford factory. This was a more complicated process than one might think. First, the B-17s and P-47s were based all over southern England, so a route had to be plotted in such a way that they all could rendezvous at some point. Second, our P-47s didn't carry enough gas at that time to stay with the B-17s all the way across the Channel to Antwerp and back. Finally, the cruising speeds of the bombers and of their escorting fighters were vastly different. On top of that were the problems that plagued every mission: weather, mechanical failures, and a host of others.

On the May 4 mission, RAF Spitfires would provide escort going in to the limit of their endurance, and then the bombers would proceed unescorted on the last leg to the target. Thunderbolts from the 4th and 56th groups weren't scheduled to meet the B-17s until after they had completed their bombing runs and were on their way home. Mac again led our squadron, and I wasn't scheduled to fly. Neither group made any claims, but Lt. Bud Mahurin, who turned out to be the hottest pilot by far in the 63rd, picked up a 20-mm hit in his tail section when he overshot a German fighter while making a diving attack on it.

I scheduled myself to fly as many missions as possible, but action continued to elude me. On the fourteenth our squadron recorded its first claims during another ramrod to Antwerp. Colonel Zemke was flying with the 61st, leading the group, and they encountered 190s just as they were breaking escort to head home. In the scrap that followed Jerry Johnson and Milt Anderson of our squadron and Zemke received credit for one German fighter damaged each, while Al Bailes of the 61st probably destroyed a 190. It was a good showing, and I was pleased by their success, but a little jealous, too. That didn't last long.

The following day's mission was a rodeo to Zanvoort, Holland, and I was assigned to lead a flight that also included Dick Mudge, Robill Roberts, and Les Smith. During this time we were flying mostly twelve-plane squadron formations, in three flights of four. We made landfall at 0930, flying at 30,000 feet. It wasn't long before I could see formations of enemy fighters in several places off in the distance. Off to my left at 9 o'clock I spotted twelve FW-190s about 6,000 feet below us flying in the opposite direction. My flight was in good position to make the bounce, so I led them in a left turn to put the sun behind us and then pushed over into a dive. My speed built up rapidly, and my heart began to pound like crazy.

Just as I was getting into position behind the leader of the 190s, he must have seen me. He rolled over and dropped away in a dive as I fired a short burst at the empty sky where he had been just a split second before. I turned my attention to the Number Two man with the same result, and then I lined up on Number Three. This guy was a little slower off the mark. I pulled to within 400 yards and opened fire just before he began his roll to dive away. Hits flashed on his fuselage about halfway back from the cockpit to the tail, and then he, too, was gone. Mudge also got off a snap shot at one of them.

I checked my altitude and position. It wasn't wise to stay down low with a flight of four and lots of Germans in the sky above, so I decided to break off the attack and climb back up to 30,000 for the trip home. It was several minutes before my heartbeat returned to normal.

It felt great to have something to report to our intelligence officer, Capt. Charles Howard, during the debriefing when we got home. The mission debriefing was a ritual I would go through many times in the future, but only a couple of them—after my first confirmed kill and my last—were any more enjoyable than this. I could claim only one enemy aircraft damaged this day, but it was the proof of the pudding for me, a sure indication that my efforts to fly with the Poles had not been wasted. Now I was a complete fighter pilot and a proven commodity in the eyes of my fellow pilots in the 56th.

More important, I felt confident in myself. I had flown the mission, led the bounce, and hit the target (if only a glancing blow). No buck fever, and I knew I could see the air battle around me now. I looked forward to my next encounter with the enemy.

Unfortunately, that next encounter was still a long time off. I led the full squadron for the first time on May 17, taking fourteen P-47s on a sweep to Morlaix, France. We had the sky all to ourselves, as we would whenever I flew for the next month or more.

On the morning of June 9 I was summoned to Zemke's office at group headquarters. I couldn't think of any trouble I had caused lately, so I wasn't concerned about the reason for the meeting, just curious. I was in for a shock.

No sooner had I presented myself with a snappy salute than Zemke invited me to take a seat. I wouldn't say he was exactly buddy-buddy, but he was more cordial than normal. Then he launched into the explanation for my visit.

The press of operations on fighter group commanders had turned out to be greater than the prewar planners had anticipated, he said. After analyzing our first two months of operations, Fighter Command had decided that its group commanders needed help. A new position of flying executive officer, more accurately described as a deputy group commander, had been created, and Loren McCollom had been given the job in the 56th. That sounded fine to me, since I had grown quite fond of Mac in our few months together. It didn't occur to me at first that the vacancy caused by his promotion was the reason for my visit.

The 61st Fighter Squadron was now in need of a new commanding officer, Zemke said, and he and Mac had decided I was the man for the job. Was I interested?

I was dumbstruck. Of course I was interested in the job, and I told him so with as much military bearing as I could muster, which probably wasn't much. Zemke said he'd have the appropriate orders cut, along with orders promoting me to the rank of major.

Think of it! A year ago I'd been a carefree second lieutenant camping out on a beach in Hawaii while I tried to learn how to fly fighter planes. Now I was to command my own squadron of P-47s, going up against the toughest opponents on the face of the earth.

CHAPTER Six

MY MIND was in a spin as McCollom and I walked back across the field from Zemke's office to the squadron headquarters. It was a lovely June morning, and the green runway seemed to sparkle as the sunlight flashed on the dewy grass.

"Okay, Mac," I said. "What have I gotten myself into here?"

McCollom, so wise and understanding for such a young man, gave me a pep talk that would help me immensely in the difficult months to come. He knew that my leadership experience was extremely limited, but he told me not to worry about that. Lead by example, he said. If the men know their squadron commander is going at it full bore, they'll do everything they can to try to keep up.

He also told me that I wouldn't have to sweat the details of running the squadron, because we had an excellent crew of support officers to do that. The key man was Capt. Ralph Eastwood, who had just taken over as executive officer the previous week after having served as adjutant since the squadron was in the States.

As executive, stern-faced Ralph actually ran the squadron. He handled all the paperwork, disciplinary actions, promotions, and a host of other things. All I had to do as squadron commander was listen to his suggestions and, in nearly every case, sign off on them. Ralph was quite a bit older than any of us pilots, and I leaned on him heavily for advice and support in the months that followed. He never let me down.

If Ralph Eastwood was a father figure, then Capt. George "Doc" Hornig, the squadron's flight surgeon, was like our favorite uncle. He had the keys to the cabinet that held our medicinal booze supply, which he parceled in two-ounce shots to pilots after each mission. But Doc would have been just as popular without the booze. He looked after the pilots like a mother hen, and the advice he gave us went far beyond medical matters.

I also had excellent officers in charge of engineering, armament, intelligence, and communications. But I needed an operations officer, since my promotion had left that slot open. Mac and I talked it over briefly and decided that Merle Eby was the natural choice. In fact, Mac told me that he and Zemke had considered appointing Eby squadron commander before deciding that my combat experience made me the better choice.

Merle had been bounced around quite a bit in the squadron since my arrival. First he had been operations officer, then he and I traded places and he took over B Flight. When Bob Wetherbee transferred to group headquarters in early May, Eby had taken his place as A Flight commander while Dick Allison took B Flight. Now Eby would move back to the job he had held before all this started. If Merle was bothered by all this, he never let on to me.

My flight commanders were all top-notch. Dick Allison had been killed in a flying accident on June 6, and Jerry Johnson took his place as B Flight commander. Everyone was saddened to lose Dick, with the possible exception of Doc Hornig. Dick was a wild character who liked to fire his .45 in the barracks, and Doc was sure that sooner or later he was going to have to patch someone up after one of Dick's shooting sprees.

I couldn't have asked for a better man than Jerry Johnson for a flight commander. His handsome, boyish face belied the fact that he had the heart of a tiger. He was a hunter through and through, with the brains to match his skills as a pilot and aerial marksman. Soon he would become the squadron's first ace.

Moving up to command A Flight after Eby was Bob Lamb. Bob, like Jerry, was a first lieutenant at the time. He was another fine pilot and future ace.

The only carryover from before my days with the 61st was Capt. Don Renwick, commander of C Flight. Don was an extremely capable pilot, very steady. He never ran up a big score of victories, but he probably had more natural leadership ability than any of us. He flew into the fall of 1943 with the 56th and then was transferred into a training outfit to put his combat experience and teaching skills to good work. By the end of the war he had moved back to the 56th, but this time he got the top job as group commander.

I'm sure there were some mixed emotions in the squadron about my selection over Eby to be the new commander, but that wasn't the case among the three men who took care of my airplane. They were clearly delighted. Staff Sgt. Ralph Safford was crew chief, and Sgt. Felix Schacki was his assistant; Cpl. Joe DiFranza was the armorer. I spent quite a bit of time down on the flight line when I wasn't flying, and I had absolute confidence in my crew.

The ground crews had a tough job. They had to keep the

P-47s in top flying condition. This meant working late into the night to make sure that everything was ready for the following day's mission. They were really the key to the performance of the airplane because of the pride they put into their work. This means they were out there polishing the airplane so I could get a little bit more speed out of it, that little advantage over the enemy. They would wipe it down and make sure the engine was running as smooth as a sewing machine. For DiFranza, it meant making sure the guns had excess oil removed from them, but had enough to lubricate them so they wouldn't freeze up at high altitude. The P-47 was a complicated machine, but they never missed the smallest detail.

In all, I had six different P-47s assigned to me during the fifteen months I flew in the 61st squadron. All were D models, and all but one carried the squadron code letters HV-A, but that's where the similarities end. Republic made continual improvements to the Thunderbolt throughout its production run, and each change brought a new subdesignation. My P-47s were a D-1 (serial number 42-7871), D-5 (42-8458, HV-F), D-6 (42-74650), D-11 (42-75510), D-22 (42-25864), and D-25 (42-26418). I flew the D-11 the longest, from December 1943 through May 1944, but I liked the last one the best. The D-25 was the only one I flew that was fitted with the bubble canopy, which was a great improvement for visibility.

By June of 1943, most of the pilots had thought up names for their planes and had them painted on the cowling or upper fuselage. I never had any interest in doing that, though I didn't have any objections to the other guys doing it. As far as doctoring up the plane, all I was interested in was having it shined up for a little more speed. But a name on the side of an airplane of my schoolteacher or my sweetheart at that time, while we were at war, just didn't fit in my territory.

My planes just carried the standard camouflage and unit markings, which changed quite a bit over the months, and a few touches that the ground crew added. Schacki was the one most interested in decorating the planes. Once I started to shoot down some planes, he would paint little swastikas on the fuselage for each one. There for a while they were adding up so fast that he couldn't keep up, so he had some decals made in London that he could just glue on and lacquer over quickly. Of course, whenever I got a new airplane he would have to start over. I didn't mind him sticking them on the planes, but it was sort of a pain to have to be careful not to scratch them up when I climbed in and out of the cockpit.

A few years ago I was at an air show in the Midwest when a fellow about my age walked up.

"Hi, Gabby," he said. "Remember me?"

I looked at him closely but didn't have the slightest idea who it was.

"It's me, Shacki!" he said.

As soon as he said that I recognized him instantly, as if he'd taken off a mask. We had a great talk over lunch; turns out he still has one of those damned decals.

McCollom had urged me to lead by example, and that's exactly what I set out to do. The 61st flew fourteen missions during June, and I went on all of them. Most of the time I led the squadron, which required a bit more skill and planning than I was accustomed to as a flight leader. I had to keep in mind that I was leading twelve planes (later increased to sixteen), and that they take up a pretty good piece of sky when they're spread out in battle formation. I had to make gentle turns and anticipate giving everyone enough time so they could hold position. Otherwise, it gets to be like crack the whip for the guys who were flying on the outside of the formation.

Squadron formation lasted only until we sighted the enemy and commenced combat. Then it was throttles to the wall, and the squadron broke up into individual flights, which often split down to pairs. I, and probably every fighter squadron commander in the 8th Air Force, harped on the pilots constantly to stay in pairs so the wingman could protect his element leader and vice versa. A fighter plane alone in enemy skies is a sitting duck. That was true in World War I, and it's still true today.

Zemke was leading the group while flying with my B Flight on June 13 when the 61st scored its first confirmed kill. Fittingly enough, the victory went to eagle-eyed Bob Johnson, who was the group's leading ace with twenty-seven kills when he completed his tour eleven months later. In making his first score, however, Bob incurred the wrath of not only me but also Zemke. Bob was flying Number Four in my flight that day on Paul Conger's wing when he sighted a 109 below us. He called in the bogey and immediately pushed over to go after it. Unfortunately, he did it so fast that no one could follow him, so he made the attack alone.

I couldn't stay mad at Bob, because my policy about air fighting was a little different than that of many squadron commanders. In lots of outfits it was strict policy that the flight and element leaders did the shooting and the wingmen protected their tails. I told my guys that once they were really working as a team, it didn't make any difference who led and who followed. If my wingman called in an enemy aircraft and I couldn't spot it immediately, I'd tell him to lead the attack. Now I'm the wingman and he's the gunner. Time was the most important element, and the few seconds it might take me to pick up the target could cost us the tactical advantage that made the difference between making the kill and *getting* killed.

I was certain that's what Bob had in mind when he broke away, but the fact was he went down alone, and Zemke didn't like it one bit. He gave Bob a pretty good chewing out when we got home. But typical of Zemke, once he'd said what he had to say, that was the end of it. No grudges. The colonel was a good judge of talent, and he knew Bob Johnson would be more valuable in the cockpit of a P-47 than in the doghouse.

In reflecting back on those first missions, Bob takes a slightly different view in a letter written in 1989:

> Basically, we had to learn combat as we went into it. One great advantage that we had was that we didn't know how great those German pilots were, and we did things that no disciplined group would ever do and that the enemy would not expect. Fortunately, it worked out in our favor. As time went on we learned how to use our weapons and could teach others to do likewise.

We flew five more missions in the next two weeks, and we learned a little more every time we went out. The doctrine of the day from Fighter Command was "stay with the bombers," and we were getting pretty good at it. By this period of the war the Germans had built up their fighter defenses in western Europe quite a bit. When they caught our B-17s and B-24s without fighter cover they could chew the bombers up and spit them out. So our orders were to stay close and block for the Big Friends. Don't let the German fighters get at the bombers. That meant maintaining your altitude even if it meant giving up a kill. It was better to chase the 109s or

190s away and return to the bombers than to follow the
Jerries down for the kill and leave the bombers unprotected,
in case some more German fighters might be lurking nearby.

That strategy made sense, but it also was frustrating for
us fighter pilots. Under those orders we were always on the
defensive, turning into an attack rather than hunting down
the Jerry fighters and making them respond to our initiative.
Under the circumstances, I think we ran up a pretty good
score. A couple of months later, when the 8th Air Force had
enough fighters to assign some to close escort and give others
free rein to hunt, the victories really started to pile up.

But for now our orders were to stay above 18,000 feet and
stick close to the bombers. The 61st was still in sort of a grace
period, since we hadn't lost any pilots in combat yet, but that
ended with a vengeance on June 26.

Our mission for the day was to provide withdrawal escort
for one hundred bombers that had attacked a factory in Paris.
It was one of the first missions in which we stopped at an
advance base in southern England to gas up before we headed
across the Channel. This meant crossing the Thames estuary
at low level, which was no problem this day but would get
dicey when the fog clung to the water.

McCollom led the group south from the RAF base at Manston into France, and we rendezvoused with the bombers near
Forges at nearly seven o'clock in the evening. Immediately
we were in the thick of the action, as flights of 109s and
190s were darting here and there, trying to get a shot at the
bombers.

Jerry Johnson was able to get behind one of them and blast
it for his first victory, but that was the only one we got.
On the other side of the ledger, we lost Merle Eby and
Louis Barron from our squadron, and Bob Wetherbee, who
had just recently transferred to group operations. Eby was

leading blue flight with Don Smith as his wingman. Smith said the flight broke up when Eby dived to avoid another formation of P-47s approaching head-on, and he never saw Eby again.

These losses were a particularly bitter pill for the squadron, since all three of the men who had gone down were well liked, and we knew that Eby and Wetherbee had married shortly before coming overseas. We hoped to get word that they had gotten down safely and been captured, but it never came. All three had been killed. We lost lots of other guys in the future, but the first losses hurt the most.

Bob Johnson also was shot up badly on the June 26 mission. He described that experience in his book, *Thunderbolt!*, far more vividly than I ever could. Justus Foster of our squadron also came home with a huge hole ripped in one wing, and Ralph Johnson of the 62nd had to bail out over the Channel and come home in a boat. It was a day to remember . . . and to inspire revenge.

The other lesson we learned from that mission was that the P-47 was one tough piece of machinery. I took a close look at Bob's Thunderbolt before they towed it away to the salvage yard, and its fuselage was shredded behind the cockpit. By all rights, the plane should have broken in two at that point. Instead it brought Bob home. Foster's airplane was even more amazing. It had absorbed five 20-mm cannon hits in the right wing, and the flap on that side was literally shot away. Yet the wing had retained enough lift to continue flying.

Early in July the 56th Fighter Group made another move. Our new base was at Halesworth, about forty miles down the coast from Horsham. The only thing we could see that was better about our new base was the fact that it was a little closer to the enemy. Otherwise, it was a mess.

Halesworth was virtually indistinguishable from scores of temporary air bases built in England during the war. After the comforts of permanent buildings at Horsham, now we were moving back into Nissen huts. They looked like over-sized pieces of corrugated drain pipe cut in half and sealed off at the ends. The buildings were spread widely around Halesworth's macadam runway, protection against air attacks that never came. In dry weather Halesworth was a dust bowl; when it rained, the base became a mud hole.

In time, we were able to make improvements at Hales-worth. Schilling even took over an abandoned farmhouse nearby for his squadron, and they fixed it up for living quarters. One thing we couldn't change at Halesworth was the width of the runway. The paved surface was only wide enough to take off two planes at a time, so it took us a little longer to form up for missions than it had at Horsham, where you could take off four or even eight P-47s line-abreast on the grass.

About this time I got word that a buddy of mine from back in Hawaii, Everett Stewart, had just arrived in England with one of the new P-47 outfits that started to show up during the summer of 1943. His group, the 355th, was stationed at Steeple Morden just north of London, and I made arrangements to fly over for a visit in a little liason plane we had at Halesworth.

The plane was an L-4, which was a military version of the Piper Cub. It had two seats in tandem and a little 65-horse-power motor that you started by hand-cranking the propeller. Ralph Eastwood volunteered to go along with me, since he liked to fly and rarely got the chance. It was a murky day, but we didn't need much visibility because Steeple Morden wasn't that far away and the L-4 wouldn't fly very high any-way. Everett and I had a nice visit, and he brought me up to date on his wife and his sister-in-law, whom I had known in Hawaii.

By the time Ralph and I were ready to leave it was starting to get dark and looked as if it was about to rain. I was in a hurry to get home, and that caused me to make a dumb mistake.

I told Ralph to sit in the front seat of the L-4 so he could turn the switch on and crack the throttle when I spun the prop to start the engine. I went out in front of the plane and grabbed the prop, which was moist. I started to pull it through, but when it got to a certain point the engine back-fired and the prop kicked back around and smacked my right hand.

The back edge of that prop caught me right at the base of my little finger and just about took it off clean. I looked down in pain and horror to see just a piece of skin and a tendon holding it on. Almost immediately the bloody finger turned from pink to purple to black.

Ralph leaped out of the plane when he saw the blood fly. He raced over to the operations office, where he procured a car to take me to the nearest hospital. Luckily for me, Diss Hospital was only a few miles away. Diss was an American field hospital set up in a big English manor house, and it had a full complement of doctors and nurses, many from New York.

My hand was throbbing something awful and I had blood all over my uniform when they took me in. A handsome young surgeon, Captain Donaldson, took a look at my black-ened finger and shook his head. He wasn't sure whether he could save it, but he said he would try. One thing he knew for sure was that I would never be able to move it normally again, so he suggested setting it in a slightly curved position so it wouldn't stick out and get in my way. I agreed readily.

Donaldson put my finger back together and slapped a cast on my hand and arm. The curved setting turned out to be the best possible decision, because I can only move it back and forth at the knuckle joint, with no other movement. Yet no one ever notices it.

They kept me at Diss for about a week, just to keep an eye on me, I think. I was free to come and go during the days, but I was still in quite a bit of discomfort, so I didn't do much except get acquainted with the hospital staff. Everyone was very nice, and I was very well treated. I suspect that hospital got quite a bit busier in the months that followed, especially after the invasion, but it was quiet and relaxed during my stay.

I was anything but quiet and relaxed when I returned to the squadron at Halesworth. More like a tiger in a cage. Day after day I had to watch the guys take off for missions without me, and then I had to sweat out their return. Capt. Don Renwick had taken over as temporary commander of the 61st during my absence and was doing a fine job. I had given Don the job of operations officer when Eby went down, with Les Smith taking over command of C Flight.

The group flew nineteen missions during July, but the Luftwaffe kept very quiet until the last few days of the month. Finally the 61st got into a big scrap on July 30 while escorting B-17s back from a mission to Kassel, Germany. Our pilots got credit for four victories, including two by a new pilot who had just joined us, Capt. Leroy Schreiber. Unfortunately, we also lost one pilot, and the 62nd another. Our loss was Lt. Jack Horton, who was one of the first replacement pilots we got and had been flying with the squadron only about two months.

The summer of 1943 was a period of much experimentation in the 8th Air Force. One of the most critical needs was to extend the range of our escort fighters. The technical types at Fighter Command worked hard on the problem, attempting to come up with an externally mounted fuel tank that pilots could jettison if combat was joined.

The first tanks were monsters, big 200-gallon bubbles that fit flush under the belly of the P-47. They had been designed strictly for ferry use, which calls for smooth flying, so they contained no baffles to keep the fuel from sloshing around inside. Once fitted with a ferry tank, the P-47 took on the appearance of a bull frog in midcroak. They were abandoned after a few tries because not only did they make the airplanes unstable but they also failed to feed fuel above altitudes of 20,000 feet because they weren't pressurized.

The next drop tank was a 75-gallon teardop model, a big improvement. These gave the P-47 an extra half-hour's endurance, were pressurized for high-altitude operations, and would drop cleanly most of the time. In time, the belly tanks increased in capacity to 108 and then 150 gallons. Some were even made of heavy paper, due to the shortage of aluminum, and they worked surprisingly well. I was ready to start flying again in mid-August, about the time we began using the 75-gallon tanks.

Before I flew any missions, however, I had a promise to keep. I had told some of the friends I made at Diss Hospital that the first thing I wanted to do when I started flying again was buzz the hospital and give them a present. On August 16 Sergeant Safford strapped me into my HV-A Thunderbolt and wished me luck as I prepared to taxi out for my first practice flight since coming back from the hospital. In my lap I carried a big can of Spam that the mess sergeant had given me. Spam was processed meat and very popular in England, where fresh meat was practically impossible to get.

I took the P-47 to treetop height as I came over the hospital, then pulled her up in a climbing turn to bleed off the airspeed and cranked the canopy open. Then I came back over the hospital a little higher, dipped a wing, and dumped the Spam can overboard. It landed in a field next to the hospital, and I watched to make sure someone ran out to retrieve it. Then I climbed on up to higher altitude and tried a few stunts. The rust melted away quickly with a couple of maneuvers, and I knew I was ready to resume operations, even though my finger was still pretty sore. Someone from the hospital called me that evening to thank me for the Spam and the show. And the next time I went back there to give Captain Donaldson a look at my finger I got a hero's welcome from the hospital staff.

My first mission back leading the squadron took place on August 17. It was a big disapointment for me, as I had problems with my belly tank and returned home early. We met the bombers coming out near Antwerp at 22,000 feet. They were under attack from German fighters, including the first Me-110 twin-engine jobs I had seen. I led the flight down for a quick bounce on two 109s I saw coming behind us, but then I glanced at the fuel gauge and knew I had to break off or I'd never have enough gas to get home. The guys who could stay and fight did well, destroying five Germans for no loss. As it turned out, however, this was one of the worst days in the history of the 8th Air Force. No fewer than sixty bombers went down that day, which was known thereafter as Black Thursday.

We were back on withdrawal support two days later for B-17s that had attacked a Luftwaffe airbase in Holland. We had a long climb out because of the distance of the target, but finally we caught up with the bombers. As leader of the 61st, I was Keyworth (code name for the 61st) White (each of the four flights had a color name) One, my regular call sign until the squadron code changed in 1944. Our red, blue, and yellow flights all got into scraps as we joined up with the bombers, but no enemy fighters came near my flight, so we held our protective position above the bombers until they cleared the hostile area, then turned for home. Again it had been a good day for the 61st, with another five kills for the cost of just one P-47, Lt. Gene Barnum's, damaged.

We said good-bye to Mac McCollom on August 21. He was transferred to one of the new P-47 groups, the 353rd, to take the place of its group commander, who had been shot down on one of his first missions. Schilling moved into Mac's old spot as deputy group commander, and Capt. Horace "Pappy" Craig took command of the 62nd squadron. Leroy Schreiber left our squadron to become Pappy's operations officer.

By then I was beginning to despair that I would never shoot down a German plane, since we had been meeting up with them nearly every day and I kept coming home empty-handed. But the day I had been waiting for since that tragic Sunday morning at Pearl Harbor finally arrived on August 24, 1943, when I scored my first confirmed victory.

My HV-A was running smoothly as we made landfall near Le Treport and continued south. At 1740 we rendezvoused with the bombers at Evreaux as they made their way toward the target, a railroad marshaling yard. Our squadron flew on the right side of the bomber formation at about 27,000 feet.

My ears were filled with the shrill wail that let us know the Germans were trying to jam our radios. It was very annoying, but there wasn't anything we could do about it, so I just lived with it. We were still able to hear each other over the racket when we used the radios, so the jamming didn't really hamper us in any way.

After a few minutes on station I spotted seven Fw-190s at 10,000 feet below us trying to get into position for a head-on attack at the bombers. This was it! I was in perfect position for the bounce, and all I had to do was execute it correctly. I glanced quickly at my wingman, Lt. Frank McCauley, and then pushed over into a dive. My speed built up rapidly as the big P-47 dropped out of the sky. I turned left, then right, and closed up behind the 190s in a rush.

I opened fire on the leader of a flight of four and could see immediately that I was hitting him hard. Pieces started flying off his fuselage and wings, and a puff of smoke burst from his fuselage. I kept firing until I had closed in to about 250 to 300 yards, just like Tadensc Andersz had advised me to do, and then I broke off to avoid running into the 190. He dropped a wing and then nosed over and dived into the ground. I saw no parachute, so I assume the pilot was killed, probably by my gunfire.

I was still moving at well over 400 mph, so I used my speed to climb back up toward the bombers. McCauley had fallen behind me in the dive, and now he was climbing in trail. As we were passing through about 25,000 feet a trio of 190s made a run at us. I broke right and lost sight of Frank, who broke left. Another pilot in the flight, Norman Brooks, stayed with me in the turn. We stooged around the area for a few minutes and then I decided it was time to go home.

We turned north, and almost immediately I saw an aircraft out in front of us heading in the same direction. Soon I could see it was another P-47, and when we got close enough I identified it as McCauley's plane. He had taken a pretty good hit in one wing, but the P-47 was flying okay and he was able to fly home with us.

That evening after dinner a bunch of us adjourned to the bar in the Halesworth officer's club to refight the day's battle. The 56th had scored three kills: one for Leroy Schreiber and one for Lt. Jones of the 62nd, plus mine. My story drew quite a bit of attention, since this was my first confirmed victory. I learned that the high speed of my attack had made it difficult for the other pilots in my flight to line up on targets long enough to do much damage, but I also knew that our attack had completely disrupted seven German fighters to the point that they had been unable to attack our bombers. That, after all, was our primary objective.

That evening before I went to sleep I thought about the implications of what I'd done that day. I had killed a man, I was sure of it. Yet I felt no remorse. It wasn't that I particularly wanted to kill people, Germans or otherwise. But this was war, and for three years I had been preparing myself mentally and physically for the day when I would begin shooting down enemy aircraft. Yes, there was a man inside of the 190 I'd destroyed today, but I never saw him, never heard him, never knew his name or what he looked like.

I just knew that the German pilots I met in the sky were up there to shoot down our bombers, and it was my job to get them before they got any of our guys. Today I had succeeded, and I felt very satisfied about it. That was all the time I could spend on the subject, because I needed to get some rest. Another mission was on for tomorrow, and I had to be ready to fly it.

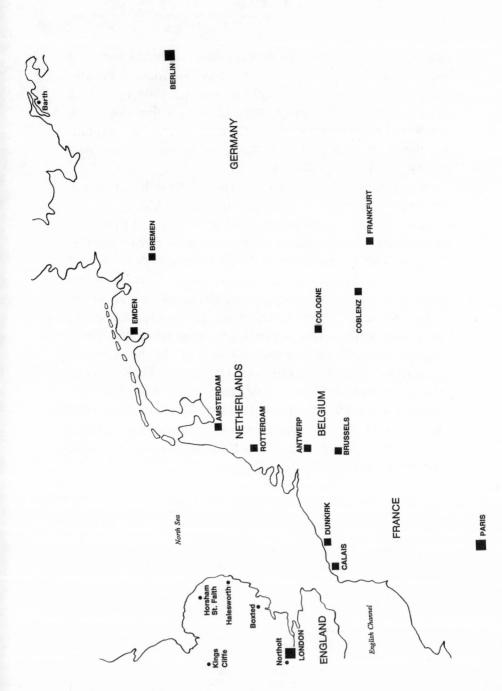

CHAPTER Seven

AS THE English summer of 1943 turned slowly into fall, the 8th Air Force's assault against occupied Europe continued to gather strength. Those of us in operational squadrons weren't privy to the intimate details of the buildup, but it was clear to see in the growing numbers of bombers and fighters we put up for missions, as well as in the quickening pace of operations. The 61st Fighter Squadron would fly no fewer than eighteen missions during September, and I got in on thirteen of them.

September opened with the 8th deeply involved in Operation STARKEY, a three-week effort designed to simulate the missions we would fly during the buildup to a cross-Channel invasion of the French coast. The bombers went after transportation facilities and defensive positions in northern France while we searched the skies expecting strong opposition from the German fighter forces.

It was on one of those missions, the September 3 morning strike on St. Germain, that I scored my second victory. We rendezvoused with the B-17s at 27,000 feet near Horney, then one of the fellows spotted what appeared to be a formation of enemy interceptors preparing to attack from above. I led our ten P-47s of the 61st up to meet them and discovered instead that they were Thunderbolts of the 4th Fighter Group. That kind of burned me up, because they were not in the position we'd been briefed to expect them.

By the time we resumed our position on the flanks of the B-17s, the bombers were nearing Paris. Again we saw enemy aircraft in the distance, and again I led the squadron up to challenge them. At 32,000 feet I could identify these guys as 190s, and we barreled straight into them head-on. Airplanes went every direction as the German formation broke up and the 190s dove for safety. I led White Flight in a circle above the bombers, and a moment later I spotted a lone 190 about 4,000 feet below me lining up for a pass into the B-17s.

I pushed HV-A over into a dive and closed in behind the 190 in a hurry. I pressed the trigger on my control stick at about 400 yards range and continued shooting until I was only about 50 yards off his tail. By this time the 190 was badly hit. As I broke off he went into an inverted spin, eventually crashing below. My wingman for the mission, Robill Roberts, confirmed the kill. Sadly, we lost Lt. Hi Blevins of A Flight, who was last heard from when he radioed to say he was on the deck and in trouble near Meaux.

As it turned out, my victory was our squadron's only score of the month, despite the fact that we flew a lot of missions and got into several good scraps. The Luftwaffe fighter pilots remained skillful, crafty foes.

It was inevitable that we would lose pilots from time to time. On top of our twin foes—the Luftwaffe and the weather—we also had to contend with the fact that we were flying sensitive, high-powered fighter aircraft day in and day out. There was no room for error if an engine quit on takeoff or if you blew a landing approach. I tried to pound safety into the heads of our pilots, but I also realized there is a fine line fighter pilots must fly between using safe procedures and becoming overcautious.

We began receiving replacement pilots almost as soon as we commenced combat back in May. In some cases these flyers were assigned to make up losses; others were simply part of the general buildup in the theater. In nearly every case, however, these pilots lacked the experience that our original pilots had. By September, some of our old hands were telling me they didn't think the newest pilots had received sufficient training in the States. In my role as squadron commander, I wanted to feel confident that every pilot I sent out was capable of flying well enough not only to take care of himself but also to provide protection for his fellow pilots. When new pilots joined the 61st, I would take them up for a practice mission.

One day in September two new pilots entered my office and introduced themselves. On these occasions when I met new pilots, I liked to put on a pretty stern face. I wanted them to know from the word *go* that this was serious business they were getting into, and their squadron commander was going to demand top performance from them.

One of these pilots was Flight Officer Frank Klibbe, a diminutive towhead from Indiana. Nearly fifty years later he still remembered that day, so I guess I made a pretty lasting impression on him, but I'll have to admit he made an impression on me that day as well. Frank tells the story this way:

I was one of several flight officers assigned to the 56th, and I think we were about the first flight officers to arrive. They weren't real sure whether we were full-fledged, certified pilots or not until they researched our records. We were noncommissioned officers with all the privileges of a commissioned officer, and oddly enough, we drew first lieutenant's pay, which wasn't bad at all.

My first impression of Gabreski came real soon after my arrival. Bob Rankin, a second lieutenant, and I were very close buddies from back in flying school (and still are today). We were called upon shortly after our arrival to fly with Gabreski. He was going to take us up on a flight and determine what our skills were with respect to formation flying, takeoff, landing, and so forth. He briefed us one morning and told us it would be a three-shift takeoff; tuck it in and demonstrate our ability to fly formation. Then he would expose us to some aerial maneuvers related to combat formation, widespread formation, as was employed by all the squadrons of the group.

So we took off and were airborne maybe an hour. We flew around in all kinds of turns, ups and downs; the normal. After we landed, Rankin and I were commenting to each other as we walked back to Operations that we thought we did a pretty good job. I was reasonably satisfied that we demonstrated to this new C.O. that we knew what we were doing.

By golly, we got in the Operations Room and old Gabby was standing there with his helmet off. He hadn't taken off his life jacket or anything else. He says disgustedly, "Where did you two learn to fly formation?"

Well I was the flight officer, so I'm scared half to death anyhow, so I let Rankin respond to that question. Rankin told him we'd had a certain amount of training, and we'd gone through the training course at Atcham. All incoming pilots would go there for about 25 hours of precombat training before being assigned to units in the theater.

Gabreski said, "Well, if you call that formation flying

you've got something to learn. Klibbe, you were out, on take-off you were too far back; you didn't tuck it in, and neither did you, Rankin. I wasn't very impressed with your formation flying. Be prepared to fly tomorrow morning. Try it again." So we saluted and left.

I remember going home, sitting on the edge of the bed, and saying "What in the hell is going on here, Rankin? I thought we were over here to fight a damned war. I didn't know we were over here for an aerial circus, for Christ's sake." Rankin agreed. He didn't think we'd done badly at all, and neither did I.

We talked about it for a while, and finally I said, "I tell you what let's do, Rankin. Let's tuck it in tomorrow to where we put our props in underneath his wings and as close as we can possibly get to his ailerons. We'll make it miserable for him. We'll cause such burbling on those ailerons that his stick will be so sloppy and he'll know we're tucked in." Bob readily agreed.

The next morning we went down and got the same thing, a little briefing from Gabreski about how we were going to do the same thing and he expected to see some improvement in us. And by God he saw some improvement because we really tucked those babies in. When those three P-47s rolled down the runway it should have looked like one plane because we were determined that we were going to overcome this criticism. So we flew for about an hour, and it got so bad up there that Gabby started waving his arms for us to move out. But by God, Rankin and I weren't going to move come hell or high water. We were going to stay right in there, and that's what we did until it came time to fly battle formation, in which you move out, of course.

We came down and landed. We met him back in the squadron Operations Room. He never said one thing with regard to our formation flying or takeoff; nothing complimentary to us at all. But he did have a lot to say about his instructions and our following them. He was referring to the time when we were giving him so much trouble and he wanted us to move out because we were in so tight.

He said, "When I tell you or motion you to move out, that's exactly what I expect you to do. I want you to follow those instructions, and don't ever forget that in the future. All right, both of you are scheduled for combat missions tomorrow." Of course, that made Rankin and me feel real good.

But we got his message. We got both of his messages. First, he demanded air discipline. He wanted you to fly just the way he instructed. And he wanted you to follow orders. That was an exercise in leadership, and it permeated all the squadrons of the 56th Fighter Group. Air discipline was a must, and Gabby taught Rankin and me that on our very first flight with him. That made him a leader, and we all respected Gabby for that during our entire tour.

Maybe the old hands were right about some of the replacements we got that fall, but there was nothing wrong with the flying skills Klibbe and Rankin brought to the 61st. They were fine pilots, and once they got some combat experience they were able to fly with the best that the Luftwaffe could send up against them. Both of them became aces, and in fact Rankin shot down five German aircraft on one mission in May 1944, the first of only four pilots in the 56th ever to accomplish that feat.

By this time, our pilots were beginning to build up a respectable number of victories. We had started off slow, but the hard-earned experience was now paying off. On October 2 Zemke got his fifth victory to earn the honors as the 56th's first ace. Bud Mahurin of the 63rd was two days behind him, and then it was our turn in the 61st. Our Johnsons, Bob and Jerry, got two kills apiece to make ace on October 10, along with Dave Schilling of group headquarters. Frank McCauley got his fifth victory on October 14 to give us three aces in the 61st.

In all, the squadron scored eleven victories during October, but I rolled snake eyes on the seven missions I flew that month. It had been nearly two months since my last kill by the time November rolled around, and I was beginning to wonder if I'd ever score again. My luck, however, was about to change.

Zemke, always the motivator, had set a goal for the 56th during October when our rising score started to draw the attention of the press corps. They had taken to calling the 56th "Zemke's Wolfpack." Zemke challenged us to reach one hundred victories by Sadie Hawkins Day, November 6. Sadie Hawkins Day was the product of cartoonist Al Capp, who drew the "Lil Abner" comic strip. On that day, the mythical maidens of Dogpatch were free to marry any bachelor they could catch. I'm not sure why Zemke picked that day, except perhaps that it was coming up soon and the strip was very popular among the pilots, especially a flight of the 62nd who decorated their P-47s with Dogpatch characters.

The reporters loved the idea and started watching our progress closely. We were pretty close to the goal by the end of October, but unfortunately it looked as if Zemke was going to have to miss his own triumph. Eighth Air Force headquarters decided Hub had to go to the States on a public relations tour, and he left for Bushey Hall October 29 to work on a movie that he would take with him to show on the tour. And who should show up at Halesworth to stand in for Hub but my old benefactor, Col. Bob Landry from Fighter Command.

Colonel Landry had no combat experience, but he was a capable pilot and a talented administrator. This meant a lot more of the responsibility for leading missions would fall on Schilling, the flying exec, and the squadron commanders. This was just fine with me, because I was anxious for every chance I could get to gain experience, and I was the senior squadron commander in the group since Phil Tukey had been transferred to training duties. Colonel Landry would be content to fly back in the formations while he learned the ropes.

Now the weather intruded. As we watched the calender move closer to Sadie Hawkins Day, the skies over northern Europe filled with storm clouds and rain. One day Zemke brought in a movie crew and we staged a make-believe mission for the cameras, but that was the closest we got to the Luftwaffe for a week.

Finally, the weather broke on November 3, and we flew a ramrod to Wilhelmshaven. Bob Johnson made the 61st's only contribution to the four kills registered that day, and our group total stood at ninety-eight with three days to go.

Two days later we were ready to go again. At the last minute Zemke showed up at Halesworth in a borrowed P-47 and bumped Schilling as leader of the mission, which was to be a ramrod to Munster.

I was Keyworth White One, leading the 61st on the left of a B-24 formation at 28,000 feet. Up ahead I could see a formation of about twenty fighters headed our way, and I headed straight for them with the throttle full forward. They turned out to be 190s.

Our head-on attack broke up the 190s. They turned away from us and dove for the deck. I followed a flight of them down, feeling the excitement build in me as HV-A closed the distance between us. I caught up with their Number Four and opened fire from about 500 yards out, closing to about 200 before he caught fire. The 190 rolled over and went into a spin, trailing thick smoke. I broke left and put a short burst into another 190, but then my guns went dead—out of ammo. I called my wingman, Eugene "Pete" Barnum, and told him to take the 190. He tacked on behind the 190, knocking him down with a deadly burst from his eight .50s.

I was tickled to fly home knowing we had reached our Sadie Hawkins Day goal. The group total for the day was six, putting us comfortably over one hundred kills. Somehow, group intelligence determined that Lieutenant Hall of the 63rd had scored number one hundred, but I always felt that it could have been any of us who scored that day. You don't have time to look at your watch when you're in the middle of a pack of 190s at 28,000 feet. But the important thing was that we had made our goal, and that Hub had been there to take part. In fact, he scored one of our kills himself. Hub left for the States on the next day.

The 56th was by now an experienced, effective fighter group. But we never stopped experimenting and looking for better ways to do things. One problem I had been thinking about a lot had to do with our guns. The November 5 mission was a perfect example of how easy it was to run out of ammunition at a critical time. I also began to think about the ammo we were using.

In the early days we didn't know what ammunition we wanted to use. We had a mixture of tracers, ball, and armor-piercing. Most of us thought the tracers would be a good way to let us know where the bullets were going. It took us awhile to figure out that the tracers didn't have a true trajectory, so they gave you a false perception of where the bullets were going. The problem had something to do with the way the outside shell burned off the bullets to create their reddish-orange color. Sometimes they would even cook off as they were leaving the gun barrel and fly off in an odd direction.

I talked with the other pilots about this, and I also had a

couple of long chats with my armorer, Cpl. Joe DiFranza. Joe normally loaded my P-47 with 250 to 300 rounds per gun for a mission. The wings would hold more than that, but I preferred to fly a light airplane that would be slightly more maneuverable. We decided to take the tracers out of the mix, and load them only for the last 25 rounds so they would be a signal to me when I was just about to run out of ammo.

Some of the pilots didn't like the armor-piercing ammunition much, either. They thought the ball was more destructive because the armor-piercing just made a little hole and penetrated the target. The ball slugs were a little more blunt, so they made a bigger hole. Then later we got some new ammunition, armor-piercing incendiary, and that turned out to be the best we ever found. With API, you could see it when you hit your target. If you fired and missed, you wouldn't see anything—and neither would the guy you were shooting at. But as soon as your bullets hit a portion of the target airplane they would give off little white puffs of smoke from the incendiary outer shell. It would go off just like a little firecracker. On the inside of the API was a good steel core that did a devastating job on the enemy's armorplate.

Another important change we made about this time was to increase the size of the drop tanks we carried, phasing out the 75-gallon models for new ones that held 108 gallons. We had a few problems with vapor locks cutting off fuel to the engines on the first couple of missions, but then the technical types figured out how to set up the pressure in the 108s so they would feed properly. The new tanks pushed our endurance another ten minutes deeper into enemy territory (unless we were jumped early and had to drop them prematurely, which rarely happened).

I finally took my place on the 56th Fighter Group's roster of aces on November 26, 1943. On this mission our job was to meet the B-17s as they withdrew from their target at Bremen, Germany, and protect them on their way home. Schilling was leading the group from the front of our squadron, and I led Blue Flight above him.

It was plenty cold in the cockpit of my P-47 at nearly six miles above northern Germany. I had the heater on full blast and, of course, I was bundled up in heavy flying gear and my thick boots. Still, I had to keep wiggling my toes and fingers to keep the blood running through them. As we approached our rendezvous I could see the rear of the bomber formation under attack from German fighters. I picked out a pair of twin-engine Me-110s below me and led the flight down behind them.

The 110s saw me coming and pushed over into a dive in hopes of escaping. That tactic didn't work any better for the 110 against P-47s than it did for the lighter German single-engine fighters. I closed in behind them rapidly and opened fire on one at about 700 yards range. Normally, I would wait until I got a lot closer before shooting, but in this case I was going so fast that I had to hurry the shot. From 300 yards away I could see both engines on fire. Then suddenly I was right on top of the 110. I just barely had time to push the control stick forward and duck below the burning German fighter. In a flash I could see oil from the 110 spattering on the left wing of my P-47, and then I could smell its smoke, which must have been sucked into the cockpit through my heater system. Now that's close—too close!

I turned left in time to watch the 110 dive straight into the ground. When I looked around, I could see my wingman, Barnum, was still with me. But we had lost everyone else. I climbed back up to 22,000 so we could rejoin the B-17s.

A few minutes later I saw another 110 below us. I led Barnum down, and again the enemy spotted my approach and also tried to dive away from us. This time I slowed my approach slightly, though we were still traveling at about 420 mph when I opened fire from 600 yards. The 110 took solid hits in its wing root and rolled over into a death fall at 14,000 feet. I saw a huge explosion below me when it hit the ground. Barnum and I rejoined the B-17s again and accompanied them to the coast, where we broke off and set course for home.

Halesworth reverberated with the joyful sounds of celebration that night after we learned that the 56th had set the record that day for the most enemy planes destroyed by a group on a single mission with twenty-three, plus two probables and seven damaged. I joined the revelry at the officers' club and enjoyed many words of congratulations for having joined the ranks of the aces. I especially noted the pleasure Colonel Landry seemed to get from my success, and I suppose he also was happy to know that the 56th was still adding to its Wolfpack reputation under his command.

More changes kept coming. About this time my operations officer, Capt. Don "Doc" Renwick, was yanked out of combat and reassigned to an operational training outfit. I was sorry to lose him, but I had to admit he was a good choice because he was so steady and competent, a natural teacher. I picked our A Flight commander, Capt. Bob Lamb, to replace him and moved Paul Conger into Lamb's old slot.

Then I got another shock when four more of our pilots also got orders sending them out. Lt. Frank McCauley would follow Renwick to the 495th Fighter Training Group, while Lieutenants Milt Anderson and Al Bailes went to the 310th Ferrying Squadron. But the biggest blow came last, when Capt. Jerry Johnson got orders sending him to the 356th Fighter Group.

I hated to see Jerry go, because we had become quite good friends. But again the logic behind the transfer was tough to argue against. The 356th was a new group in the theater and had gotten off to a slow start. They needed someone with combat experience and fighting spirit, which made Jerry a perfect choice. In his place, the 356th sent us Capt. Joe Bennett, who assumed Jerry's duties as assistant operations officer. Joe turned out to be quite a fighter pilot in his own right, joining our roster of aces a quick four months later. At the same time, I moved Jim Carter up to Jerry's other former job of B Flight commander.

On November 29 we went out again, this time escorting B-17s in toward their target at Bremen. I was leading White Flight of the 61st on the left side of the Fortresses at 30,000 feet above a solid overcast when Blue and Red flights radioed that they were being bounced.

I called for White Flight to break into the attackers and turned sharply to find myself nose-to-nose with about *forty* 109s. I looked around and saw that only my wingman, Joe Powers, had followed. Forty to two, not my kind of odds, but there was nothing to do but keep going. We went through and then turned to attack eight of them about 2,000 feet below us. Just as I was getting into position for a shot, Joe called in that there were more 109s behind us and coming fast. I pulled up out of the dive and used my airspeed to zoom away from the 109s. As soon as we were clear I picked out eight more 109s below and turned to try another bounce.

This time we had clear sailing. I picked out a straggler and opened up on him at 600 yards. He still was carrying his belly tank, and it burst into flames when my shots hit it. I continued firing short bursts until I was about 200 yards away and could see that he was a goner. Smoke and flames belched from the 109 as it spun down into the clouds, obviously out of control.

I swung away to the right and picked up four more enemy fighters. I was dead astern when I opened fire on another one carrying its belly tank, and again it burst into flames. Smoke and glycol poured from the 109 as it dove at a slight angle for about ten seconds; then at about 24,000 feet it rolled over and dove straight down into overcast trailing smoke and fire. Another sure kill.

About this time I saw a flash out of the corner of my eye. I looked back to see that Powers had caught a 109 trying to jump me and blasted him off my tail. That was typical for Joe. He was as good a wingman as ever flew with me, and I flew with some great ones. Sadly, Joe was killed in action while flying a P-51 in Korea early in 1951.

November had been a great month for me, but the first day of December nearly brought my combat career to an end. On this day I was leading the full group on a ramrod to Solingen. Lt. Norm Brooks was my wingman. We made landfall over the Dutch island at 27,000 and rendezvoused with the B-17s at 1142. About half an hour later the action started.

We could see lots of contrails around us, and I began to hear calls from a bomber box that was under attack in the rear of the formation. I turned our fighters back to help them, and before long I spotted seven 109s below us lining up for an attack. I led White Flight down after them, but they spotted us quickly and dove away. We gave up the chase at 22,000 and climbed back up to the bombers. As we approached them I spotted an Me-110 and attacked it from above. I saw no hits from my gunfire, but the 110 rolled over and dove away vertically.

I chose not to follow him down when I spotted a lone B-24 under attack by a mixed group of 109s and Junkers 88s. The Ju-88 was a twin-engine light bomber; very fast. The Luftwaffe was beginning to use 88s as interceptors, often armed with rockets. Like the Me-110, the Ju-88 carried a rear gunner. Again I made a diving attack. I opened up on an 88 at about 600 yards and fired a burst at him with no visible effect as I closed in to point-blank range. Suddenly he whipped over in a snap turn that carried him under me to the right. I was so close that his turbulence rocked my plane, and I broke off the attack. In seconds I could feel my engine lose power and see oil spattering on my windshield. The 88's rear gunner had hit me!

I throttled her back and dropped down to 12,000 feet. Brooks stayed with me, weaving above as we headed back toward the coast. My heart was in my throat as I watched the oil pressure gauge and listened for signs that the engine was failing. Instead, the engine held together and I was able to climb slowly back up to 24,000. In about forty-five minutes we reached the coast. Then I got another shock.

Brooks called to say that *he* was having trouble. It seems his propellor had become stuck in high pitch, which meant that he wouldn't last for the flight home across the North Sea. He was going to lose a little altitude and then bail out while he was still over land. Jeez, what next? I felt bad for Brooks, but I was also worried about myself. What would happen if my engine failed while I was over the water? Normally, my wingman would be there to help the air-sea rescue guys find me, but now I didn't have a wingman. There was nothing to do but go it alone.

It was a long flight across the water at 180 mph, but my trusty P-47 carried me home. I sadly reported on Brooks's fate but was pleased to be informed that he, too, had made it back. He had been able to regain his prop control after he left me, and had come home alone.

Later, when my ground crew was going over HV-A, they dug a 20-mm slug out from between two of the engine cylinders. It was an explosive bullet, but for some reason it hadn't gone off. Someone grabbed a camera to snap a picture of Doc

Hornig and me looking at that slug and marveling at my good luck. I was glad to accept a shot of Doc's postmission "medicine" that day, too!

By this time the winter weather was upon us, making operations very difficult. The 56th flew only five missions in the first two weeks of December. Either the weather would be too bad over our bases to get in and out, or it would be too bad over enemy territory to allow an effective mission— sometimes both. But one of those five missions, an escort to Emden on the eleventh, would prove memorable to our squadron and especially so for me.

I was flying as Keyworth Blue One in one of the P-47s, 42-7871. The group was attacked over the Frisian Islands at 30,000 feet before we had even reached rendezvous with the B-17s. The 62nd took the brunt of the attack, and our other two squadrons pressed on toward the bombers. By the time we spotted them the Big Friends were already under attack.

Our squadron approached from the rear of the formation and saw about forty Me-110s between us and the bombers, lining up to make rocket attacks. It was the kind of setup a fighter pilot dreams about: We were above and behind the enemy, flying a superior aircraft, and we had a full load of ammunition. All I had to do was turn our fighters to the right and lead them down.

Nothing is ever as simple as it looks, I guess. Just as I was turning in behind the 110s I saw a bright flash above me to the left. We've been jumped, I thought. Two P-47s were falling in smoke and flames, and I wasn't about to be next, so I broke off the attack and zoomed up and away. When I looked back at 30,000 feet, I realized I was alone. Later I found out there had been no bounce. The two P-47s, flown by Lts. Edward Kruer and Lawrence Strand, had collided in the turn. Because of my position out front, I was the only pilot in the squadron who didn't see what happened. The rest of them continued their bounce on the 110s, and they shot down a bunch of them.

I knew it was dangerous to fly alone in a battle area, so I started looking around for some P-47s to tag along with. Instead, I spotted three more 110s flying in string formation about 5,000 feet below me. I couldn't resist the bounce, even though I knew better, so I pushed over and dove after the last one. I opened fire and kept shooting until I was close enough to see the crew bailing out. I was about 50 yards behind when they jumped from their burning plane, and it fell away trailing thick smoke.

I recovered at 23,000 and spotted a formation of P-47s; at least they looked like P-47s to me. But when I drew closer to them I could see they were 190s. Their radial-engine profile had fooled me. Lucky for me, they must have been looking the other way, because I was able to turn tail and get away without them chasing me.

By this time my fuel supply was getting seriously low, so I decided it was time to head home. I turned westward and flew for a few minutes before I spotted an Me-109 passing below me in a direction about 75 degrees from me. I held my breath, hoping he wouldn't see me, because I didn't have enough gas to stick around and fight with him. I was almost ready to breathe easy when I saw him make a sharp upward turn and start coming toward me.

I was so low on gas that I felt I shouldn't try to run at 100 percent throttle, which was 52 inches of manifold pressure. So I said to myself that I would try to run this guy out of ammunition. Pretty brazen of me, but I felt the best I could do was present him a difficult shot. As he closed in behind me I nosed the P-47 down to pick up some speed with the throttle at 43–44 inches. When he got close behind me, I would pull up and then kick the airplane over about the time I thought he was ready to shoot. When I saw the muzzle flashes from his guns I would present him with a 90-degree deflection shot, about the most difficult there is.

It worked the first time. I made kind of a chandelle, came down again in sort of a lazy eight as I watched what he was doing. I didn't look into my cockpit at all then. I just kept watching him, making sure he didn't get too close. I made another turn with my nose down, picked up speed, and went back up again. He did the same thing. It worked again. He had fired twice and not hit me, so he was running himself out of amunition.

The third time I came up, kicked it off from the side, and he started firing again. But the moment he started shooting I realized he had his bead right on, because I heard an explosion in the cockpit. He hit my rudder pedal and shot it away. Part of my flying boot was shot up, too. My engine lost power, so I figured it had been hit, too. I said to myself, well it's the end of the road, I'd better get out of this mother.

I was at about 20,000 feet. I didn't look at the gauges, but it appeared to me that my engine was dead. I nosed the plane down to keep up my airspeed and began to roll my canopy back so I could bail out. The canopy was open about a foot when I looked at my gauges and saw that I still had some manifold pressure, and that my rpms were still up about 1,500. As it turned out, he had hit the turbocharger unit and knocked it out, which had caused me to lose power at high altitude. Once I realized I still had some power I gave up the idea of bailing out and decided to try again at getting home. The guy in the 109 had other ideas, however.

About this time I realized my foot was numb and I began to worry about how much that exploding shell had injured it. I didn't want to look at it, because I was afraid I might pass out if there was a lot of blood. My first job, though, was to get away from that 109. I pulled the canopy closed and pushed over in a dive toward of a bank of clouds I could see below me. It didn't make any difference what those clouds had in them—hills, mountains, or whatever. I was going to get into them before the guy behind me could finish me off.

I reached the clouds just in time, as the 109 was closing in on me. I immediately went on instruments and turned west toward England. Periodically I would come up out of the clouds to see where the 109 was. He wasn't giving up, but he was way back there skirting around the clouds looking for me. Finally I ducked back into the clouds and stayed there for about twenty-five minutes. I didn't know if I'd have enough fuel to get back to England, so when I got out over the water I called Mayday and raised air-sea rescue. A controller told me they had a radar fix on me and advised me to maintain my present heading.

So I kept going for all I was worth. By that time I was pretty low, so I couldn't really tell where I was. I just kept looking for landfall and hoping the controller was giving me good directions. I leaned out my fuel mixture, decreased rpms to the minimum, pulled my manifold pressure all the way back to 26 inches, and prayed. Eventually I saw the English shoreline ahead, and within minutes I landed at Manston, an RAF recovery field on the coast near Margate.

I got the P-47 down okay and taxied in just as the engine quit. Only then did I work up the nerve to take a look at my foot. I wore fur-lined boots like the bomber crews had, and the one that was hit had a big gash across the bottom of it. But my foot wasn't injured at all! The impact of the shell hitting my boot had numbed my foot, but no shrapnel had hit me.

I hadn't made it back to the tower when the engine

stopped, so a lorry drove up and a guy shouted up to ask if I was having any trouble.

"Absolutely!" I replied. "I'm having all kinds of trouble. First of all I can't move this airplane. You'll have to tow it off."

My foot was still numb and was starting to sting, so he gave me a ride to the little RAF operations tower. One of the people there called the 56th at Halesworth to let them know I'd gotten down okay, and someone else made me some tea. I had some time to kill before the people from Halesworth could get there to pick me up, so I chatted with the people in operations for a while, then went back out to look at my plane. It had holes in the cockpit, the turbocharger unit down under the fuselage, and the oil tank, which was practically dry. So if I hadn't gotten down when I did, chances are the engine would have burned up about the time I ran out of gas.

I thought about the events of the day: out of fuel, out of oil, a hole in my turbocharger, and my boot ripped by a 20-mm shot. That was one of the most devastating, exciting missions I ever flew. Eventually, a Jeep from Halesworth arrived to pick me up, and I went home with nothing but my parachute.

The excitement generated by the December 11 mission carried our squadron through the end of the year. We had scored no fewer than fourteen kills that day, including three each by Don Smith, Bob Lamb, and Paul Conger.

Christmas passed pleasantly enough. Our squadron had a big party for all personnel, enlisted and officers, on the twenty-seventh with the Halesworth dance orchestra ("The Jivin' Yanks") and lots of English girls. Some of the guys showed signs of homesickness, but I fought it off. I knew I couldn't let my mind get occupied with the things back home, not even Kay. She and I kept up steady correspondence, but if I let myself think about home too much I might get despondent and emotional. I couldn't afford that in my position as squadron commander.

I thought mostly about the job that had to be done and enjoyed camaraderie with the guys who were there. We were making the best of the situation, so the Christmas party was a happy day. In any case, I think Christmas has different meanings for different people. In my case, I relate more with the Navity, the religious portion of it.

Not that we had much time to think anything about Christmas. The party was just a very short period of time taken out of our operational activities. The next day we could be flying again. If the weather was good, you had to be ready to get out on the mission.

So my Christmas with the 56th Fighter Group came and went in 1943. I didn't make the next one.

CHAPTER *Eight*

THE NEW year of 1944 started off with a bang, but the action wasn't in the air. In fact, after the mission of December 11, 1943, I didn't score another victory for nearly six weeks.

The excitement was on the ground at muddy Halesworth. We were all heartened to learn shortly after New Year's Day that Zemke was back in England and would rejoin the group shortly. It wasn't that we had any misgivings about Bob Landry's leadership. He had made a number of important organizational changes in the group and was even beginning to develop into a pretty good fighter pilot. In fact, he had scored a confirmed kill on our December 11 mission.

But Zemke was something different. He was a fighter through and through, whether he was in a P-47 taking on the Germans or down at Bushey Hall scrapping with the paper pushers at 8th Fighter Command. And he usually came out on top. As good a man as Bob Landry was, the 56th just seemed to come on a little stronger when Hub Zemke was running the show.

Zemke's return precipitated a change in jobs for me. When word arrived that Hub would be returning, Landry was reassigned to Fighter Command and Dave Schilling was left in charge of the 56th temporarily. Schilling needed another lead pilot to help him run the group, so I was named assistant executive officer of the 56th, and Maj. Jimmy Stewart took my slot as commander of the 61st Squadron. Up to that time Jimmy had been the group operations officer, a job I inherited when Zemke returned on January 20. I was promoted to lieutenant colonel that same day.

I've never been sure why Schilling made the switch. There was really no reason for it. Dave and I weren't particularly close. I was still sort of an outsider at that time, except in the squadron. The 61st knew me, and I knew the 61st. My squadron had good momentum going. Maybe Stewart had Schilling's ear and wanted the experience of running a squadron. I know he wanted the opportunity to score. We all did.

In any case, the new assignment didn't change my life a lot. I had enjoyed commanding the 61st and took great pride in our accomplishments, but my main responsibility was flying P-47s. That didn't change after I moved to group. I continued to live in the same quarters, and most important, I continued to fly nearly all my missions with the 61st.

My duties on the ground didn't change very much, either. The only responsibility I had as group operations officer was overlooking the people who worked in the Ops section. They were responsible for getting the frag orders from higher headquarters and turning them into specific instructions for our pilots. They determined the number of fighters needed, take-off timing, the routes to and from rendezvous with the bombers, the altitudes, fuel loads, and dozens of other little items that direct the timing of the mission up to the point of rendezvous. Then it was up to the individual squadron operations staffs to take it from there and work up the final details, such as which pilots would be flying, and which planes would be used. It was all mechanical, strictly routine. We had special guys who had that task, and they kept doing it.

During January 1944 we began to take advantage of two important changes that were made in our P-47s. The first was water injection for the engines. All the P-47s built from the D-10 series and beyond had water injection built in, but our older planes had to be retrofitted with the device.

The concept behind water injection sounded goofy—spraying water into the engine's combustion chambers with the fuel-air mixture to allow the engine to produce more power—but it really worked. The water helped cool the engine so you could run a much higher manifold pressure, up to about 60 inches of mercury. That gave you a couple of hundred more horsepower, so at 2,700 rpm a P-47 could fly on the deck at 335–345 miles per hour. That was moving back in those days.

The other change they introduced about this time was the paddle-blade propellor. We used them for the first time on the January 4 mission. I noticed a little more vibration with the paddles, but what an improvement in performance, especially in the climb! Previously, we found the fastest way to gain altitude in combat was to dive and zoom, and the German pilots were well aware of it. Now we could pull the P-47's nose up and keep on going after them.

I had just started flying a new P-47D-11, and it had both features. It was a fine ship, and later my crew made it even better by putting a wax finish on it. The wax not only made it a little prettier (or at least as pretty as a P-47 could be) but it also improved the speed slightly. My crew chief, Ralph Safford, remembers what a big job that was:

When I was first assigned as crew chief of Gabby's plane I wasn't sure how it would work out, because he was very picky about every detail concerning the aircraft. As I look back on it, he was right. All surfaces (wing, empennages, cowling, etc.) had to be absolutely smooth; nothing loose or out of position.

The P-47D-11 was a good example of that. We sanded the paint until it was perfectly smooth and then gave it six coats of hard paste wax that Schacki had found somewhere in England. I'd say it took about two months off and on to complete the task, and then, of course, there was touching up to do.

The technical advances sometimes turned out to be a two-steps-forward-one-step-back sort of thing, though. Frank Klibbe tells a good story about his experience with an early water-injection P-47:

There came an occasion when I was to get a new airplane, a later model. In those days, the airplanes came over [by ship], were assembled up in northern England, and then flown down to the units. And the engines had to be slow-timed. This meant you had to fly 10 hours of time at low rpms on the engine before you could really open it up to its maximum. So, after each mission I'd jump into this new P-47 and go up to put on an hour or two.

This one day I was going to put on the last hour of slow time on the plane. I couldn't wait. I was flying along and looked down to see a bomber base below me, which was Bungay. I decided that as soon as the clock ticked around to that last hour I was going to bring this baby up to 62 inches of manifold pressure, then kick in the water injection and dive down over the bomber base and give them a thrill; you know, right on the grass. So time ticked down and the hour was up. I poured the coal to it, dived down, and was going like a scalded eagle on the deck. But just before I reached the base the engine shuttered, the cowling rotated, the engine started misfiring, and then it quit.

I must have been going close to 500 mph, so I attempted to fishtail the airplane to slow it down so I could make a 180-degree turn and perhaps land on the bomber base. But the speed was such that as I reached the other side of the field, I didn't have enough airspeed to make the turn, so I had to quickly pick out a field ahead of me and prepare to make a belly landing. I spotted the field I needed ahead of me, and I had sufficient time to lower the wing flaps slightly to slow me down a little bit. When I got closer I could see there was an English farmer out in the field plowing it. I also noticed that I had run out of gas in one of my internal tanks. So I switched it over to another tank and tried to restart the engine. It didn't restart.

I bellied the aircraft in, and we slid across the field and in through some trees. It did very little damage to the airplane, because the P-47 was built like a battleship. Once I came to rest I thought, "well, shall I make up a story or shall I tell the truth?" In the meantime, the farmer I'd just missed on his tractor came running over, screaming at me. Of course, I was disgusted and mad as hell that I'd pulled such a thing. Anyhow, some guys from the bomber base pulled up in a Jeep and took me back.

I thought this was the end of my career with the 56th right here, because this was just a head-up sort of a thing, running out of fuel with the water injection on. Because with the water injection on and no fuel to the engine, the spark plugs would foul, so the engine would never have restarted.

But something good came out of this. The water-injection switch was on a toggle on top of the throttle. This toggle could accidentally be tripped getting in and out of the airplane. And on the other hand, you had to trip it yourself at maximum manifold pressure and then turn it off manually as well. As a result of this accident they modified the P-47s by putting a microswitch in there so that once you got to 62 inches, just moving the throttle forward would start the water injection. By the same token, when you retarded the throttle, the microswitch would release and shut the water off. If I had had such a system instead of the toggle switch, I might have been able to salvage my airplane.

Stewart was the squadron commander at the time, and I explained to him what happened. He advised me that he was going to take no more action than to recommend a $25 fine. Well, that went up the line, and by the time it got to 8th Air Force headquarters, General Spaatz and his staff apparently decided it was worth a $75 fine and an official reprimand. I didn't mind the $75, but I was concerned about that reprimand because I didn't know whether it would come back to haunt me someday. As it turned out, it didn't have too much of an effect. At least I was able to serve out thirty-one years in the Air Force without too much of a penalty.

The other major change that came along at this time was the introduction of A and B groups within the 56th. We had built up the numbers of pilots and planes so much by now that it was possible to send about two thirty-six-plane formations at once, and we did it for the first time on the January 11 mission to Halberstadt. Schilling, the squadron commanders, and I took turns leading the groups until Hub got himself resettled and up to speed to the latest combat developments.

This growth in strength also brought about a much-awaited change in tactics. Up to this time, 8th Air Force policy had been very clear about the priorities of fighter escorts: Bring the bombers back first, and worry about shooting down German fighters second. That translated into orders not to leave the bombers in order to chase fleeing enemy fighters down to the deck. It's hard to tell how many German pilots in damaged fighters lived to fight again another day because of this rule, but we accepted it as best we could.

Now our new boss in command of the 8th Air Force, Gen. Jimmy Doolittle, had a change of heart. All the German fighters were to be chased to their destruction, wherever they may be, wherever we could find them. Even more than that, we were told to strike anything we could see in Germany— airfields, staff cars, trucks, trains. We still were supposed to stay with the bombers on escort until we were relieved by another group, but then we were free to drop down and hit targets of opportunity on the way home if we had enough gas and ammunition.

That put a very different complexion on the whole war. It became a real free-for-all. There were airplanes all over, and some days 8th Fighter Command was able to destroy a couple of hundred German planes. On the ground or in the air, it didn't make any difference. And we were blowing up trains all over the place.

We flew whenever the weather allowed, and I got in seven missions during January. Finally on the twenty-ninth I shot down a 110 while leading B Group, and the very next day I got a 210 and a 109. Earlier that month I had written Kay to tell her that the next victory I got, my ninth, would be dedicated to her. But by the time I wrote her again a week or so later, I had to admit that I'd already scored numbers ten and eleven as well. That's just how it went during those hectic days.

Occasionally on my days off I'd go into London or over to Northolt to visit my Polish friends. London was a very exciting place, even with the war on. The place just didn't shut down. It was all blacked out at night, and you might think that the place would close up and nobody would be out. But that wasn't the case at all. The 61st Squadron pilots had pitched in to rent an apartment in London so they would be certain of having a place to stay when they got to the city. I stayed there several times, but Jim Carter remembers London better than I do. Here's how he describes it:

The squadron had an apartment in London (on James Street) about four blocks from Buckingham Palace. It was about two blocks from the Women's Army Barracks, which was destroyed with great loss of life by a VI buzz bomb. It was probably this event which caused us to terminate the lease.

As I recall, there was a small kitchen, a bath with tub, three or four rooms with beds or cots. The whole thing was sparsely furnished and poorly at that. I think the rent was about seventy-five pounds per month. The apartment was thought necessary when England became overcrowded with Americans as the preinvasion buildup began. Officer and enlisted billets often were not available (in London) after mid-1943.

Our usual itinerary on visits to London seems pretty dull on looking back, but it was a treat then. There were several clubs that admitted U.S. officers with dancing available with girls considerably above the caliber of those met on the streets. There were stage plays and movies, and NAAFI wagons; also Regent Street, Harrod's, Selfridge's, and Bond Street for shoes, boots, uniforms, and gifts. There were restaurants with fare superior to the base mess.

One day I flew HV-A over to Northolt to visit my old Polish friends in 315 Squadron. Tadensc Andersz was still in the outfit, but his spirits weren't as high as I had come to expect. He told me the whole outfit was in the dumps because the daylight fighter action had moved beyond the range of their Spitfire IXs. When I thought about it, I could see why.

Even a year earlier when I had been flying with 315, the Spitfires had insufficient range to penetrate very far into France. At that time, the Germans had their fighters stationed right along the French coast to challenge us, but there was a whole new ballgame now. Our bomber formations were pushing deeper into Germany every day, and the drop tanks allowed our P-47s and P-38s to go most of the distance with them. The Germans had been forced to pull back their fighters so they could concentrate on hitting our bombers when they ventured beyond the protective cover of our fighters. The introduction of the P-51 Mustang long-range fighter into our forces at this time was only adding to the pressure on the Germans to pull their fighters back even farther.

The result was that the RAF Spitfire squadrons, including 315, were pretty much out of the fight, at least the main event. That just didn't sit very well with the aggressive Poles.

Not long afterward, Hub Zemke and I were having one of our skull sessions in his office. He was concerned that some of our most experienced pilots were approaching the ends of their combat tours and we seemed to have a lack of qualified men to replace them. At that time, fighter pilots were eligible to go home after two hundred combat hours. We were running down a roster of guys who were approaching the magic two hundred when an idea struck me: We have need of experienced pilots, and the Poles of 315 have experience but aren't getting any action. How about bringing some of them over to Halesworth to fly P-47s with us in the 56th?

Zemke said he couldn't see anything wrong with the idea, as long as they came on a voluntary basis. We wouldn't be able to pay them or anything, but we could give them a place to sleep and a P-47 to fly. He ran the plan up the command ladder to 8th Air Force and no one kicked. We went ahead. I don't know if there was any paperwork even, because it didn't change anything except the individuals who were in the cockpit flying. Eventually, I think we got about five Polish pilots: Mike Gladych, Thaddeus Sawicz, Witold Lanowski, Zbigniew Janicki, and of course, Tadensc Andersz.

During my tenure they were mixed in with the flight leaders and did a fine job. Later on they may have formed their own flight in the 61st. I felt real good about bringing those guys in to fly with us. I owed them a lot, and this was a small way of repaying the debt.

One problem we encountered was that the RAF was unwilling to pay these Polish pilots while they were flying with us. We tried to get American pay for them, but the bigwigs said no. Finally, we established the practice of passing the hat among our pilots on payday to collect enough money to keep our Polish friends going. It was a heck of a way to have to operate, but it gives you an idea of how keen the Poles were to keep fighting.

Toward the middle of February came a series of missions into Germany that have come to be known as the Big Week. That name was cooked up later, but it fit pretty well. We had some big targets, because 8th Air Force headquarters decided that we needed to spend a week just pounding

Germany's aircraft production plants, and of course the Jerries were going to fight back with all they had. And we ran up a big score. That was the week that made the German high command squirm, particularly Goering because his Luftwaffe really took a licking. Goering could not tolerate such losses—the 56th alone destroyed fifty-nine German aircraft in just five missions—and they were right in his front yard. That meant he couldn't support his people on the Eastern Front.

My own contribution to Big Week was three kills. On February 20 we carried new 150-gallon drop tanks for the first time and headed for Leipizig. We caught up with the bombers and took up station on the left side of their formation at 22,000 feet. All was quiet until we were ready to break off escort about thirty miles west of Hannover.

I was leading the last run along the flank of the bombers when Lt. Justus Foster called in a hostile formation below us at 7 o'clock and suggested a 180-degree left turn to bounce them. That sounded fine to me, so I turned us directly up sun from fourteen Me-110s and dove from 22,000 feet. White Flight spaced out nicely around me, and we really hit those 110s hard. They were divided into two sections, and I attacked the 110 that was second from the right on the rear group. He exploded when I was about 50 yards behind him, with his tail and one wing separating from the rest of the plane, and went down spinning.

I let my speed carry me on to the front formation of 110s, and picked out the guy on the extreme right. I started shooting at 500 yards range with the same result. I saw strikes all over the fuselage and wings before I broke off at 50 yards, only to see this plane explode, too. Pieces of the plane fell away as if in slow motion.

I pulled into a climbing turn and looked around. The sky

was littered with burning 110s and the parachutes of their crews. It looked to me as if only one of them had escaped. He was at 7,000 feet and running for all he was worth, so I pushed over into a dive from 12,000 in hopes of catching him before he reached the clouds below us. I closed to within 1,500 yards and snapped off a burst just as he disappeared into the clouds. Once more I climbed back up. We were able to reform the squadron into two flights of six for the long ride home. When I filed my report that evening, I included the statement: "It must have been the most perfect show that I have been on."

On the twenty-second I scored again, this time getting a Focke-Wulf over Arnhem and then resuming station with the bombers until we reached the limit of our endurance. Flying my wing was Lt. Col. Gil Meyers, commander of a P-47 group that had just arrived in England and an old friend of Zemke's. By the time we broke off to come home, the two of us were separated from the rest of the squadron.

As we approached St. Anthonis, Holland, I spotted a new airfield below us. I could see what appeared to be a Dornier bomber sitting next to a control hut. It was a pretty good setup to try out General Doolittle's new instructions, so down we went. We came across the airfield low and fast. I put a burst into the bomber while Meyers sprayed a hangar. We could see a lot of ground fire coming up at us and dodged it as best we could. I decided it was best to leave well enough alone, even though I couldn't claim more than a damaged on the Dornier. Ground strafing was a sure way of blowing off steam and it was a lot of fun, but I couldn't see any point in pushing my luck.

February 22 was a special day for more reason than simply the fact that I had made my first strafing attack. It was also the day that the 61st Fighter Squadron scored its one hundredth victory. I still felt a special attachment to the 61st, which made it especially sweet to know that it was the first squadron in the European theater to accomplish the feat.

We had another big mission to Schweinfurt on the twenty-fourth, and it was a tough one. Hub Zemke came home with one wing on his P-47 riddled by shell splinters. I took one look at his airplane and said to Hub, "By God, if they'd put a hole like that in the other wing too, you wouldn't be here now!"

The last day of Big Week was the twenty-fifth, when we escorted the bombers back from their mission to Regensburg. I led A Group while Jerry Johnson led B. Much to my delight, Jerry had transferred back to the 56th earlier in February and now was commanding the 63rd Squadron. In contrast to the previous missions, we sighted only a few German fighters, destroying three for no losses. Then the weather closed in, and the Big Week was over.

With March came the target we had all been waiting for: Berlin. The bombers hit it for the first time in a daylight raid on the Fourth, and we got into the act two days later.

Then on March 8 we went back again and set a new ETO record with twenty-seven victories in the air and two more on the ground. One of the ground kills was mine.

On that day I led B Group off a few minutes behind Jerry Johnson, who was leading A Group. They got into a big scrap ahead of us between Dummer and Steinhuder lakes, and we could hear their chatter on the radio. After we joined up with the bombers we got a report of fifty-plus coming our way. I led the group out in front of our bomber formation and then saw about twenty Fw-190s coming through the task force ahead of us. They turned to make a stern attack on the bombers they had just hit, and I led our P-47s down behind them. A huge dogfight ensued. I chased one 190 after another, but there were so many airplanes around that I couldn't stay in position long enough to get off a shot. Finally the 190s dove for the deck.

Near Hannover I saw below me an enemy airfield with activity on it. I dropped down low about eight miles away so I could come in at low level and fast. Before going down, I picked out my target. About six 190s were sitting there being refueled and reloaded, with men stooging around them. Evidently I caught them by surprise, as no one hit the dirt until my eight .50s started firing. It was perfect. The planes were lined up well for my angle of approach. I could see hits flashing on nearly all of the aircraft down the line. The hits concentrated on three aircraft, while two others were caught in the line of the spray. As I broke away I could see one fighter on fire and two others smoking. It was all over in a flash. I kept on going and climbed to 10,000 feet, then hit the deck over the Zuider Zee and stayed low all the way home.

The ace race was really heating up in the 8th Air Force now. I had fourteen aerial victories, but I wasn't even close to the leaders. Bud Mahurin took over the lead from Walter Beckham of the 353rd on March 8, when he got his twentieth kill. Then a week later old eagle eyes Bob Johnson scored a triple to pass Mahurin with twenty-one. By the end of the month my score stood at eighteen, with doubles scored on the sixteenth and twenty-seventh. I also shot up four steam locomotives during March. They made great targets, because they would give off a big belch of steam and smoke when you pierced their boilers with gunfire.

The March 27 mission was a pretty easy one for us, but it also served as a reminder of how dangerous this ground strafing business could be. I was one of the few pilots to encounter any enemy fighters, and the first one I shot at, a 109, took no evasive action at all. He just sat there and let me pound API into him until I saw a slight explosion in the fuselage and he went down trailing gray and black smoke. I broke off to the right and pulled in behind another 109. The same thing happened, only this time I was almost hit by debris flying off the 109 before he went down. I had used only about 800 rounds of ammunition to score two kills.

I was in for a shock when I got back to Halesworth. Word spread quickly across the base that German flak had knocked down two of our best boys that day. Not only was Bud Mahurin missing but so was my pal Jerry Johnson. We were pleased to learn later that both had survived. Bud evaded capture and returned to England, while Jerry became a prisoner of war. Their losses were a real sobering development for the group, since these guys were both top aces. We were supremely confident of our ability to dish it out against the German fighters, but it was clear now that ground attack required almost as much luck to survive as it did skill.

Dangerous or not, we continued to pound ground targets. Anything that moved, and a few things that didn't, got our attention when we dropped down off escort to come home. On April 6 I was leading three pilots from the 63rd Squadron out of Germany when I spotted about six seaplanes anchored on a lake a few miles east of Schleswig. I took the flight down to strafe, and we put on quite a show. I had a good line on the seaplanes, and my gunfire kicked up big spouts of water as it walked into the closest one. The plane was an He-115, and I put a burst dead into its cockpit and engines with a heavy concentration. Next in line was an airplane that looked like the China Clipper. I put a burst into its engines, too, but saw no fire or explosion.

Now I could see light-arms fire coming at me from the banks of the lake dead ahead. Red streaks of tracer reached out toward me. I'd never seen so many tracers in my life. I sprayed the banks with my guns and kept on going. When we got home, Lt. Harold Matthews, my wingman, reported that he had a runaway gun that wouldn't stop firing, so he banked as he went over the seaplanes and could see smoke and flames coming from the one I'd hit first.

I also remember shooting at a staff car in Germany during a mission about this time. At first it just looked like an ant—a sort of shadow—going down a road. I came down to a lower altitude and identified it as a staff car. I was real green at this type of work and decided to attack it from the side, rather than from the front or back. I came down on the car at a steep angle and fired too long. In fact, when I pulled out, my own bullets ricocheted off the pavement and punctured the wing of my plane. I pulled back for all I was worth just to keep from hitting the ground. It was a real close call. After that I changed my mind about how to attack targets on the ground. From then on I used a flatter approach so I could open fire at longer range. We never did get any instruction in this; we just learned as we went and hashed it out in bull sessions in the evenings.

Toward the middle of April Jimmy Stewart completed his two-hundred combat hours and was transferred to a desk job in Fighter Command operations. Zemke asked me if I was interested in resuming command of the 61st as well as continuing to serve as assistant group flying exec. That sounded fine to me, so we made the switch.

An even bigger change came a few days later when the 56th Fighter Group moved from Halesworth to its new base at Boxted. About the only advantage the new base offered was its location. Not only was it close to Colchester, a good-sized town in its own right, but it also was half the distance to London.

The former residents at Boxted had been a 9th Air Force

P-51 group, so it was pretty well set up for us when we arrived. It had two hangars on opposite sides of the field. Other buildings skirted the tarmac perimeter. Farther back from the action were the administrative buildings, mess halls, and eight clusters of Nissen huts for living quarters. I lived in the "wheel house" with the other squadron commanders, Zemke, and some other key officers. It was a pleasant stucco farmhouse not far from the field.

My next score came on May 8, the same day Bob Johnson got two to bring his total to twenty-seven victories. That made him the top-scoring American fighter pilot of all times, with one more than Eddie Rickenbacker had shot down flying Spads during World War I. Everyone made a big deal out of it, and within days he'd been shipped home to go on a bond tour. That put Zemke, Schilling, and me at the top of the scoring heap among the pilots who were still active, but I didn't give much thought to catching Bob or beating out those other guys for the top ace slot. I just wanted to fly and fight and stay alive to fly again.

Still, I had some good days ahead of me. The best ever was May 22, 1944, when we escorted about three hundred heavies to Kiel. This was one of our first uses of the "Zemke Fan," a tactic Hub cooked up to spread the group over a wider area than we had previously covered on our missions.

We left the bombers safely on their way home, and I led the 61st on a 30-degree vector to twenty miles east of Bremen, where someone spotted a couple of locomotives through the clouds. I sent Evan McMinn's Yellow Flight down after them, while the rest of us waited up at 15,000 to provide top cover. We hadn't been circling long before I spotted a camouflaged air base down below us with quite a few planes coming and going. About the same time McMinn radioed to say he could see some Fw-190s taking off from the base.

I felt the familiar surge of excitement as my P-47 hurtled down toward the 190s. When I got closer I could see sixteen of them flying line-abreast. They had enough altitude and speed up now to be able to turn and fight, but maybe they didn't see us coming because I was able to lead White Flight right up behind eight 190s that were holding steady formation. Ten or twelve others were off to the left, presenting similar targets for the rest of our boys. I picked out one guy in front of me and let fly. My API ammo flashed all over his fuselage and wing. The 190 fell away and burst into flames as I pulled up and got behind another one. Again, I got good hits on the fuselage, but this time I could see the canopy flying off, and a moment later the pilot bailed out as the 190 fell off smoking.

I looked over my shoulder to clear my tail and there big as life were two more 190s coming in for the kill on me. I broke to the right and up, depending on that big paddle prop out front to pull me out of trouble. It didn't fail me. I made two turns, which was enough to shake off the 190s, but when I looked back I could see a P-47 going down in flames. It was my Number Three from White Flight, Lt. Richard Heineman. I also saw another P-47 trailing heavy smoke. This was either McMinn, who got home safely, or Lt. Cletus Nale, who was lost. In either case, seeing two of our P-47s in trouble sort of shook me.

I climbed back to 12,000 while calling the squadron to regroup over the airfield. Within five minutes we had six P-47s together. Then I saw about twenty more Fw-190s below us coming our way. But as they crossed their airfield, the gunners on the ground opened up at them. The 190s went every direction then and one of them fired a green flare, which must have been a signal to tell the gunners to cease fire. I took that as my cue, too, but I had another thought in mind.

I led our six P-47s down behind six 190s that were flying in string formation. When I got into range behind their tail-end charlie I gave him a long burst. The 190 slowed way down, gave off a cloud of black smoke, and then rolled straight into the ground. I closed up behind the next one, but I knew I was low on ammo so I held my fire while I sneaked a look off to my left. There below was another 190 trying to sneak in behind me for a shot.

I yanked back on the stick as I cut my throttle, slowing the P-47 down to a near stall. The 190 had no choice but to hop over me, unless he wanted to ram. Luckily, he didn't. Now I was behind him, but without any airspeed I was in no position to take a shot. The 190 turned tightly to the right, and as I turned behind him I saw five more 190s joining in our chase. That was enough to scare the bravest man, and I never claimed to be that guy anyway. I poured the coal to HV-A and made three steep climbing turns with the 190s hot on my trail. Then another 190 came in on me and made a 60-degree deflection shot that missed. I kept turning and climbing. By the time I reached 10,000 feet the 190s had all dropped away. Again, the paddle-blade prop had saved my skin.

I spotted three P-47s and joined up with them to head home. I wasn't finished yet, however. In about five minutes one of the other pilots called in twenty-plus bandits close by to the northeast near Bremen. We turned back over the area of my last fight, and I spotted a lone 190 below us in the clouds. He zipped into a cloud bank, so I flew on the other side and circled, waiting for him to emerge. Sure enough, he popped out a few moments later and I tagged on behind him at about 3,000 feet. My first burst went high, but the next shot banged him hard amidships. He snap-rolled to the left and went straight down, trailing thick black smoke.

That was enough for me. The telltale tracers had told me I was nearly out of ammunition, so I set course for Boxted and headed home, exhausted. Three kills in one day, plus a probable: May 22, 1944, turned out to be the most productive mission I ever flew. It was one of the toughest as well. Not only had we lost two pilots from my flight, but my wingman, Lt. Joel Popplewell, also had suffered serious damage. He recalls:

> I was hit over a hundred times. One cylinder was knocked out; the horizontal stabilizer practically destroyed. I recovered my aircraft at treetop level—when I was hit in the tail section my nose went up. I kicked right rudder and recovered. I slowly climbed to 8,000 and came back to base last, of course.

I'll never understand how that P-47 brought Joel home. When the engine stopped you could see that a hole had been blown clear through one of its prop blades. Joel said he never felt any vibration from the damaged prop, however. That's the kind of toughness that endeared the P-47 to the men of the 56th Fighter Group.

Nine

JUNE 6, 1944, will live for-
ever in the annals of military history as D-day, and I am
proud to be able to say I took part in the Normandy invasion.
But to be perfectly honest, D-day itself was something of an
anticlimax for most of us fighter pilots who flew cover over
the beachhead that day.

We had been watching the buildup for the invasion all
spring long. Our targets had gradually switched back from
Germany to France, and all the papers were full of speculation about when the big day would arrive. I figured we fighter
pilots were in for the air battle to end all air battles. The
weatherman, however, had other ideas.

To put it simply, the weather was lousy on D-day. For the
generals in charge, June 6 was now or never, because they
couldn't wait any longer without losing the favorable tides or
whatever. For the Allied fighter pilots, it was much the same.
Maybe the bad weather meant we couldn't give adequate air
cover, but we were going to try.

We weren't briefed on any of the details of the invasion

until early on the morning of the sixth. We knew that it was programmed to occur soon, but we also knew that the weather was a real stinker over England and Normandy right then. There was solid overcast in layers, with the bottom about 2,000 feet. This was enough to get the fighters off, so we were given specific sectors to patrol.

It was still quite dark when we went out to our planes for the first mission a little after 3 A.M. During the night, all of the P-47s had been painted with black-and-white bands around the fuselage and wings to help with identification. That way, everyone on the ground and in the air would know instantly if a plane was friendly or not. My crew chief, Ralph Safford, remembers:

I think that period stands out as the most exciting time. We started about 3 P.M. (on June 5) with routine maintenance of the plane plus painting the stripes. When we painted the invasion stripes we used a British paint that was very heavy in texture and hard to spread. We had to hurry the job; even so it took us about four hours to complete. I thought it was a sloppy job, but I guess it answered the purpose.

Then we did a special inspection, went to late chow, and only got about one hour's sleep before it was time to do the preflight checks and warmup at 2:30 A.M. The sky was full of aircraft—bombers, transports, gliders, etc. At dawn our planes took off, and to me that was the longest day.

My P-47 was heavily loaded for that early mission, and I couldn't see very well as we flew across the Channel, but I could tell that the water was literally covered with ships between England and France. It was one of the most spectacular sights that I have ever seen, a massive demonstration of power.

I think I flew four times that day. We would go out and patrol our area as best we could until we were about out of fuel. Then we'd come home, load up again, and go back out. We flew between layers of clouds. Sometimes I could barely make out the ground through light spots in the overcast, but that was all. I don't suppose we were very effective at cutting the Germans' supply lines to their defenders at Normandy, but at least our own guys weren't bothered by German air attacks. The weather must have kept the Germans from putting up their airplanes almost entirely.

The weather improved a little on June 7. On my second mission of the day, our P-47s were loaded with a bomb under each wing. I took off at 1043, leading the 61st Squadron to bomb railroad targets near Chartres. Conditions were hazy, and the P-47s were slow and unwieldy with the bombs hanging under them. We made the drop successfully about noon, and then made for Dreux Airdrome to see if we could scout up any action. Sure enough we did.

After one orbit of the field at 10,000 feet, I spotted two Fw-190s below and led White Flight down after them. We were down to 2,000 feet when I looked up and saw about twenty fighters above us flying in beautiful formation. At first I thought they were Spitfires, but then I identified them as a mixed group of 190s and Me-109s. I broke off the original attack and led our flight up after the bigger gaggle. As I pulled up behind two 109s, one saw me and broke away. The other guy kept going, so I opened fire on him. He broke left, and I followed, shooting all the way. I saw hits on his tail just as he slowed down abruptly, causing me to overshoot. I cut my throttle, then climbed up above him to prepare for another run. However, I saw the pilot bail out, saving me the trouble. Back up I went.

Soon I saw four 190s off the right and about 1,000 feet below me. Throttle full forward, and down I went again. I slowly closed on one of them, and for a moment I thought he was going to get away by ducking into the haze. I opened fire and almost immediately saw an explosion in his fuselage. He dropped off to the left and crashed into the ground. I returned to base a tired but satisfied pilot. Not only had I participated in the greatest military action of all times but I had also added to my score of enemy planes destroyed.

Those victories brought my total to twenty-four, and I started thinking seriously about going home. The invasion was a success, and I'd been there to see it. I'd been flying combat for well over a year. Plus, I wanted to get married.

My intent ever since I left Hawaii had been to marry Kay. Once I got involved in combat, of course, I was completely involved in the mission, the work at hand. I'll have to admit I didn't write to Kay nearly as much as I should have. But I never did forget the idea that one day I'd like to get back, whether on leave or permanently, and marry her. In May I had written to suggest that I would be taking leave soon, and perhaps we should get married then. She agreed and started making arrangements as best she could, considering we didn't know exactly when I would be arriving. After D-day she wrote that she had her trousseau and the approximate date pretty well established.

I had something else on my mind at this time, too. I was very well aware that I had a shot at becoming the top ace in the ETO. Bob Johnson had gone home with twenty-seven victories, so naturally I felt that before I went home I would like to have a record that was better than anybody else's. I didn't set any number goals, but that was my general intent.

That went along with the job, and I didn't feel I was quite finished.

So I continued to fly as often as possible until my leave orders came through. In fact, June was my busiest month of the war, with twenty-two missions recorded. Nearly all of them went to France, where we were heavily engaged in supporting the invasion troops. Sometimes we would load up with bombs and act as fighter-bombers; other missions were ramrods in which we escorted the heavies as they attacked airdromes, railroad yards, and other targets that would cripple the Germans' efforts to support their forces in the field.

My next scores came on June 12 as I was leading the group in an afternoon mission over northern France. We were patrolling about ten miles east of Paris when our radar controller, code-named "Colgate," reported over the radio that the 353rd Fighter Group was heavily engaged with a formation of German fighters west of the city. I immediately turned our planes west, hoping to get in on the action, but when we arrived in the area I couldn't find anything.

I was about to leave when Steve Gerick, flying Red Three, called in aircraft flying north on the deck. I couldn't pick them up, so Steve suggested I make a 180-degree turn and look directly below. I did so, and sure enough, there were twelve Me-109s down there at about 3,000 feet. I pushed over, and we started down from 14,000 out of the sun.

My speed built up in a rush, and I was almost on top of a 109 on the edge of the formation when I opened fire. I gave him one good burst and saw hits from the API flash all over his fuselage and tail. Flames erupted from his fuselage and pieces began to fly off, nearly hitting my plane. The 109 slowed down so quickly that I nearly ran into him from behind, but I was just able to duck below at the last split second. Then to my horror I saw the dying 109 above me start to nose over on top of me. I shoved the stick full forward and zoomed out of the way with no more than a few yards to spare.

By now I was low and slow, but I still had my wingman, Lt. Art Maul, with me. Normally in that situation I would have started grabbing all the altitude I could get, but just then we spotted four more 109s ahead of us and a few thousand feet below. I pushed the throttle through the gate and went down after them.

We caught up just as the German formation was breaking up, and I followed a 109 through a steep right turn before I started shooting. My fire hit him hard in the fuselage and cockpit. I pulled off to the left, but then the 109 fell off to that side and nearly rammed me before it went down trailing fire and smoke. I pulled up to the left, and as I did so I spotted a 109 approaching us from the rear and below, obviously trying to sneak in for a shot. I held my P-47 in a climbing turn, thanking God for the guy who invented the paddle-blade prop, and kept the 109 out of range for about thirty seconds. Then Bill Heaton of our squadron showed up and made a run on the 109 chasing him off.

Lieutenant Maul confirmed both my kills when we got back to Boxted. Now I was just one behind the record.

My chance to tie came on the twenty-seventh, during a dive-bombing mission. Again I was leading the group as Whippet White One, for an attack on Connantre Airdrome in France. The 61st was assigned to bomb first while I stayed on top with the other two squadrons to cover until they finished.

Red Flight of the 61st went down first, and as they completed their runs the four P-47s were met head-on by ten Me-109s that bounced them out of a cloud. No one was hit, and the 109s scattered back into the clouds. Blue and Yellow flights proceeded to make their bomb runs as I led White Flight on several unsuccessful attempts to bounce the 109s.

Finally, our gas was beginning to get low, especially for White Four, Jim Jure. We made one last run over the airdrome. I saw one 109 moving on the runaway in his landing roll and two more that had just come to a stop, so I knew there was a chance that a few more might still be in the pattern. I didn't look long before I saw a 109 pop out of the clouds at 4,000 feet and begin a dive toward the field. The chase was on.

I had a hard time keeping the 109 in sight, because its camouflage blended very well with the clouds around. Finally I lost it entirely down on the deck and pulled back up, disgusted.

Then, as if by magic, I saw four more 109s directly ahead and above us. I picked out a target and pulled in behind, but he spotted me and broke off sharply as I opened fire. Rather than chasing him, I decided to go after another one that was a couple of hundred yards to my right. I started firing while still out of range, but I closed rapidly and saw hits in his wing roots at 300 yards. A violent explosion followed in his fuselage, and then flames seemed to melt the tail clean off the aircraft. The 109 went down in pieces and I flew back to England with my twenty-seventh victory, tied for the honor of top ace in the 8th Air Force.

I was pleased to accept everyone's congratulations when I got home, but I was more proud of the 61st Fighter Squadron's success than my own. The June 27 mission had resulted in five kills for the squadron, which brought its total to 230, the best in the ETO. In fact, five full fighter groups in the 8th Air Force scored fewer kills during the entire war than our squadron had at that time. The 61st also boasted seventeen aces on its roster, and six pilots had been awarded the Distin-

guished Service Cross. The 61st certainly had lived up to the
bulldog face we proudly displayed on our squadron insignia.

Early July brought more action over France. On Indepen-
dence day, the group scored twenty kills in two missions for
the loss of one pilot. It was becoming increasingly evident
that the quality of the Luftwaffe pilots we were facing now
had deteriorated markedly from the tough guys we had faced
in these same skies the previous summer. Of course, that year
of hard-won combat experience hadn't hurt us, either.

On July 5 our job was to escort a formation of B-17s that
was returning to England from Italy and planned to bomb an
enemy airfield in France on the way. We flew south into
France to the rendezvous point, then turned around and
headed back toward England with the bombers.

I was leading the group with one of our Polish pilots,
Lanny Lanowski, as my wingman. The escort was uneventful
until we got to Evreux, and I was beginning to get frustrated.
I had missed out on the action the previous day, and now it
looked as if this mission would be another goose egg.

We were just about to break escort when I spotted a lone
Me-109 below us, heading eastward. This was it, my chance
to break the record! I dropped down through a hole in the
clouds, setting up a bounce on the guy, but then I lost him
in scud at 5,000. I made one orbit to look for him and realized I'd lost my wingman as well as the 109, so I began
climbing back up to a safer altitude. About that time, I heard
Red Flight call in many 109s engaged near an airdrome somewhere in the area.

I circled some more, looking for the action, and finally
picked up a 109 being chased by a P-47 below me. I figured
I might as well join the pursuit, but before I could catch up
with them, the other P-47 (which turned out to be Lanowski's)
but a good burst into the 109, and its pilot bailed out as I

broke out under the clouds. Once more I climbed back up and circled. This was getting frustrating.

My day wasn't over, however. A few minutes after I began circling, I spotted three more 109s on the deck. Down I went again, determined to do the job this time. As always, my speed built rapidly as I dropped down for the bounce. In fact, it built up too much, and before I could do anything about it, I had overshot the 109s. This left me in a pretty uncomfortable spot. There was nothing to do but turn into them and try to fight my way out. One 109 had broken away in my initial attack, so I concentrated on chasing the other two. Then I saw the single 109 climbing to my left, and I broke off to chase him instead.

We made three turns together at 3,000 feet. I fired several bursts at him, but the angle of deflection was extreme and I saw no hits. This joker was pretty good, but he made the classic mistake when he tried to break off by diving out of the fight. I followed him down, and my P-47 rapidly overhauled him.

I was closing up nicely when the 109 made a sharp turn to the left. I was ready for him, though, and stuck on his tail with no trouble. I led him two rings of deflection in my gunsight, which placed him out of sight under my nose, and opened fire. After my first burst I eased off the back pressure on my stick and the 109 danced back into my line of sight over the nose of my plane.

The 109 was smoking badly as he eased out of his turn and leveled off. Then it was fairly simple for me to line up behind him and let him have it with another burst of my eight .50 calibers. I was real close, and hits flashed all over the 109. Again I was in danger of overrunning my target, so I did a quick 180-degree turn, all the while keeping my eyes on him through the top of my canopy. As I watched, the pilot bailed out and the 109 crashed into the ground from about 200 feet.

So there it was: number twenty-eight. I was the top ace in all American forces at the time. The pressure I had placed on myself to set the record had paid off. But not long after I returned home to Boxted I began to feel pressure of a different kind. Previously I had lived in the shadow of our earlier top aces in the 56th. Now I was on center stage.

The publicity about me went right across the United States. Ted Malone, who was a radio commentator on the Westinghouse Network, asked me to come to London for an interview on his nationally broadcast show. The public relations troops at 8th Fighter Command were only too anxious for me to accept the invitation. So that put me right out of the cockpit and into a situation that was not very comfortable because I didn't know how to handle it. I got through the interview by giving Ted simple, direct answers to his questions and not trying to make myself out to be some big hero. He said it went very well.

Pretty soon everyone wanted to interview me or take my picture. I hardly had a moment to spare doing what I was in England to do, which was fly airplanes. I felt I had an obligation in the war, just like everyone else. But I was being taken out of that environment and put on a little pedestal. It was an awkward position for me, and I never did fit into it very well. I felt I had a responsibility to the men and to my country, but I was being used for public relations purposes, something that was out of my character.

It became clear very soon that the air force wanted me off operations and safe at home to sell war bonds, rather than continuing to fly missions. The same thing had happened to Bob Johnson when he set the record. So the wheels got in motion between the group headquarters and 8th Fighter

Command. They had me scheduled to leave sometime toward the latter part of July, depending on the availability of flights and so forth. I wrote Kay and my parents to let them know I'd be home in late July or early August, and the wedding plans shifted into high gear.

Back in Oil City, the word spread quickly that I would be coming home soon. Civic groups began preparing for a big celebration to mark my arrival, including a parade and a round of banquets and luncheons. The town even raised $2,000 as a wedding present for Kay and me. Unfortunately, it would be quite some time yet before we could collect it.

CHAPTER Ten

I AWOKE a happy man on the morning of July 20, 1944. Later that day I would be leaving Boxted airbase, heading for the United States. Within a week or so, Kay and I would be married. All I had to do was get myself home.

As I dressed, I thought about the hectic events of the past sixteen months since I had joined the 56th Fighter Group. We had grown from an inexperienced unit flying an untested aircraft into the most formidable fighter group in the 8th Air Force. A year ago, the 8th Air Force's B-17s had gotten creamed when they ventured beyond our escort range; now we could stay with them all the way to Frankfurt and beyond. At the same time, I had grown from an insecure "outsider" into the top ace and, more important, a leader of men. I couldn't help but smile.

Soon my uniform was straight, my duffle bag was packed, and I was ready to roll. I had orders to fly out that day with Capt. Jim Carter, one of the last remaining original pilots of the 61st. We had been flying together for a long time, and I was pleased to know that I would be traveling with him.

After breakfast I dropped by group operations to kill some time, and I found Lt. Col. Dave Schilling sitting at his desk there looking over the field order for the day's mission. He would be leading the group on a ramrod escort to Russelheim, near Frankfurt, Germany, and he was pretty excited because the weather was good and it looked like the kind of mission that was liable to stir up some action. I asked him to let me take a look. He handed the field order to me.

Schilling was right; this was the sort of mission that might give a guy the chance to score a kill or two. Almost before I knew what I was saying, I told Dave I wanted to go along. He looked up at me as if I was crazy. What do you mean go along? You're supposed to be going home. But Dave was a tiger, and he understood what I was saying. One more shot, one final mission to close out my tour with a bang. He called over to the 61st Squadron and told them to chalk me in on the operation board for one last trip in HV-A.

Carter was amazed when I told him what was up. He recalls that day this way:

> Gabby and I were to be picked up from Boxted . . . for a flight to Valley, Wales, where we would be flown to the U.S. for thirty days' leave.
>
> Our bags were on the airplane and Gabby said, "Just a minute, Jim, while I check the field order." Gabby disappeared into operations and soon came running back with a big grin on his face.
>
> "Throw the bags down, Jim," he said. "We can't miss this one. We can get home later."
>
> I stayed on the transport and handed only Gabby's bag to him and said that I would see him when I got back.

I had to get into my flying clothes in a hurry, since the mission was due to take off soon. I strapped on the .45 pistol that I always carried on missions, grabbed my helmet, goggles, and Mae West, then trotted out to the flight line. I barely had time to walk around HV-A before I had to strap in, but that didn't worry me. I knew I could depend on Safford, Schacki, and DiFranza to have her in perfect condition.

Safford jumped up on the wing next to me and pulled the safety harness over my shoulders, latching it snugly to the lap belts. I attached my oxygen mask and checked to make sure it was in working order. Ralph and I checked all the switches to see that they were in proper position, and then he hopped down off the wing and took his place by the energizer in front of the right wing. I switched on the gunsight, and its ring glowed brightly on the glass. In all my missions I never had a gunsight failure, thanks to DiFranza's careful attention to the details, but I always checked before each mission.

It was time to fly. Mission number 166 for me.

I raised my arm out of the cockpit and twirled my index finger in the air, our signal to start the engine. Safford acknowledged with an okay signal. I hit the ignition switch, primed the engine with a couple of strokes, then toggled the starter switch to "energize" and held it for about fifteen seconds.

"Clear!" I yelled, then toggled the starter to the right and held for a few seconds as the prop began to turn. The engine started with its customary gurgling roar, then smoothed out as I switched the mixture control to "auto rich." Safford unplugged the external power unit from the right side of the fuselage and gave me a thumbs-up signal, smiling all the while.

On my signal, Safford and Schacki pulled the chocks away

from the wheels and scampered back beyond the wingtips. I gave them both a wave, then rolled out of the hardstand and onto the taxi track toward the end of the runway. Along the way my wingman, Lt. Stuart Getz, and my second element, Lieutenants Cleon Thomton and Bill Barnes, fell in behind me. Thomton was easy to spot because he was flying Frank Klibbe's old plane, which had a big Indian head painted on the cowling.

We were on our way toward Germany by a few minutes after 9 A.M. I was leading our squadron from the center of White Flight. Capt. Don Smith, another of our old hands, led Blue Flight. He was flying his new bubble canopy P-47, HV-S, which sported a painting of a rooster on the cowling and the name "Ole Cock III." Lt. Praeger Neyland was leading Yellow Flight. Slightly ahead, I could see Dave Schilling, the mission commander, leading the 62nd Squadron.

We crossed the enemy coast near Blankenberge, Belgium, and rendezvoused with the B-24s we were to escort about twenty minutes ahead of schedule. I'm sure the fellows in those Liberators didn't mind. All was quiet as we took up position on the B-24s. I could hear the irritating wail of German jamming in my headphones, but we maintained radio silence. I swiveled my head in every direction, scanning the sky with practiced eyes for a sign of enemy fighters: perhaps a short spurt of contrail or the flash of sun reflecting off a canopy. I saw nothing but open sky.

An hour or more passed this way. We stayed with the bombers while they made their run over the target, some railroad marshalling yards near Frankfurt. The weather report had been right. It was beautiful. I could see the target clearly and the city of Frankfurt beyond. When the bombers turned for home I relaxed a little and began to scan the ground below for targets of opportunity. We had plenty of gas and a full load of ammunition. I didn't want to waste it.

We hadn't gone far before I saw an airfield below us about seven miles west of Koblenz. To the north ran the Rhine River; to the south was the Mosel. I called Neyland and told him to take Yellow Flight down for a squirt to size the place up. His four P-47s rolled over and dropped away. A few moments later he called in to report some He-111 bombers and Me-110 fighters parked on the field, and light flak. That's what I had been hoping for, so I sent Blue Flight down next to give it a shot while I held my flight above for top cover. By the time Neyland's flight had regained enough height to take over as top cover, Smith's P-47s had started a couple of fires down on the airfield. Now it was my White Flight's turn.

We dropped down to treetop level a couple of miles north-east, picking up plenty of speed in the process, and headed straight for the target. I wanted to maintain what little element of surprise might be left after the other flights had come in from other directions. In a few seconds I cleared the edge of the field and could see several undamaged He-111s dispersed around the runway, and three others burning to my left. I picked out one of the bombers and gave it a long burst. My gunfire walked across turf and directly into the bomber. I looked back over my shoulder as I passed over to see the Heinkel explode in a cloud of flames and black smoke. The plane must have been fully loaded with fuel when I hit it.

This was great. I could see the boys in my flight also got some hits, but there were a few undamaged bombers still sitting there. I decided to buck the rules and make another pass. At that time, our policy was to make one pass on an airdrome and get out, because the flak gunners were always ready and waiting if you tried to come back for more. But I figured the flak had been so light that I could get away with another pass. And besides, this was my last mission. What was Zemke going to do about it? Send me home?

I was still way down on the deck when I called the squadron and told them I was going back in. I whipped the P-47 around in a tight 180-degree turn. This was a mistake because I was strictly as low as I could be over the trees. I completed the turn and leveled off. In a flash I was heading back toward the field on a reciprocal course from the first pass. I wanted to stay low because I knew the element of surprise was gone and I needed to make myself as difficult a target as possible for the gunners on the field. I guess I didn't realize how low I really was.

Again I was able to pick up a 111 to shoot at. The gunners around the field were ready and waiting for me, and I could see a few tracers arching toward me out of the edges of my vision. I pulled the trigger and HV-A shook as its guns spat out a burst of fire. With disgust I saw that I had aimed high and my bullets were carrying over the parked bomber. That's when I compounded my first mistake. Without thinking I twitched the stick forward slightly to drop the nose for a better firing angle.

The nose came down, but then I felt a thump that seemed to bounce me off the ground. It wasn't a severe jolt, but it was enough to make my heart jump something fierce. The bottom of the aircraft hadn't hit the ground, but the propellor had. It must have bent the tips somewhat, and it definitely stripped the prop's control mechanism, because in a split second hydraulic oil sprayed back all over my windshield, and the engine began to vibrate badly. I could just barely see out, and I had no idea how badly my P-47 was damaged.

Here is Cleon Thomton's account of how it looked from his cockpit:

We found this airfield, and we couldn't believe our eyes, as these planes were lined up on the field like they were on parade. What had probably happened was that they had been on a night bombing mission and there hadn't been time to disperse them yet.

The field ran east and west with the planes lined up on the south side, and there was one lone bomber sitting in front of a hangar on the west side. Gabby told me to take that one, and he would take the ones on the south side. I had just completed my pass at this target, and as I pulled up I saw this streak of dust going across the field. At first I thought it was somebody's bullets, but it turned out to be Gabby's plane. Someone asked who that was, and I said I thought it was White Leader. . . .

I have always had a theory about why an experienced pilot like Gabby would have this happen. He was flying the first P-47D-25 model with the bubble canopy we got in the squadron. These planes carried 270 gallons of gas in the main tanks instead of the 205 gallons in the razorback P-47s. We had just dropped our wing tanks, so our main tanks were full. That additional gallonage added over 400 pounds of weight, and definitely changed the mushing characteristics of the aircraft. I think it mushed right into the ground when he pulled up.

My first instinct was survival. What was the best chance of getting home? I throttled back quickly in order to keep the plane from shaking itself to pieces, and it helped a little. But I realized I was hundreds of miles deep into Germany and there was no way HV-A was going to be able to fly me out. I had to make a decision instantly before the airplane made it for me. I was too low to bail out, and I didn't have enough power to climb. I figured my chances would be best if I belly-landed the plane in an open field somewhere. But open fields were few and far between in this corner of Germany. I called the squadron and told them I'd had it.

The airfield was behind me now, and I couldn't turn back to get in there. I still had pretty good airspeed, and the prop was still turning over. I squinted through the oil-smeared windshield and looked for some place ahead of me that would be adequate to sit the P-47 down. Beyond a clump of trees appeared a wheat field. It wasn't very big, but it would have to do. There wasn't enough time left to get picky about a parking place.

I felt that if I dumped the airplane in on its belly it would decelerate very rapidly with its wheels up. As soon as I crossed over the trees I shoved the stick forward and pushed the P-47 down into the field nose first. I guess I was doing about 160 miles per hour when I hit the wheat and started skidding through it. I held the stick forward and was able to maintain slight control of the rudder and elevator until I slowed below flying speed.

The trees at the far end of the field were looming closer, so I kicked the right rudder pedal hard. The airplane skidded crossways with the left wing forward as the slide continued. I knew that if I hit any hard object the wing would take the impact and crumple. Now I crossed my arms in front of my face and grabbed the bar that was above me on the lower portion of the canopy to keep my head from banging into the gunsight if we jolted to a stop.

The jolt never came. Instead I felt a sudden forward motion as the nose and wing dug in. The tail section rose behind me, and for a second I thought HV-A was going to flip over onto her back. But just before we reached vertical the motion stopped and the tail flopped back onto the ground. I found myself sitting quite still on the ground, all in one piece.

I only had a second to collect my wits before I realized the plane was smoking, probably from the broken oil line and perhaps a severed gas line as well. My greatest fear was fire. I tried to open the canopy, but it wouldn't budge. The fuselage had warped in the crash landing, bending the rails that the canopy was supposed to slide back on. I began to panic. I hadn't flown 166 missions just to burn up in my plane after such a successful crash landing on the last one. I braced both feet against the instrument panel, grabbed the cross bar that was supposed to open the canopy, and pull back for all I was worth. I guess the adrenaline was really pumping right then and gave me a little superhuman strength. The canopy opened just far enough that I could get my head out. That was all I needed.

I figured if I could get my head out of the cockpit, I could get the rest of my body out, too. I released my parachute. I took my leather flight jacket off and pushed it out. I picked up my ration kit and I pulled myself up through that very small opening. Once I was clear of the cockpit, I jumped down onto the wing, pulled my jacket back on, and looked around for a few moments. It appeared quiet in every direction.

I still had my .45 strapped on. After I jumped down to the ground I took it off and tossed it under the plane, which was continuing to smoke. I figured the gun wasn't going to do me any good, but it might be of use to some German if he picked me up and wanted to use it on me. If the plane continued to burn, the gun would go up with it.

In the heat of excitement, I looked around to get my bearings and decide which direction I ought to run. To the west was a little forest, with some tree cover, a lot of underbrush, and foliage. I began to trot toward it. As I ran I began to hear these little clicks. They didn't bother me at first. But then I heard another click that was followed by somewhat of a whistle going by me. I looked back to my left and saw two soldiers across the field who were getting down onto their knees and firing their rifles at me. Obviously, what I had heard was a bullet whizzing past my head!

I played cat and mouse with the two soldiers. As they went down on one knee to fire at me, I would hit the dirt. When they jumped up and began running toward me, I would get back up and start running away from them again. I outran them by a considerable margin. Finally, I made it into the cover of the woods. I kept running and soon found myself on a well-worn path. It had little shrines every so often along it. They were like little chapels with statues inside them sitting on a level wooden floor.

After I had passed several of these shrines I decided the next one would make a good place to hide. I figured I could wedge myself between the floor and the ground, and that's exactly what I did. I just had time to pull a little brush over me before I heard the soldiers coming up the path behind me. They were making quite a bit of commotion, looking up the path and off to either side, as they talked back and forth.

I can vividly recall the soldiers passing right by the shrine, just a few feet away from me. They were older men, probably some sort of home guards and not first-line troops. I was just scared to death, and I was sure that my pulse was beating so loudly that they would be able to hear it. And then they were gone, moving on down the path ahead of me. The remarkable thing is that they never backtracked. They just kept on going and didn't re-search the ground they had covered. I don't know where they went, but I never saw them again.

By now it was just past noon. While I had been running through the woods, Don Smith had sent two members of his flight down to strafe HV-A so it wouldn't be captured, and then the squadron had set off for England without me. I decided it would be best for me to stay put until dark, even though it meant spending the entire afternoon and evening in my hiding place under the shrine. Periodically I would hear the sound of a small airplane engine and look up to see a small German observation plane, probably searching the area for me. They kept it up all afternoon.

During that long afternoon I took stock of things. I had a small compass and a map in my escape and evasion kit. I also had a water bag and a tube of concentrated milk, but not much else. I wasn't worried about eating at that time, though. I just wanted to put as much distance as possible between me and the crash site.

Finally it began to get dark. Quietly, I extracted myself from my hiding place and started out through the woods again. After I had tromped along for a while I came to a dirt road, which I decided to follow to the west since I knew that any other direction would soon lead to a river. Before long I came to a small village, maybe four or five homes on each side of the road. The track was quite narrow as it came between the houses, and I could see the women of the families talking to each other back and forth from the second-story windows. I figured I would be able to walk right through unnoticed, even though there were a lot of men in and around the buildings. So I dragged one foot as if I had been hurt in the war and was no longer capable of being a combat soldier. I wanted to look like an invalid. I walked slowly down the street dragging my foot behind me, and it didn't take long to get through the village.

The houses were still in sight behind me when I heard a commotion coming from that direction. I looked back and saw a group of men coming together, waving their arms and talking frantically about something. I strongly suspected that something was me. Someone had figured out that I didn't belong there, and these guys were going to chase me down and find out what I was doing in their village. Pretty soon I could see them marching up the road in my direction. I knew I had to do something quickly, so I started running as fast as I could down that dirt road.

A short distance ahead was a slight knoll. Once I made it over the crest, the knoll blocked me from view of the men chasing behind. There were cornfields on either side of the road, and I decided I would be better off hiding in a cornfield than continuing to run on the road. I raced down one of the rows of shoulder-high corn to the right until I was about 150 feet from the road, being careful not to break off any plants to leave a trail. Then I lay down among the corn stalks.

Then I was in hiding. I pulled up into a little ball to make myself as small as possible and pulled the closest stalks around me as best I could to provide a little coverage without breaking them off. Pretty soon I heard my pursuers come over the rise. There were about six of them, all talking excitedly. They must have figured out I was in one of the fields because they split up, some of them going into the field to the left, and the others coming into my field. They really ripped through that corn, spreading it this way and that. The more they broke up the cornstalks, the more secure I felt because they were tromping over their own clues. I lay there absolutely motionless, and if I could have quit breathing right then I would have, just to keep quiet.

Before long, one of the searchers found his way into my section of the field. I listened intently as he came closer and closer. Finally, he couldn't have been more than three feet away. I'm sure that in my anxiety at that moment, my pulse rate must have gone well past the red line. I could hear my pulse beating behind my ear. Finally he moved past me and went on to another section of the field. Just then it started to rain lightly, and it was getting quite dark. That was the end of the search. After a while I could hear the men heading back to the village.

As I look back on it now, I can see that they probably weren't all that anxious to come face to face with me alone in that field. They didn't know who I was—maybe an escaping forced laborer or an army deserter, maybe even a desperate Allied aviator trying to save his skin. These were farmers, not soldiers, and they knew they stood a good chance of getting hurt out in that dreary cornfield. Had I been in their shoes, I would have gone home too.

Once I was sure my pursuers had departed, I started moving again. This time I decided to stay off the road and work my way through the woods on the far side of the cornfield. When I got into the woods, however, I found that I couldn't make my way through it in the dark. The underbrush was so thick that I couldn't see it before I ran into it. I might have been okay on a moonlit night, but this night was overcast and raining, absolutely pitch dark. So I sat myself down against a bush as gracefully as possible and tried to sleep. I doubt that I was successful at sleeping, but at least I got some rest. It had been a long day.

I've been asked over the years if I spent any time that first day reflecting on the nasty turn of events in my life and feeling sorry for myself. After all, I should have been on a transport plane heading home across the Atlantic instead of hiding out like an escaped criminal in a miserable forest in the center of Germany. But I can say in all honesty that I didn't do that. My every thought was on how to avoid capture, and I simply didn't have time to do anything else. I can't, however, say that that thought never crossed my mind in the months that followed.

At first light, I started walking again. Before long I found that I had a new problem. I was wearing my black flying boots, and they weren't designed for this sort of use. What was worse, they had become wet during the previous night's rain. This made walking increasingly difficult. During this day I walked through the fields instead of staying on the road. As long as it was light I had little difficulty staying out of sight as I continued moving.

I came to two fields that were separated by a hedgerow and small trees. Across one of the fields I could see a farmer heading in my general direction leading a horse that was pulling a wagon. I couldn't keep moving without him seeing me, so I decided to hide in the underbrush of the hedge. When the farmer got closer I could see he had a boy with him, perhaps nine or ten years old.

I could see them clearly from my hiding place as they approached. The farmer had a ''P'' on the lapel of his shirt. I didn't know what that meant, but when they got within earshot I could hear that they were speaking in Polish. I was thirsty. I hadn't eaten anything since breakfast the previous morning at Boxted. I decided to take a chance.

As the man and boy passed by my hiding place, I called out to them in Polish, asking if they could spare me some food and water. My call startled them, and they stared in my direction until they figured out exactly where I was. Then they walked over to me. I explained I was a flyer who had crash-landed near the airdrome. Oh yes, the farmer said, he had seen the plane that went down. I repeated my request for food and water.

He looked at me intently, obviously considering his options. He was a displaced person—forced labor—so he had no loyalty to the Germans. On the other hand, he was putting himself in a very precarious situation if he were to be seen by

Paul Conger was one of our most aggressive pilots. He flew two tours with the 56th and ran up a score of 11½ victories. Here he sits in the cockpit of his "Hollywood High Hatter" P-47. (Paul Conger)

Sharing a toast are three pilots of the 61st Fighter Squadron who were credited with no less than 58 German aircraft destroyed during the war. They are, *from left,* Joe Powers (14½ kills), Bob Johnson (27), and Jerry Johnson (16½). Bob Johnson had the best eyes in the outfit, and Jerry was the best marksman.

I first ran across Col. Bob Landry while I was stationed in Hawaii. He commanded the 56th Fighter Group from October through December 1943, then went on to Eighth Fighter Command. (Paul Conger)

One of the fine Polish pilots who joined the 61st Fighter Squadron in 1944 was 1st Lt. Witold Lanowski. Lanny flew with the Polish Air Force and the RAF before joining us. (Carl Westman)

My sister Lottie, Mom, and Dad enjoy the front page coverage that the Oil City newspaper, the *Blizzard,* gave the story when I scored my 28th kill on July 5, 1944, to become America's leading ace at that time. (UPI)

I was a skinny bird when I was released from the German POW camp at Barth and returned to the 56th Fighter Group briefly in May 1945. Here I enjoy a reunion with Jim Carter, Ralph Eastwood, and Joe Perry. They all had served with me in the 61st Fighter Squadron.

I posed for this formal portrait shortly after the end of the war. Of note is the Polish Cross of Valor above my wings. It was awarded to me in April 1943 by Gen. Wladyslaw Sikorski, the prime minister of the exile Polish government in London.

Kay and I were married on June 11, 1945, at Prairie Du Chien, Wisconsin. Much to our surprise, the press gave the ceremony a lot of coverage. (UPI)

An F-86A Sabrejet of the 4th Fighter Wing stands on the ramp at K-13 in South Korea during the summer of 1951. I'm standing at the wingroot in flight gear, talking to Capt. Jimmy Jabara, *far right,* and another pilot. Meanwhile, Col. George Jones, *second from left,* faces the camera. (George Jones)

Capts. Richard Becker and Ralph "Hoot" Gibson, who, along with Jimmy Jabara, were the first aces of the Korean War, discuss a mission with me and Capt. Arthur Beckwith, intelligence officer with the 4th Fighter Wing, in September 1951. (UPI)

I give a briefing to Gen. Matthew Ridgway, the overall commander in Korea, and Lt. Gen. Frank Everest, commander of the 5th Air Force, on the ramp at K-13 in 1952 while I was commanding the 51st Fighter Wing. My group commander, Col. Al Schinz, stands at left. (U.S. Army)

Two of the key officers I brought with me to the 51st Fighter Wing when I transferred from the 4th were Maj. Bill Whisner, *center,* and Col. George Jones. Behind us is Whisner's F-86, which displays 5½ victory marks below the cockpit, Bill's final score in Korea. (George Jones)

Probably the best thing that happened to me in Korea was "Operation Happiness," in which the 51st Fighter Wing took on the job of sponsoring an orphanage at the Yongjoo Jahae Buddhist temple near our airbase. Here our wing chaplain, Father Mike Finneran, passes out goodies to some of the orphans.

East and West meet in friendship. The priest at the Yongjoo Jahae orphanage thanks me for the contributions of "Operation Happiness" in the spring of 1952.

President Harry Truman welcomes me home from Korea during my visit to the Oval Office on June 24, 1952.

Our entire family went overseas with me during my assignment as commander of the 18th Tactical Fighter Wing on Okinawa. We posed for this picture in January 1962. *Top row, from left,* Djoni (age 15), Debbie (4), Mary Ann (12), Francie (10), and Donnie (13). *Bottom row,* Kay, Linda (6), Jimmy (7), Patsy (8), Robert (2), and me.

any Germans talking to me, much less giving me assistance. I suggested he duck into the bushes with me so we could talk without the chance of being seen. He told the boy to wait in the wagon, and then he joined me. He asked me about the war. How was it going? Would the Germans win? I told him it looked as if the Allies would win by Christmas. I told him about the Normandy invasion and that we had already established air superiority over Europe. This pleased him greatly, because he had been in forced labor here since shortly after the Germans overran Poland back in 1939. He agreed to help me, but he said it would take a while to bring me any food without arousing suspicion. They would have to work their way back toward the house, then find an excuse to come back to where I was hiding.

After he left, I began to worry. What if he changed his mind? Did he really intend to bring me some food, or would he return with a couple of German soldiers? I decided to move forward where I could keep a better eye on them when they returned. Also, that way I wouldn't be a sitting duck if trouble developed. Then I waited. It must have been two hours before I saw the two of them coming back across the field, leading the horse and wagon.

When they came abreast of me, I called out to them again. They turned around, and I could see they were carrying a jug of water and some bread with a little margarine on it. The farmer said he was sorry, but that was all he could spare me. I couldn't have been happier with a porterhouse steak and a beer.

Again the farmer joined me in the hedge, and we talked some more. He wondered what would happen to him after the war. I told him Poland would be liberated and given its land back. He said he was worried about the Russians, too. I said I didn't know anything about that. He was obviously a man of some intelligence, probably in his midthirties. I asked him how far he thought I was from Belgium or Luxembourg, but he didn't have much idea of that. He was confined to this small area of Germany. He was a farmer. I only wish I had his name now. If he was still alive I'd certainly enjoy getting back to him.

The farmer's visit, and his food, gave me a new lease on life, a little bit more confidence. Maybe I had a chance of getting away after all. We parted as friends, and I continued my westward trek.

The next four days were mostly a blur. I took to walking only in the low-light periods of early morning and toward evening. During the middays I would hide in the woods. My biggest problem wasn't food so much as it was water. As I walked, I became dehydrated. The more I walked, the thirstier I got. I took advantage of every opportunity. I drank water out of any stream I came across. At one point, I even got down on my knees and drank water out of mud puddle that had formed in a rut of a dirt road. I didn't even hesitate. The water looked clear enough to me, and I was so thirsty that I had to have it. I was lucky. It wasn't contaminated, because I didn't get sick at all. For food, I picked sugar beets, berries, and anything else that looked edible.

The farther I went, the more fatigued I got. At one point I approached a farm with the idea of going into one of the outbuildings to sleep. It turned out to be a chicken coop, and when a rooster started raising a ruckus I had to take off. By the fifth day I was weary, unshaven, and looked like a tramp. I was also getting restless, wanting to cover more ground. I figured I was still four or five days from the Moselle River, and I didn't know how I would cross it when I got there. My first desire was to reach it. So I started walking longer into the day.

I was on a path that wound around bushes and trees. I could see a valley below me on one side, and a hill rose up on the other side. I planned to climb the hill and hide up there for the day. But it was late enough in the morning that people were already out and about. I couldn't see forward very far because of the winding route of the path.

I rounded a corner and found myself face to face with a man and a boy who were leading a cow. It was too late to duck out of sight because they were only about one hundred feet away and I was in plain view. There was nothing to do but keep walking toward them. I nodded as we passed, and they responded in kind. We both kept moving.

When I got out of sight, I dodged off the path and into the underbrush. I wanted to see what would happen next. In a few moments the two of them returned up the path without the cow. The fellow called out in German to other farmers nearby. The boy walked right up to my hiding place and looked directly at me. Our eyes met, and I'll never forget how blue his were. He called to his father, who rushed up to us. I had no hope of getting away now, so I agreed to go with them.

The farmer took me to his home, which was a nice farmhouse. When we got inside I noticed a crucifix on the wall. Maybe there was hope here, after all. I pulled out my rosary and pointed to his religious artifacts. Would he help me? He didn't speak English, but he got the gist of what I wanted. He shook his head sternly: no way. Then he turned to his hand-crank telephone and made a call. In a short time some policemen arrived and escorted me to the local jail. That was it. No excitement. No fight to the finish. Just a clean cell with a sliding cover over the window in the door.

All day people would come by and open the window to take a look at me. At one point the jailer brought me some ersatz tea and a chunk of *kriegsbrot,* or "war bread." It looked like sawdust and had a hard crust to preserve it. I practically needed a saw to cut it open, but eventually I broke off a piece. I soaked it in the tea to soften it up so I could eat it. There would be a lot more *kriegsbrot* in my diet in the months that followed. My days of freedom were over.

CHAPTER *Eleven*

I SUPPOSE my period as a prisoner of war actually began on the morning of July 25, 1944, when I was collected at the little German jail by two Luftwaffe airmen. They carried their rifles right into the cell where I was being held and escorted me out.

One of the men could speak a little English. He told me they were taking me to Oberursel, an interrogation center on the outskirts of Frankfurt. I left the jail with one guard on either side, and we walked a couple of miles to a railroad stop to wait there for an eastbound train. It was just a sign next to the track where the country folks could catch a train to the city, no station or anything. A steam locomotive finally appeared in the distance, and not long afterward we got aboard a car bound for Frankfurt. We couldn't have been too far from Frankfurt, because it took only about an hour and a half to get there. And this train was definitely not an express.

When we got to the Frankfurt station, the place was a disaster. The rails were all torn up except for a very few that the Germans were able to keep in operation. The station building itself was a pile of rubble, obviously the victim of some accurate Allied bombing. Evidence of the devastation continued after we left the station and began to walk through the city. Some streets were barely passable. That kind of worried me because I was an enemy airman, so I could be considered responsible for the damage. Many of the people we passed gave me dirty looks. One of the guards made note of the obvious hostility toward me. He said they would try to take care of me if anyone got nasty, but they wouldn't hurt their own people to protect me. Luckily for me, no lynch mob formed. Eventually we reached a streetcar stop where we could catch a ride to Oberursel.

Once we arrived at Oberursel, my guards turned me over to the authorities at the Auswertestelle-West interrogation center and departed. After the standard name-rank-and-serial-number routine, my first introduction to military captivity was a 14-by-10-foot cell. It contained nothing more than a sleeping bench against one wall and a heater next to it. Even though this was late July, the heater was just as hot as you could get it. Whether that was by accident or by design I don't know, but I do know that cell was some kind of a hot box. I hardly slept that night.

The following morning I was taken from my hot box, allowed to shower, and then introduced to my interrogator. I couldn't tell his rank by looking at his uniform, but he was very well turned out. He introduced himself in perfect English as Hanns Scharff. I decided to come on strong, so I started right in to complain about the heat in my cell. What were they trying to do, cook me?

Smooth as silk, Scharff apologized for the thoughtless treatment. It must have been an accident, he said. He would take care of it immediately. So now he took on the role of the good guy.

Scharff's first remark was to ask what had taken me so long to get there. He said the Luftwaffe had expected to capture me long ago. He said that they had my friend, Maj. Jerry Johnson, up at Stalag Luft I. He mentioned other pilots I knew who were prisoners and said they were all okay and getting good treatment.

Scharff talked some more, and then he got up from his desk. You know, he said, there were some real fine pictures of you in *Stars and Stripes*. Then he pulled out a complete copy of the newspaper and read its account of my twenty-eighth kill to me.

"You see, we know who you are," he said. "As a matter of fact, we know more about your organization than you probably even think about. We know where the pilots come from and we know what they're doing. We have a clipping system, and we have our own little ways of getting information.

"What we really have you here for is just one thing. We want to know if you are *the* Gabreski."

"What do you mean?" I asked.

"You say you are Francis S. Gabreski, but we are looking for Francis E. Gabreski," Scharff said.

It was a pretty simple ploy to get me started talking, and I saw through it right away. I don't know where he got the "E." I just told him that I was Francis S., and I couldn't help him beyond that. We parted amicably, and he said we would continue the conversation later. That went on for quite a few days.

One day Scharff asked me if there was anything I would like to do during my stay at Oberursel.

"Well, yeah, I'd like to go to church." I replied.

Scharff said he could arrange that, but I would have to promise that I wouldn't try to escape because he would be held responsible.

"I'm not promising anything," I said. "But my only motive is to go to church."

Before long, Scharff and I rode out the gates of the center in a staff car, heading for a nearby Catholic church. When we arrived, he walked me up to the front door but didn't go in. He told me he would meet me there when the service ended.

I listened carefully to the Latin portion of the service, which of course I could understand. The sermon was in German, and I couldn't follow that. But I felt much better for having gone. I didn't entertain any thoughts of escape. I just wanted a little time alone with the Lord above, and that's all I was interested in at the time.

As the days passed I began to feel more comfortable with Scharff, in spite of myself. He would go on and on about how he couldn't understand why Germany and the United States were on opposite sides of the war, since our countries were so much alike.

Another time he took some other captured American fighter pilots and me to a public swimming pool in the city. He told us to keep quiet so no one would know we were Americans. There were all kinds of people there—girls, mothers and fathers, and so forth. But what impressed me were all the young guys with arms and legs missing who were there, former soldiers who had been grievously wounded in battle. That had a real impact on me.

This was a reality of war that I had been shielded from until now. War in the cockpit of a fighter was impersonal. We weren't shooting at people. We were shooting at machines, destroying machines. We saw the pieces flying off an airplane. We didn't see the gory end of it, the bloodshed. I was a little bit shook by the swimming pool visit.

Scharff's specialty was fighter pilots, so there were quite a few of us at Oberursel. He arranged for some of us to meet one of the top Luftwaffe aces once. I was pretty ambivalent about the idea, but I wasn't about to fight it, either. I don't know who the pilot was, but he was a nice enough guy about my age. I didn't have that much to say to him, and he didn't have that much to say to me.

But that was how Scharff operated. The interrogation was very spotty, mixed with niceties. Scharff was an internationalist, not a Nazi. He was very suave, and his English was superb. His wife was an English girl, and he had been an Opel car representative in Johannesburg, South Africa, before the war.

Finally, I guess Scharff figured he had squeezed all the information out of me that he could. But instead of sending me straight to a prisoner of war camp, he arranged for me to go to Hohe Mark hospital, where many Allied flyers who had been badly burned and otherwise injured were being treated. I spent about five days there, mixing with the guys and getting to know Col. Charlie Stark, who was kind of the overseer of the Americans there.

When Scharff came back to Hohe Mark, I told him I wanted to be sent to the POW camp at Sagan, Poland. I figured that I would have a better chance of mixing in with the population there if I could manage to escape. Scharff wasn't too hopeful about that idea. He said the Germans were filling up camps one at a time. First I would be sent to Dulag Luft, the POW distribution center at Wetzlar. Then I would go to a Stalag Luft, which would be my permanent home.

About twenty of us left Oberursel together. As we were leaving, Scharff handed me a box containing ten rolls with some sort of dressing on them. I split them up among the men, and all of us appreciated the gesture. We ate them as we marched to the railroad station for the first leg of our trip to Wetzlar. We carried Red Cross provisions kits with us on the march. One thing I'll never forget was that during the march a German soldier came up to me and insisted on carrying my package. It was one soldier's gesture of respect for the achievements of another. He knew who I was and the record I had compiled, so he was going to give me a little special treatment by carrying my bag. That really flipped me. It was extraordinary and amusing to me. But it was a good example of the complex thinking of a soldier.

The train trip to Wetzlar, about fifty miles north of Frankfurt, was uneventful. The Dulag Luft was a miserable place: bare wooden barracks and minimal sanitation. It was just a steppingstone to prepare us for permanent captivity. I was deloused again and given my prison clothes. They were rough khaki, just like army clothes. Through it all, I was allowed to hang onto my flight jacket.

I was only at Wetzlar about four days, but during that time I experienced one of the most frightening events of my life. Wetzlar was a small industrial city. These days it's famous as the home of Leica cameras, but back then I'm sure they were turning out more volatile products there. Because of this, Wetzlar was on the 8th Air Force's target list.

I was unfortunate enough to be at Wetzlar on a day when the B-17s came over for an unfriendly visit. First we heard the air raid sirens begin to wail, and soon we could see a whole formation of B-17s above us on their target run. We were supposed to go to shelters in the camp, but a good many of us decided to stay outside and watch the show. We thought we would be pretty safe in the camp.

But as we stood there looking up at a formation of B-17s going over, we could see them release their bombs directly over the camp. I stood there frozen for a moment. It was too late to run, and I didn't know where to go anyway. Then someone made a break for a nearby revetment, and soon all of us were stampeding into it, trampling over one another trying to get there first. Of course, the momentum of the B-17s carried the bombs over the camp and onto their target in Wetzlar. Later the Germans reprimanded us for not obeying orders to go to the shelters. I guess they didn't like the idea of having a bunch of cheerleaders out there in the yard during a raid.

Finally, they passed out Red Cross parcels to us and sent us on our way. My group's destination would be Stalag Luft I at Barth, a lonely outpost on the Baltic Sea coast north of Berlin. The train trip took all day and well into the night to cover the four hundred or so miles to Barth. The train stopped several times because of Allied air raids nearby, and each time I could feel the tension rise among us. All of us knew there was no way a P-47 pilot up there could tell our train was carrying a bunch of "Kriegies," as we POWs called ourselves. And we all knew how much damage a P-47 could do to the train—and us. Luckily for us, the train wasn't attacked.

Finally, the train rolled to a stop at Barth. A single track led into the small station. It was practically the end of the line, because you couldn't go much farther without running into the Baltic Sea. German guards gathered us into a loose formation and marched us out of town.

My first view of Stalag Luft I was anything but encouraging. As we marched up the road toward the camp, I could see the mass of barbed wire that formed the outer perimeter and the tall guard towers at all four corners. The searchlights and machine guns in each tower were mounted conspicuously and aimed down into the camp. As in Dulag Luft, the barracks were shabby one-story affairs. Beyond the camp I could see a scraggly forest on one side and to the north an open plain that led to the sea. It didn't occur to me on that

August day just how nasty the winter winds would be blowing in off the Baltic. I didn't expect to be there much beyond Christmas, anyway. I thought the war would be over by then.

We passed through several gates and then went through a check-in area where they set up our identifications and assigned us to one of the compounds. Rather than pitching the Kriegies all into one big camp, the Germans had split up Stalag Luft I into several compounds, the divide-and-conquer theory at work, I suppose. They had well over five thousand POWs in the camp at that time, and by the end of the war the number topped nine thousand.

I was first assigned to North Two compound. One of the first guys I saw when I walked through the gate was Jerry Johnson. This cheered me up considerably. He said they had received word in the camp that I had been taken prisoner, but they didn't know I'd be coming to Barth. Before long I found Mac McCollom there, too. He was one of the long-timers at Barth, having arrived way back in January. We had quite a jolly reunion. I brought them up to date on the happenings in the 56th, and they briefed me on what to expect there at Barth.

It was pretty simple, really. The Germans kept the Kriegies locked up in the compounds, and we ran things from there. It was just like any other military organization, with rank and time in grade determining the command structure. The senior officer in charge when I arrived was Col. J. J. Byerly, a former B-17 pilot. His position was the equivalent of a wing commander. Below him, each compound was the equivalent of a group and each barracks was a squadron. We had a full organization, with sections for intelligence, supply, and all the rest.

We had a roll call in the morning and another in the evening. We would line up in the exercise area, and the Germans would come in with their head-counters to make sure no one was missing. We would stand at attention until they finished. Then we would exchange salutes and they would leave. If someone was missing, they would check his barracks and elsewhere until they were satisfied he hadn't escaped. We never did have anyone disappear while I was in charge. Other than that, the guards left us alone except for an occasional shakedown search or something like that.

The days quickly blended into a dull routine. The most important times of all were when a load of mail arrived. I didn't receive any mail at first, because it took a while before my family and Kay got the word on how to reach me. My parents had been notified of my capture soon after my first visit with Hanns Scharff, but Kay learned about my fate almost by accident when someone asked her about a newspaper article reporting my capture. Once the letters began, they were a great source of strength to me.

The first biting winds of winter were just beginning to blow through our rickety barracks when we got word that another well-known fighter pilot had just arrived at the camp. It was none other than Hub Zemke. Like me, he hadn't been shot down; his undoing was a nasty storm cloud that knocked his fighter out of the sky.

Hub had a few days' seniority over Colonel Byerly, so he assumed the job of camp commander. A few weeks later the Germans finished construction of a new compound, North Three. Hub assigned me the job of compound commander. I used what little privilege this job accorded me to make sure Jerry Johnson came with me to North Three, and we lived in the same barracks for the rest of our stay.

I think my most enduring memory of Stalag Luft I is one of increasing hunger. The most important part of camp life was food. It wasn't too bad at first, because the Red Cross supplied us with care packages on a regular basis. These packages contained food, smokes, and other items that augmented the basic German-supplied diet. But as the war continued to go worse for Germany, the food they supplied us became more meager, and the Red Cross parcels had to be stretched further and further. Eventually, the parcels stopped coming altogether.

I tried to encourage the men to stay active. I thought it was better for them to be busy than to sit and stew over their predicament. It was easy to start feeling sorry for yourself and your family, but that just led to a deterioration of mind and body. The activity was strictly what you made of it, because nobody was going to force you to do anything, not even take a shower or brush your teeth. I encouraged them to walk a lot and do calisthenics, as I did.

The YMCA supplied us with some recreational equipment, like playing cards, footballs, and softballs, bats, and mitts. We organized card tournaments and athletic games to pass the time and try to maintain our physical condition. Still there were some guys who would rather just spend their time lying in bed. We didn't have too many of those, though.

Another activity that consumed a lot of time and energy at Barth was escape planning. I didn't participate in this personally, since my position was too visible and I had plenty of other things to worry about. They say that the earth under our camp was virtually a honeycomb of tunnels, but to my knowledge no one ever succeeded at getting away.

Actually, as the war progressed into 1945, the consensus in the camp was that it was wiser to wait out the surrender in the camp than to try to get out. We didn't issue any instructions to this effect, but most of us felt that we had a better chance of getting home quickly and in one piece by staying put. The German populace at that time was very hostile and in disarray, so the likelihood of our getting away alive was very, very slim.

I picked up one bad habit in North Three that it took me years to break. As commander, it was my responsibility to make sure that the Red Cross parcels were distributed properly by my barracks commanders to the 2,300 men in the compound. Included in each parcel was a box of cigars, but very few Kriegies smoked them. Some of the guys started giving me their cigars, even though at that time I didn't smoke. I didn't want to turn them down, so I graciously accepted the gifts. Then I got to thinking that maybe smoking a cigar would enhance my image as commander, since I was still pretty young (twenty-five) for a lieutenant colonel. So I started smoking cigars. I was well hooked on them by the time the war ended, and I stayed that way for twenty years. It was rare to see me during that time without a cigar in my mouth. But finally I decided it was ridiculous to keep up such a dirty, smelly habit. I quit smoking in August 1964.

We lived from news to news. Somewhere in the camp, the Kriegies had a radio hidden that provided us with information from the BBC. We had a camp newspaper, the *Pow Wow,* which was edited by a captured war correspondent and hand-printed. It contained war news and camp news, such as it was. We passed that around, and it was read closely by virtually every Kriegie.

Now and then, something exceptional would happen. One day a small plane roared low over the camp. It didn't sound like any airplane I had ever heard, making more of a booming noise than a roar. We could see a nacelle sitting up on top of the fuselage, but it had no propeller. I figured out years later that it was a Heinkel He-162, one of the earliest jet fighters. It caused quite a stir.

But probably the most memorable event of my eight

months in captivity was the morning Russ Spicer told off the Germans. Russ was a full colonel who had been commander of the 357th Fighter Group when he was shot down in March 1944. He was an aggressive character with a big mustache and a deep hatred for the Germans.

One day in December someone stole one of the metal crossbars off a bathroom window. I never knew what the Kriegie intended to do with it, but Kriegies were extremely inventive, and metal was a precious commodity for making tools and other things. The Germans discovered that the bar was missing, and during roll call one morning they announced that if it wasn't returned they were going to cut off the coal ration. That would have been disastrous, because we needed that coal to heat our barracks and stay alive.

That really got Spicer hot. He turned to the troops standing in formation and gave them a speech that was guaranteed to infuriate the German major who was standing there. The more he talked, the nastier he got. He criticized the Germans for their activities in Holland and Belgium, and wrapped it up by calling them a bunch of murderous, no-good liars. The men were cheering by the time he finished.

The German major stalked away, but an hour or so later he returned with some guards and took Spicer away. Russ was held in solitary confinement for months on end, and there was a rumor that he'd been sentenced to death. He was the talk of the camp. We were all very remorseful, but there wasn't anything we could do to help him. He finally was released at the end of the war. Russ made a career of the air force, and I ran into him on several assignments over the years.

Winter and spring of 1945 were probably the roughest months of my life. Our food supplies seemed to drop with the temperature. We couldn't stand to be outside for long in the icy wind, so we couldn't keep up our exercise. Our roll calls became an exercise in misery. All of us lost weight dramatically.

Toward the end of April, the German commandant called Zemke into his office and told him of plans to move the camp south. He wasn't talking about a minor move, either. The plan called for us to go all the way to Odessa on the Black Sea, nearly one thousand miles away—on foot! We had heard rumors by then that Hitler wanted all the POWs killed, and perhaps this was how he intended to do it. Zemke told the commandant that none of us could survive such a march.

Whatever their plans might have been, the Germans never moved us. On April 30 we began to hear the boom of the advancing Russian army's big guns. That night, our German captors packed up quickly and moved out. It was a pitiful sight. They piled their belongings on carts that normally would have been drawn by horses, and pulled them away by hand. They probably had eaten all the horses by then. The next morning we looked up to see the guard towers were empty. It was a wonderful sight.

Zemke was quick to try to organize us in light of this turn of events. Lots of the guys wanted to open the gates and take off, but Hub called everyone together and told them they were forbidden to leave the base. He said he was arranging to have the 8th Air Force fly us out in short order, and in the meantime we would be safer inside the fence than outside. Some of the guys grumbled about it, but Hub was still Hub. They did as they were told.

We sent out scouting parties to check the immediate area. They found an airfield south of Barth, so we organized work parties to go out there and clear it of obstructions so it could be used to fly us out. That night, we saw our first Russians. They rode up to the camp on horseback, just like you would expect of the Cossacks. They were big, brutal guys, but very helpful to us. They recognized us as Americans, and they were determined to do everything possible to get us food. But the food had to come from the local area. They confiscated everything they could find and brought it back to us. Once they herded in some cows, which were quickly slaughtered and cooked. It was a hilarious time, a busy time, a happy time.

But then we sat and waited. Apparently the Russians held up matters for several days while the 8th Air Force tried to make plans to come pick us up. Everyone started to get antsy.

Adding to our gloom was a sight several of us discovered one afternoon while we were reconnoitering the area outside the camp in a car the Germans had left behind. We rounded a corner and saw in the distance what looked to be another POW camp, with its unpainted barracks and barbed wire fence.

But as we drew closer we could see there was a ghastly difference between this camp and ours. Corpses were hanging on the electrified fence, where the people had died trying to get out. The bodies were skin and bones, as were those of the people we found inside a little later. We had stumbled across a German forced labor camp, where political prisoners had been sent to build aircraft components. As at our camp, the Germans had pulled out. But here they had locked the gates and charged the electric fence when they left, a final act of brutality.

We found some people who weren't dead yet, but it would be stretching the point to call them alive. They stared at us with blank eyes that could see but not register. Their quarters reeked of dysentery, for they had grown too weak to even go outside when their bowels erupted. I recall a dead body lying flopped across a table where the person had died while trying to eat a final crumb of bread. It was a horrifying sight that has not faded in my mind through all the years since that day.

This validated the war for me as no propaganda campaign ever could have. Here was proof that the Nazis had been enslaving people and working them to death. The practical side of me told me I was lucky to have been an American POW with the Geneva Convention accords to protect me from my captors. The patriotic side told me to feel proud for having played a part in defeating the Germans.

When we got back to our camp, we alerted the Russians to what we had found. They did a good job of reviving as many of the people as possible.

On May 12 we heard the drone of B-17 engines in the sky, and we knew the long-awaited liberation day was at hand. A Fortress landed to check out the field, then took off with a few lucky Kriegies aboard. The next day, American planes started coming in a steady stream—B-17s, B-24s, C-46s, C-47s. They took out about six thousand that day and the rest of us the next. The pilots never even shut down their engines. They would just taxi to the end of the field, pick up a full load of Kriegies, and go right back out again bound for Camp Lucky Strike near Le Havre, France.

North Three compound was the last to leave, since we were the newest section of the camp. I think I went out in a C-46, because it was a more comfortable flight than I would have gotten in a bomber.

Lucky Strike was really a conglomeration of camps. Something like 100,000 former prisoners congregated there. It was very temporary, with people living in tents, but even then there wasn't enough room for everyone. They gave us new uniforms and fed us well, then did interrogations. All of us had the same question for the interviewers: When am I going home? Of course, no one had any answers to that.

In all that turmoil, I decided I would be better off to try to get back to the 61st Fighter Squadron at Boxted and make arrangements from there. I was permitted to catch a flight from France to England, and then I made my way to Colchester and Boxted.

I had left quite a few things behind when I went down, and I thought they might still be in storage at the base. I didn't find anything that I was looking for, because my stuff had been boxed up and shipped away. It was either in a warehouse somewhere, or my parents had it. Wherever it was, it wasn't at Boxted. Eventually, some of my clothes caught up with me, but none of my combat film or any items of a personal nature ever arrived in the United States. Over the next few years I was able to get duplicates of my pictures and films made up, but the other stuff was gone for good.

I also was curious to see if any of the old gang from 1944 was still around the 56th Fighter Group. Not many were, but I did get to say hello to Jim Carter, Joe Perry, and Ralph Eastwood. Don Renwick was the group exec now, and another old-timer, Pete Dade, was the C.O. Pete got on the phone and put in a good word for me at Transport Command. Within three or four days I was aboard a C-54 flying across the Atlantic.

The destination of the C-54 was LaGuardia Airport, New York. Up to now I hadn't had an opportunity to get in touch with my family or Kay because things had been in such a turmoil. I did, however, nab a parachute at Boxted to bring home with me. I had an idea that Kay could have a wedding dress made out of the silk in it, even though I knew she already had a trousseau. I lugged the parachute off the plane and into the LaGuardia terminal, where I set it down to find a telephone so I could call Kay. I got through to her on the phone, and we had a wonderful conversation, as you might imagine. Then I called my sister, Lottie, to let the folks in Oil City know I'd made it home in one piece. But when I remembered the parachute and returned for it, the darned thing was gone. I guess someone needed it more than I did.

I made a quick trip to Washington D.C., where the War Department was conducting interviews with higher-ranking POWs to determine what kind of treatment they had received. It was short and sweet. I collected my back pay, which amounted to a nice bundle for those days, and departed for Prairie du Chien, Wisconsin. Kay had been living there with her aunt for the past year. I wanted to get married as soon as possible.

Kay and Mrs. Bush met me at the train station. As soon as I saw Kay's pretty, smiling face I knew everything was going to work out fine. Her embrace as I stepped off the train confirmed it. The hectic days in combat, the dreary months in the POW camp were all behind me now.

There was no question in my mind that Kay was still my number-one girl, and I suppose there was no question in her mind that I was still her number-one guy. So we went ahead and made plans to get married there in a couple of weeks. A day or so later I got back on the train; next stop, Oil City.

I had a wonderful reunion with my family and friends in Oil City. They had a celebration to honor my return, though it wasn't the big shindig they had planned back the previous summer before I went down. They had a dinner in my honor at the Polish Club, and we announced my wedding plans that Sunday at church.

Kay and I were finally married in Prairie du Chien on June 11, 1945. Her mother attended, as did my old pal from Hawaii days, Johnny Thacker. My big brother, Ted, was best man. Even though the war in Europe had ended by then, I was still pretty big news. There were all sorts of news photographers outside the church when we came out, even one from a newsreel company.

We spent the next two months getting to know each other again. I wasn't the same carefree junior lieutenant she had known in Hawaii, and Kay had grown from a pretty high school girl into a mature young woman. Luckily, the war hadn't changed our affection for each other. We stayed a short time in Miami, and then we went on to Cuba, where the congressman from my district in Pennsylvania had arranged a marvelous visit for us. Kay has kidded me ever since about all the cemeteries I filmed there. I had a new movie camera, and I got fascinated by the Cuban cemeteries, so I shot roll after roll of pictures. Then it was back to Miami to complete my rest and recuperation. During our stay there the Japanese signed the surrender documents aboard the USS *Missouri*.

World War II was over.

CHAPTER *Twelve*

I LOOKED out of my office window at the F-86 Sabrejet fighters on the ramp at Selfridge Air Force Base in Michigan. The sign on my desk said "Col. F. S. Gabreski, Commander, 56th Fighter Group." In every way, this had been a dream assignment, but now it was ending in favor of something even more exciting. I had just received orders assigning me to the "police action" in Korea. It was April 1951.

It had been an eventful six years since the day I walked out of Stalag Luft I in Germany and went home to marry Kay.

My first postwar assignment took us to Wright Field in Dayton, Ohio, late in 1945. I was assigned to the flight test division, and I was very happy to be getting into the fighter test business. Kay and I rented a nice house in town, and for the first time we had to shift ourselves without family and friends around. We shifted pretty well.

Everything looked rosy, but that wasn't quite the case. The flight test division roster contained several top aces from the ETO, including Don Gentile and Johnny Godfrey from the 4th

Fighter Group and Chuck Yeager of the 357th, in addition to me. Even Bob Johnson was there, though he was a civilian working for Republic Aircraft. The colonel in command of flight test apparently wasn't too comfortable with having high-profile guys like us around, and he gave us a real hard time. I've never understood why.

In order to become a full-fledged member of flight test, you had to complete a school for test pilots. I asked the colonel when I could start the class, and he hedged. He said he wasn't sure whether he wanted to send me or not. Godfrey and Gentile were getting the same treatment. The three of us were reduced to doing a little bit of flying and a lot of public appearances to sell bonds. Johnny and Don started talking about leaving the service to get into the civilian aviation business.

Before long, Col. Al Boyd was assigned to Wright Field and cleared the way for me to attend test pilot school, which was located right there on the base. My promotion to full colonel came through, and when I completed the school Boyd put me in charge of the flight test section.

At this time, the flight test landscape was changing. Our job was to do operational testing, checking such items as fuel consumption and climb and dive rates on current aircraft—fighters, bombers, and even transports. It was pretty tedious. I got to fly the first American jet fighter, the Bell P-59, once. It was underpowered and not much to remember, but it was the closest thing to a thrill I got.

The advanced engineering testing was moved that year to Muroc Dry Lake, California, later to become Edwards Air Force Base. Out there in the desert, the weather and terrain were better suited to flying ultra-high-performance experimental aircraft. Chuck Yeager left us to fly the X-1 rocket plane at Muroc, and suddenly my plans for the future started to change.

Gentile and Godfrey resigned from the service in January 1946 to join the Globe airplane company in Texas, which had just introduced a pretty little light aircraft, the Swift. We had done a lot of talking about our futures, and I began to think they had the right idea. I was still determined to finish my college education, and I couldn't see much chance of that happening in my present job at Wright Field. Besides that, Kay was pregnant. It was time to get serious about my life.

Into my life came Vic Bertrandias, whom I had met a few months back while he was a general commanding the safety office in San Bernardino. Vic had just gone to work in sales for the Douglas Aircraft Company. He had served in World War I, worked with Rickenbacker between the wars, and then gone back into the service during World War II. He called to say he was taking over the foreign sales section for Douglas, and he offered me a job.

Kay and I talked it over. She had spent most of her life on military posts and was comfortable with that life. On the other hand, she understood my desire to finish college, and it looked as if I would have a better chance of doing that as a civilian. The Douglas deal looked too good to pass up, so we decided to go for it. I left the Army Air Force in May 1946, the month after our first child, Djoni Marie, was born.

We settled in Santa Monica, California, but I had hardly unpacked my bags before I had to say good-bye to Kay and Djoni. My first business trip took Bertrandias and me to South America.

We made a whirlwind trip through Mexico, Argentina, Brazil, and Chile. Vic figured that all these countries would be good prospects to buy the new Douglas transport, the

DC-6. It was a pressurized version of the four-engined DC-4, which made it an ideal aircraft for crossing the great distances and high mountain ranges of South America. We spent time in each country, touting the DC-6 to government and business officials.

It was a super experience, if not particularly successful. Everyone we met was enthusiastic about the DC-6 except when it came to the price. The DC-6 was a very expensive airplane for its day, and we were dealing in a quasi-socialistic environment. Military juntas ruled in Chile and Argentina. When Vic and I returned to California, we assessed the prospects and had to admit they didn't look too good.

Others trips followed, and we had a few successes. But I wasn't really comfortable with my life. For one thing, the travel was keeping me away from my family. For another, the travel was making it impossible for me to pursue my education. I would need some sort of regular schedule if I ever hoped to finish college, and I was afraid that if I didn't obtain a degree I wouldn't be able to advance in the coming years. And I definitely would need to advance, because Kay was pregnant again. However, the rumor around Douglas was that cutbacks were in the works. That worried me, since I had so little seniority with the company. Kay and I talked some more, and I decided to look into the possibilities of rejoining the military.

My timing couldn't have been better. The army had reduced its flight personnel after the war, but now heightening international tensions were creating a need for more pilots. Regular commissions were being offered, and I decided to apply for one. I told Bertrandias about my decision, and he offered to help me. He called a friend of his, Gen. Bobby Burns, who was the deputy chief of staff for personnel. General Burns said the army would love to have me back. On

April 7, 1947, I rejoined the Army Air Force with the permanent rank of lieutenant colonel. Five months later the U.S. Air Force became a separate armed service.

My first duty station was Shaw Air Force Base, South Carolina. I was given command of the 55th Fighter Squadron, which was flying P-51 Mustangs at the time. My boss was Col. Archie Knight, commander of the 20th Fighter Group. I knew immediately that I had made the right decision in rejoining the service. It was great to get back into the cockpit again, and it was great to be a squadron commander in peacetime conditions. The P-51 was a beautiful airplane with a lot of range. It was a joy to fly.

Much as I enjoyed working with Archie and flying the Mustang, I still had it in mind to go back to school. Besides, our family had experienced a sad shock that summer when our son died a few hours after Kay delivered him. We needed a change. I checked with the 9th Air Force personnel office, and they referred me to the Air University at Maxwell Field in Alabama. I flew down there to check out the programs, but all slots were filled for the coming year or more. I asked if there were any other possibilities and learned about a program at Columbia University in New York City studying the Russian language and culture. It prepared officers for air attaché duties. That sounded pretty interesting to me, and I decided to go for it. Orders were cut for me to begin school in September 1947.

I wanted to live near Mitchell Field on Long Island to make it simple for me to do my proficiency flying while I attended classes at Columbia. Kay and I started house hunting as soon as we got to New York, looking for somewhere to rent, but nothing really appealed. Then we came across a development of new homes in Hempstead. This was just what we wanted, and we bought one of the houses. It was our pride and joy.

I started commuting into the city for classes, sometimes by train but usually driving.

I had to work like a dog to keep up with my studies. Most of the classes were graduate level, and the meager study skills I retained from my Notre Dame days were rusty at best. I stuck with it, however, working ten to twelve hours a day. The work paid off in good grades.

After the end of my first year at Columbia, word came down that the air force was canceling my air attaché program. That didn't exactly break my heart, because I really wanted to continue operational flying. But I also wanted that bachelor's degree. I flew down to Maxwell and convinced the Air University to allow me to continue at Columbia until I completed the requirements for my undergraduate degree. I graduated in August 1949 with a Bachelor of Science degree.

Imagine my delight when I received word that my new assignment would send me to Selfridge AFB to command my old unit from the war, the 56th Fighter Group. This soon brought a promotion to full colonel as well.

In the time that I had been away at school, the air force had made a change in its command structure. Now there was a wing commander who was the big cheese, and the group commander was in charge of operational activities. My boss at wing was Col. Bill Hudnal. He was a tough bird, but we got along fine.

The first few days with the 56th were like déjà vu because I kept running into guys who had flown with me in the group during the war. Joe Perry, whom I'd last seen when I returned to Boxted after release from the POW camp, was my group operations officer. Ralph Johnson was one of the squadron commanders, and Mike Jackson was there, too. They explained that Dave Schilling had packed the outfit with them while he was group commander in 1946–47.

The other thing that stands out about this assignment was that it was my first command of a jet outfit. The 56th was equipped with Lockheed F-80s, and we got a few two-seat T-33s not long after I arrived. My only jet experience up to then had been the single flight in a P-59 back in early 1946, so I flew a lot that fall to build up my proficiency.

The F-80 was the air force's first operational jet fighter, and as such I suppose it was pretty crude by modern standards. But in 1949 it represented a great leap forward from prop-driven fighters, and I really enjoyed flying it. The jet engine made it entirely different. For one thing, the fuel consumption differential between high and low altitudes was very pronounced. Down low, a jet engine really gobbles the fuel. Thank God I never had to bail out of the airplane because I had run out of fuel, but I came pretty close to it. We did lose a few airplanes that way, though, when the pilots came down too low and then couldn't find their way back to base quickly enough. Later, they installed radio compasses in the airplanes, which pretty much solved that problem.

The acceleration of the early jets was absolutely slow, because of the power-to-weight ratio, and the F-80 was no exception. Its engine had only about 4,500 pounds of thrust. And there was another idiosyncrasy of the early jets that was particularly critical on the F-80. You could not advance the throttle rapidly without getting a compressor stall. The engine would get too much fuel before it was ready, causing it to lose power.

Our mission in the 56th at that time was air defense for the industrial areas around Detroit. We were fair-weather day interceptors. Our job wasn't really much different from what the RAF did during the Battle of Britain, except, of course, that we weren't in a shooting war. But we flew practice missions under the direction of ground radar just like the Spitfires and Hurricanes did in 1940. One change I made was to insist that our pilots got plenty of practice flying in bad weather, because the conditions were so lousy around Detroit much of the time. My guys needed to build up confidence in their ability to get home if the weather closed in on them, and the only way to do it was to practice.

We also did quite a bit of air-show work, sending formations of fighters to do fly-bys, and the highlight of each year was the air force–wide gunnery meet at Nellis Air Force Base in Nevada.

June of 1950 brought big changes. Over in Korea, the Communists attacked south across the 38th Parallel, kicking off a shooting war that quickly involved U.S. forces. That same month at Selfridge, the 56th Fighter Group began to trade in its F-80s in favor of new North American F-86A-5 Sabrejets. This was very exciting for us, because the F-86 was the hottest fighter in the air force inventory. Only one other outfit, the 4th Fighter Group in Delaware, got Sabres ahead of us.

We worked up on the F-86s as quickly as possible while continuing to fly the F-80s. It took each squadron about four weeks to become completely equipped and qualified with the new planes. This process was hindered somewhat by shortages of specialized ground equipment for the F-86s—engine stands, auxiliary power units, tow bars, etc. North American was not turning these things out fast enough at first, but eventually we got what we needed.

The F-86 gave us a tremendous boost in performance. It was capable of Mach .92, nearly the speed of sound. Its engine had more thrust than the F-80's, but it also had swept wings, which was a major aerodynamic advance. The only thing that kept us from breaking Mach 1 in a dive was the design of the horizontal stabilizer. That was changed in later models.

I really enjoyed flying the F-86. It was fast, climbed well, and was very responsive to the controls. The cockpit was placed out in front of the leading edge of the wings, so the pilot had to swivel his head way around even to see the wings. It made you feel as if you were flying a rocket with no wings at all. The cockpit position also gave the pilot an excellent field of vision. The F-86 was a fighter pilot's airplane in every way.

George Jones, who had replaced Joe Perry as group operations officer by that time, recalls those days at Selfridge:

I got to know Gabby fairly well at Selfridge. He was deeply interested in the flying we were doing and gave us the impression he wanted a "crackerjack" outfit. His status as a top World War II ace was admired by all, but fighter pilots being what they are, what mattered most was not what you did but what you do daily. He did well and was respected for it.

The transition from F-80s to F-86s was a time of great enthusiasm for the pilots. Going to Los Angeles to pick up the new aircraft at the factory and flying them back to Selfridge was super for those of us in the program. Gabby, of course, was well known to the people at North American Aviation, and they leaned over backward to help us with the transition.

One day Gabby called squadron operations and said to set him up on a flight with two of the best pilots we had. All of the pilots had been flying the F-86s for a while and felt comfortable in them. [Major Bill] "Hawkeye" Hawkins, commander of the 63rd Fighter Squadron, said he didn't know of a pilot better than he was, and I said, "I feel the same. Put my name on the flight, too." So we took off, Gabby the group c.o., Hawkins the squadron c.o., and myself the operations officer.

We climbed up through a light overcast in formation, then rat-raced [in-trail maneuvering and acrobatics] for a while. Hawkins and I stuck to Gabby like ticks. Gabby signaled close formation, and we returned to the base and landed.

At the debriefing, Gabby said, "Good flight. We don't need much debriefing. You got any questions?" We didn't. Everyone laughed and relaxed.

All of us watched the events in Korea closely during 1950. After the initial advance by the Communists, Gen. Douglas MacArthur was able to turn things around with the Inchon landing. Soon the United Nations forces had pushed the Communists all the way back across the 38th Parallel and well into North Korea toward the Yalu River. American air power also played a role, first by sweeping the skies of the North Koreans' meager air force and then by providing close air support for our ground forces. It looked like everything would be over in a matter of weeks.

Then November came, and with it two events that would change the lives of millions of people, myself included. Most shocking was the entry of the Chinese into the Korean War. Hundreds of thousands of Communist troops plunged into the fighting, and again the Allied forces were forced to retreat. At about the same time, our fighter-bomber pilots began to report sightings of a new enemy aircraft of superior performance. These swept-wing jet fighters were able to attack and break off engagements at will. The plane would soon become world famous as the MiG-15.

Within weeks, the air force decided to respond in kind by sending F-86s into the fighting. The group chosen to go was our old rivals, the 4th. The entire 4th Fighter Wing was loaded up and shipped out. The 4th flew its first mission on December 13, 1950, and began scoring against the MiGs almost immediately. Their success was the talk of the air force.

I was a regular air force officer, and I had combat experience in World War II. On top of that, I was proficient at flying the F-86. I became very anxious to test these fighters myself, jet versus jet, in the Korean conflict. In fact, I think I may have entertained that thought once too often and just a bit too loud, because somebody conveyed the message up the line to the commanding general of the 1st Air Force. The next thing I knew, I had a set of orders sitting on my desk assigning me to the 4th Fighter Wing in Korea.

Kay didn't like it at all. We had three kids by now, and she didn't relish the thought of raising them on her own for a year, which was the standard tour of duty in Korea. On top of that, she was pregnant again and due to deliver within a few weeks. We compromised. I convinced the air force to delay my departure until after the baby came, and we moved the family to Battle Creek so she could be close to her aunt and their friends. I left a few days after our new daughter, Francie, was born.

When I reached the West Coast I stopped by North American Aviation in Los Angeles to get the word on any modifications that were in the works for the F-86. There I ran into Bud Mahurin, who had been one of our top aces in the 56th during the war, and George Welch, an old pal from back in the Hawaii days. George had become an ace in the South Pacific during the war. Now he was the chief test pilot for NAA, so he had the inside scoop on everything. He told me that the engineers were working on a new tail for the F-86 that would cure its control problems at high speeds.

My route to Korea took me through Hawaii. It was there that I ran into Col. J. C. Meyer, who was on his way back from Korea. J. C. was a high-scoring Mustang ace in the 8th Air Force, and he had commanded the 4th Fighter Group during its initial months of combat in Korea. We had dinner together at a military club overlooking Diamond Head, and he filled me in on what to expect.

J. C. told me that Korea was entirely different from World War II, except that people were shooting real bullets at each other. The equipment, the mission, and the politics were all changed. He cautioned me that it was easy to get too eager and lose yourself in a skirmish that could defeat your whole purpose in going out. Moderation was the key to success. I recall him saying something about a dead hero. The fate of the world wasn't at stake.

I pondered J. C.'s advice on my flight across the Pacific. I'm not a fatalistic person, so I never expected to be killed in combat. On the other hand, the aggressive style of combat flying had always worked best for me. Pull in close, give the target a heavy blast, then get out of the way. I decided good tactics were good tactics, regardless of the rules of the game. I would keep J. C.'s advice in mind and see for myself what developed.

I reported in to the 4th Fighter Wing rear echelon at Johnson Air Force Base, Japan, in May 1951. The wing headquarters and heavy maintenance were located there, while the fighter group flew combat missions out of K-14, an airbase at Kimpo near the South Korean capital of Seoul. I spent several days at Johnson taking care of paperwork, and then caught a transport flight across the Sea of Japan to Kimpo.

My second combat career was about to begin.

CHAPTER *Thirteen*

K-14 AT Kimpo came as a shock, after the relatively peaceful surroundings in Japan. The Korean landscape was brown and battered from the ravages of war. The base had a single macadam runway that was in pretty good shape. But everything else showed the scars of war. Kimpo had been held by the North Koreans for some weeks prior to the Inchon landings, so our planes worked it over thoroughly before it was recaptured. The hangars were all burned out, the results of bombing and shelling. Our quarters looked more like temporary storage sheds than actual barracks. All along the road to Seoul you could see burned-out tanks and other military vehicles abandoned where they had been shot up.

I reported in to the 4th Fighter Wing commander, Col. Herman Schmid. He told me my job would be deputy wing commander, which suited me fine. The 4th Fighter Group's commander, Col. Glenn Eagleston, was another top ETO ace. I looked forward to working and flying with him. My job was primarily to fly with the group and learn all I could about

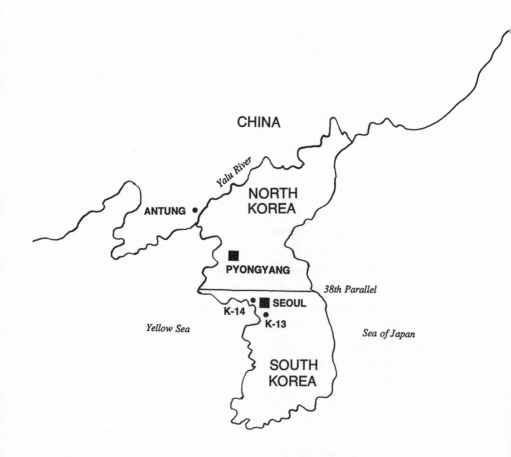

CHINA

Yalu River

ANTUNG ●

NORTH
KOREA

■
PYONGYANG

38th Parallel

K-14 ● ■ SEOUL
        ● K-13

Yellow Sea

Sea of Japan

SOUTH
KOREA

tactics and techniques. I would be the pilots' connection to wing headquarters, because Colonel Schmid concentrated most of his efforts on administrative matters. It was a real occasion when he flew.

I spent the first week or so familiarizing myself with the outfit and the local surroundings. I flew F-86s locally until I got up to speed on the idiosyncrasies of the area. I wanted to make damned sure I could find my way home before I started flying up north. The more I saw of the landscape, the sadder it looked. The hills were dotted with burned-out reminders of the recent fighting. Not far to the north was the 38th Parallel, where the fighting seemed to have stabilized after the second Communist push into the south was turned back that spring.

If my surroundings were depressing, my companions were anything but. The pilots of the 4th were a healthy mixture of World War II combat vets and bright, young officers eager to make their own marks. They were confident of their F-86s and of their ability to fly them. Just the previous month they had cheered Capt. Jim Jabara when he shot down his fifth MiG to become the first jet ace in U.S. history. Several other pilots were close behind him.

My bull sessions with Eagleston and his pilots soon gave me a clear picture of our air war in Korea. The F-86 was the only fighter available that could mix it up effectively with the MiGs, but we had fewer than fifty Sabres at K-14. The MiGs were based at Antung in Red China, just across the Yalu River, which forms the border between North Korea and China. Most of the 4th's missions were patrols along the south side of the Yalu, which came to be known as "MiG Alley." The assignment was to stop the MiGs from interfering with our bombers and fighter-bombers as they pounded targets in North Korea.

Officially, China was not involved in the war, so our pilots were forbidden from crossing the Yalu and invading Chinese airspace. In reality, we knew that the MiGs were being flown primarily by Chinese and Russian pilots. They could climb up to altitude above us and circle in perfect safety on their side of the river, then drop down on top of us when they thought the time was right. If the F-86s started to get the best of them, they could break off and run for sanctuary on the north side of the Yalu . . . at least, most of the time they could. Such were the politics of flying F-86s in Korea.

As for the relative performance of the MiGs and our F-86s, I got mixed signals. Everyone agreed that the MiG could out-turn and out-climb the Sabre above 25,000 feet, and it could operate at higher altitudes. On the other hand, the MiG's superior performance was a product of its lightweight construction, which also made it unable to sustain much damage without going down. If you hit a MiG, you were liable to hurt it, the pilots told me. They also felt that the F-86's greater weight gave it a speed advantage in a dive.

The final factor, and probably the most important one, was the pilots. So far, our guys hadn't been impressed with the quality of the MiG drivers they had encountered, which was a great confidence builder. They felt that any time they could draw the MiGs into a fight, they had a better than even chance of coming out on top. Our pilots knew the F-86 could take more punishment than a MiG if they got hit, and they preferred their armament of six quick-firing .50-caliber guns grouped in the nose to the MiG's three slower-firing cannons.

On June 17, 1951, I suited up for my first combat mission in Korea. Flying gear had advanced since my P-47 days, and now I found myself encased in an olive green G-suit that inflated automatically in high-G manuevers to help prevent the pilot from blacking out. The old leather helmet of 1944 had been replaced by a hard plastic model with built-in radio earphones. At least the yellow Mae West life vest looked about the same.

At the appointed hour, we climbed up into the cockpits and took off. I looked over at Eagleston's aircraft from my wingman position. It was a beauty, with black and white stripes around the fuselage and wings, plus a reddish brown band around the nose. We climbed to 30,000 feet as quickly as possible, then went to cruise setting for the trip up north to MiG Alley. Within half an hour we crossed the Yellow Sea coast near Sinuiju heading northeast, and the MiG hunt began.

I searched the deep blue sky for signs of enemy fighters and began to wonder if I still had what it took to fly combat. I was thirty-two years old now, and my eyesight might not be as sharp as it was in Europe. Had my reflexes slowed? Would I still have the old fire in my belly that made me want to climb right up their tails before opening fire? Only time would tell.

I got one of the answers right away. Someone called in contrails ahead of us at 10 o'clock, and I picked them up immediately. Scratch one worry: The eyes still had it.

Eagleston led straight toward the MiGs and began to climb, but I soon experienced one of the frustrations that dogged Sabre pilots throughout this period of the war. The higher we went, the more unstable the aircraft became. I could see the other guys feeling their way along like I was, being careful not to stall. As we went up, so did the MiGs. It was just like playing cat and mouse, except I wasn't sure who was whom.

We were real close to the Yalu River by now. Eagleston led us in a wide circle, trying to entice the MiGs to come down and play, but they weren't going for the bait. After about twenty minutes, a light began to blink on my instrument panel warning me that my fuel supply was getting low. Moments later Eagleston called off the game and led us home to K-14.

We didn't have much to say at debriefing. One of the guys began to complain that the mission had been a waste of time, but Eagleston cut him off quickly. Remember, he told the pilots, while we were dancing the minuet with the MiGs up there, our F-80s and F-51s were pounding ground targets south of us with no MiGs to bother them. We might not have scored any kills, but we did accomplish our mission.

Still, it was a hell of a way for an air force to have to fight a war. Every man in the room would have given a month's pay to be allowed to chase those MiGs back to their base at Antung.

I flew a lot in the weeks that followed, and on one trip we finally got into a tussle with the MiGs. Two guys got kills. I never got into a position to fire, but I could feel that I made the right moves for the situation. Scratch another concern: My reflexes were still up to the task. This was the first time I got close enough to a MiG-15 to see its distinctive tail grouping. The horizontal stabilizer was mounted way up near the top of the fin, which made it easy for us to identify a MiG from ahead or behind.

The mission of July 8 was something new for me, and I expected it to be an easy one. Our F-86s were assigned to provide area top cover for F-80s that were attacking ground targets near Pyongyang, the North Korean capital. This would take us quite a distance south of MiG Alley, so I didn't figure we were likely to run into any trouble.

I was leading a flight of four F-86s. We cruised into the area at 15,000 feet, and I enjoyed watching some fighter-bombers below us hitting some railroad marshalling yards. It felt like I was back over Germany for a moment. We were about to turn north for the Yalu when I spotted an air battle in the distance. F-80s and MiGs were going round and round at about 10,000 feet. This was it, a perfect setup for us!

I barreled down into the fight with my flight holding perfect position. As we got closer, I saw a MiG break away from the melee, and I turned to follow him. My wingman, Lt. Bob Makinney, stuck to me, and the other element continued into the rest of them. I held my fire as the MiG's tailpipe grew larger in my windshield.

I was only about 300 yards behind the MiG when I pulled the trigger. The six .50s barked beside me in the Sabre's fuselage, and I quickly saw hits from the API slugs sparkle on the MiG's fuselage and wing. The MiG began to trail flames from its fuselage, and I could see pieces of it breaking away in the slipstream. He slowed rapidly, and I began to overshoot him. I racked the Sabre around in a hard climbing turn and came back in for another pass. I felt my G-suit put the squeeze on my body as the turn tightened, not allowing the blood to drain from my head and black me out.

By now the MiG had nosed over and was going down smoking. I dove in behind him for another run, and opened fire in a steep decelerating turn. Again my burst hit his fuselage, and this time the MiG erupted in flames. Part of his tail section blew off, and the MiG rolled over into an inverted spin. He never pulled out, and I saw him crash near Pyongyang.

There it was, the answer to my last question about myself. The spirit was still willing to get in close and make the kill.

This mission marked the beginning of a new phase in the air war over Korea. Our pilots had begun to report different markings on some of the MiGs they encountered in recent scuffles, and some thought that the MiG drivers were displaying more skill than those previously seen. Now we saw evidence of new tactics to match. Were we now going up against Russian pilots? No one could say for sure, but we had a pretty good hunch.

Colonel Schmid and I talked about this new wrinkle in the air war and its connection to the sanctuary problem. I told him that our pilots were frustrated by not being free to chase the MiGs home, and this was compounded by the evidence that a higher quality of enemy pilot was being encountered. Our boys needed any edge we could give them. All Schmid could do was relay the message up the line to 5th Air Force, and again the instructions came back to us: "Don't cross the Yalu. If you get caught over there we can't help you."

So we used our own discretion. I never indiscriminately crossed the river on purpose, and I don't think many of the pilots did. But there were lots of instances when a Sabre pilot in hot pursuit of a MiG would cross over if he thought he could catch the target and shoot it down without getting too far into China. Usually he made it back out, but sometimes he didn't.

We continued to send Sabres to MiG Alley nearly every day. The operations were limited by our numbers, since we only had three squadrons of twelve planes each. When I first got to Korea we flew at group strength in a big formation, but we found that if the MiGs didn't engage, we were done for the day after just a very short time on station. We decided we could be just as effective over a longer period of the day if we broke down into smaller formations and shuttled our planes in and out. The typical formation became one squadron of twelve, and later we broke down even smaller. This proved effective at stretching our Sabre force to its maximum, but what we really needed was more Sabres.

My next crack at the MiGs came on September 2. This was a rare mission for us at the time, in that we put up twenty

F-86s for a sweep through MiG Alley. On the way north we passed several fighter-bomber flights working areas around Pyongyang. I led the formation northeastward up the alley at 29,000 feet, just under the altitude where our engine exhaust created contrails, then turned 180 degrees and headed back down.

Suddenly, someone yelled, "Break." I looked up to see a gaggle of about eight MiGs coming right for us, firing all the way. I snapped into a left-hand turn and dumped my drop tanks. Somehow, the MiGs missed everyone. They pulled up and hauled ass back north. I tried to chase them, but within a few minutes they had climbed way ahead of me, and I wasn't closing as we crossed the Yalu. I broke off and recrossed the Yalu.

I checked my fuel and saw I had a little time left before I needed to head home. A few moments later I spotted an F-86 heading south, but before I could call him to form up for the trip home, I saw a MiG-15 below me at 10 o'clock heading north. It was a perfect opportunity for a bounce, and I took it. He didn't see me at first, but before I could get into firing position he turned steeply into me. This was the logical move on his part since I had the speed and altitude advantage, but I was able to cut inside his turn and get the pipper of my gunsight on him for a short burst. My deflection angle was so great that I couldn't actually see the MiG when I hit him, but one of the other pilots in the flight saw it snap roll and fall into a tight spin. The MiG crashed about five miles northwest of Taechon.

I knocked down another MiG on a similar mission October 2, and if the truth were known I believe I was on the Manchuria side of the Yalu when I made the kill. It was one of just two victories we registered that day, though most of the pilots on the mission were engaged. That was the nature of

225

combat in MiG Alley then: a series of quick skirmishes in which a pilot was lucky to get off a quick shot at the enemy before having to break off. Victories came slowly, but when they came it was usually our guys who got them.

Then we started to see the MiGs using a new tactic. Taking advantage of their numerical superiority, the MiG pilots would form up in two long lines of fifty to sixty planes each and head south on parallel courses into North Korea. One string would come down the west coast of the peninsula and the other would come down the middle. Their objective was to bounce our fighter-bombers or even F-86s that were heading home from the Yalu. We called these strings "MiG trains." They were a further indication of how badly the 4th Fighter Wing was outnumbered.

Finally, the Pentagon figured out what we already knew: We needed more F-86 outfits in Korea. The air force reassigned the F-86s from two air defense squadrons to the 5th Air Force and loaded them on an aircraft carrier bound for Korea.

This was about the time that Colonel Schmid was due to complete his tour, and Col. Harry Thyng arrived at K-14 with an assignment to the 4th Fighter Wing. Harry was another ace from World War II, with six kills while flying Spitfires in the Mediterranean theater, and a fine fellow to boot. Maj. Gen. Frank Everest, commander of the 5th Air Force, called the two of us in for a chat.

General Everest told us that the new F-86s would be used to reequip the 51st Fighter Wing, which until now had been flying fighter-bomber missions with F-80s. He also mentioned that some of the pilots who had flown with me in the 56th were on their way to Korea with the Sabres. He needed two F-86 wing commanders now, and we were the two. He asked if either us had any preference which wing we got.

I was tickled to finally get my shot at commanding a wing. Logic seemed to indicate that I should take the 51st. Harry was senior to me, but I had more combat experience. And I had converted an outfit from F-80s to F-86s once before. I told the general I would take the 51st, but I asked him to let me pick some key personnel from the 4th to go with me. He readily agreed.

My transfer to the 51st Fighter Wing was made effective November 8, 1951. Two of the pilots I took with me from the 4th were Lt. Col. George Jones and Maj. Bill Whisner. George had been my operations officer in the 56th, and Bill was yet another 8th Air Force ace. Then when I arrived at Suwon, where the 51st Wing was based at K-13, I was pleasantly surprised to find that my old pal Johnny Thacker was commander of the 51st Fighter Group.

Johnny, who was a lieutenant colonel at that time, had been flying F-80s for a couple of months. He recalls:

When we switched to F-86s, Gabby came in as wing commander. He moved me "up" to be his wing exec and made George Jones group commander. George had considerably more experience than I on the F-86, so it was a wise decision. Combat against the MiGs over North Korea and up to (and perhaps beyond) the Yalu required considerable skill.

The 4th Fighter Wing had already established a terrific record against the MiGs; the 51st, under Gabreski, added icing to the cake. He was aggressive both in the air and on the ground. He attended to the details of aircraft maintenance, supply (spare parts for the aircraft in particular), morale of the troops, conditions of the barracks, the messes, and spiritual guidance. His devotion to God and the Catholic Church was ever apparent.

Our new F-86s were offloaded in Japan at Johnson Air Force Base, where they could be prepared for combat after the long sea voyage. Most of them were new E-models, which featured the improved tail surfaces I had heard so much about. They called it the "all-flying tail" because the entire horizontal surface pivoted, as opposed to the more traditional hinged arrangement in which the stabilizer was fixed and just the elevators pivoted. With the new fighters, the new pilots, and new leadership the 51st Wing was practically an entirely different organization. Some of the hot new flyers I got from Selfridge included Bill Wescott, Don Adams, and Ivan Kincheloe. All three would become aces in the months to come.

K-13 was very similar to K-14 in that it was a muddy smudge of an airbase that obviously had been scratched out of the ground in a hurry. The runway and hardstands consisted of pieced steel planking (PSP) laid on bare dirt that had been scraped flat. The base's biggest drawback was the fact that it was twenty miles farther south than K-14, so we had that much farther to go each way on missions to the Yalu.

I had been at the base only a few days when General Everest called to ask how long I thought it would take to convert the 51st to F-86s. He suggested that I stand down from operations for a month or so while everyone got familiar with the new aircraft and mission. I had other plans, however. I told the general that I thought we could continue operating our F-80s while we built up our F-86 capability. The two squadron commanders, Don Adams of the 16th and Bill Wescott of the 25th, had supported the idea when I first mentioned it to them. Now General Everest bought it as well. We spent the month of November busily making the conversion.

The task wasn't accomplished without problems to overcome. I decided to send the first twenty Sabres to the 25th,

228

and then convert the 16th. At first we seemed to be short of everything, especially people since many of the pilots and technicians were completing their tours at this time. We also lacked sufficient tech orders, engine buildup kits, and spare parts. But somehow we got the job done. Later, the 51st received a commendation for accomplishing the feat.

The wing flew its first F-86 mission on December 1, 1951. It was the beginning of a new era for the 51st.

CHAPTER *Fourteen*

At K-13 in December 1951 I learned what many thousands of American servicemen already knew: Korea is a cold, nasty place in the wintertime. We in the 51st Fighter Wing were anxious to start hunting MiGs in our new F-86s, but the weather limited our flying.

I flew all of our early Sabre missions, because I wanted to check out the quality of our pilots firsthand. Those early missions consisted of eight aircraft, because that's all we had. I needed to get a good idea about who were going to be the leaders, the aggressive types, and I wanted to weed out any laggards quickly. I simply didn't have enough F-86s in the outfit to waste them on pilots who weren't going to come to grips with the enemy. Luckily, I found few, if any, of this type of pilot in the 51st. Those who came from Selfridge were already proficient in the F-86 and adapted quickly to combat operations. The holdover pilots in the 51st had been flying F-80s, so they were comfortable in jet aircraft and already knew the score in Korea.

I had to admit that North Korea was a lot prettier in the winter when viewed from the cockpit of an F-86 at altitude. The storms blew in from the north and turned the brown terrain of summer into a snow-covered wonderland. The storm track presented a problem in weather forecasting for us, because we had no intelligence up north in China and Russia where the storms originated. On the other hand, we did get a break from the fact that the jet stream flowed strongly from the north in the winter. It reached an intensity of 150 to 175 mph, which was quite a tail wind to help us on our way home from MiG Alley. You could stay on station to a lower fuel state before breaking off to return to base. Normally it took us about twenty minutes to get back from the Yalu, but with that tail wind the time was cut nearly in half. It wasn't unusual for our guys to run out of fuel on the way home and glide in with no trouble.

Actually, the weather presented more of a problem for our ground crews than for the pilots. We simply didn't fly when the weather got bad. The F-86 was a fair-weather fighter, so we needed a ceiling over the base in order to operate. But the ground crews had to contend with every type of inclement weather. We didn't have covered hangars at K-13. The planes were maintained in their revetments, and most of the work on them was done out in the open. One of my biggest jobs as wing commander was to keep the men motivated under those conditions. I spent a lot of time out on the flight line talking with them and looking to see what they were doing. I had a special red Jeep that I drove, and part of the reason for the paint job was so that the men would be able to tell I was out there among them, even if I didn't happen to stop in their particular revetment every day.

Johnny Thacker moved in with me when I arrived at Suwon. Our quarters were heated by a makeshift potbellied stove that some previous lodger had built. It was an oil-fired gadget with a sandbox underneath to catch any dripping oil. One particularly cold night that winter we cranked the stove way up before we went to bed. Sometime after midnight I rolled over in bed and noticed a small flame flickering from the sandbox, which apparently had become saturated with oil and ignited. The room was filling up with smoke.

I jumped out of bed and then shook Johnny awake. We quickly opened the door and all the windows, then extinguished the fire. As the room aired out, it also got quite cold. We dressed warmly and spent the rest of the night shivering in our cold beds. At least it was better than being asphyxiated.

The next morning we started tinkering with the stove, thinking we could fix it ourselves. We checked the oil on-off switch, but that was in good working order. In fact, everything looked okay except that the stove wasn't burning properly. That seemed to indicate the draft wasn't working right. I suggested to Johnny that he get up on the roof of the building and look down the stack to see if it was plugged. He went outside, and in a few minutes I could hear his footsteps above me on the roof. I continued to fool around with the switches on the stove, and I decided to light the fire in the potbelly and see what happened. I never gave a thought to Johnny up on the roof.

I lit a match and stuck it into the opening. *Whoosh!* The fumes from the oil exploded, blowing me back from the stove. But most of the force of the explosion went straight up the stack. The fireball blew a tremendous cloud of soot out the top just as Johnny was bending over to take a look down the pipe. His head and shoulders were absolutely black when he descended from the roof. He was pretty shook up, as you might imagine, but I could hardly contain my laughter when I looked at him. We decided to turn the stove repair job over to the engineering department. That was as close as the two of us ever came in Korea to meeting our Maker.

Almost as soon as the 51st began flying the F-86s, visitors began to show up at K-13. The first was Bob Johnson, who had flown with me in the 61st Fighter Squadron. He came as a representative of Republic Aircraft, which made the F-84 fighter-bombers that were coming into service in Korea at that time. Then George Welch, North American Aviation's test pilot, came to observe our F-86 operation. Of course, both of them wanted to fly missions, but I had to turn them down because they were civilians now.

One visitor I didn't have to turn down was Col. Bud Mahurin, who wangled a temporary assignment in Korea to escape a desk in the Pentagon. He recalls arriving in Korea this way:

> I finally was transported by DC-4 to Korea, landing at K-13 after dark. I remember lowering myself to the ground from a knotted rope attached to the door of the DC-4 and finding myself standing in mud about ankle-deep. I didn't know anything about Korea, but I did know that I was to report to 5th Air Force headquarters in Seoul. However, the weather was too bad to land at K-16, the Seoul City airfield, so we came in to K-13.
>
> When we went into Base Operations, I was surprised to find that Gabby now had the 51st Wing and was on the side of the base where the transport had landed. I called him immediately. When we were settled in at the "O" Club, such as it was, Gabby said he would call B. Gen. James Ferguson and have me assigned to the 51st Wing until time to go home. He would call me the deputy wing commander for lack of any other title, especially since he didn't have a deputy at that time.

I don't remember any specific advice from Gabby, but he did assign me to the 25th Squadron for flying duties. As usual, it was necessary to fly a couple of missions up above the bomb line to get acquainted with the territory, but that was about all the indoctrination anyone got.

Gabby and I decided that I would fly his wing for my first few missions; first so I could see firsthand what was going on, and second so we could prove to the younger hands that we were still capable of flying good formation and engaging the enemy. I can't remember exactly how many missions we flew together, but I do know that I was shot at from behind on eleven of my first twelve missions.

On one specific mission Gabby and I were flying toward the north when the group encountered many, many bandit flights. (I remember hearing our radar station calling in as many as thirteen bandit flights on one mission we were on.) The radar station didn't indicate how many aircraft were in each bandit flight, but there were always upwards of twenty or so. Anyway, we began to tangle with the MiGs, and at one point I looked past my right wing to see a great number of little flashes just off the wing. I knew these were cannon shells from MiGs exploding out there. I immediately called for Gabby to break left, and both of us broke away from the exploding shells. Thank God Gabby didn't question my call and did as I had yelled out to him.

I'll never forget that day. It would have been a heck of a note for the both of us to get shot down on the same mission, but that's almost what happened. Later, Bud got himself assigned for a full tour in Korea. He was shot down on a dive-bombing mission with the 4th Wing, and spent sixteen months as a prisoner. I had found him so helpful as deputy wing commander that I decided to retain the position when he left. His replacement was Col. Al Schinz, who filled Bud's shoes nicely.

While Bud was with us in the 51st, I began to host informal bull sessions in the evenings at my quarters. A group of pilots would gather, and we would discuss every aspect of combat flying, looking for new ways of getting at the MiGs. Not only did the sessions boost the morale of the pilots, but they also yielded some good ideas. Here are two examples, the first from Bill Wescott:

> The one encounter with Gabby that was of some significance involved the use of tracer. Gabby was dead set against it because if you missed, the tracer would alert the bad-guy pilot that he was being had. The MiGs' use of 30-mm tracer ammunition probably is a major reason I am still around. One day two MiGs crawled up my tail and opened fire. I became aware of this when their shells went past my canopy (and broke away). You might say "I was alerted."
>
> I had a single purpose in pursuing the tracer issue with Gabby. That was to verify your gun harmonization at the bomb line on your way in. This was accomplished by taking a "sighter burst" and noting where the tracer trajectory was in relation to the pipper gunsight set at 1,000 feet range, or whatever range the pilot desired.
>
> Well, the issue was raised during a steak-fry at Gabby's quarters. I reluctantly pointed out that most of the pilots needed tracer because they weren't all "Gabreskis." The 51st got tracers (loaded one-to-five with API) shortly thereafter.

A second memory of those bull sessions comes from George Jones:

All of us were constantly trying to figure out ways to shoot down more MiG-15s, both from an individual pilot standpoint and for the highest total for the 51st. Bill Whisner and I came up with an idea for different flight spacing. Instead of flying in masses of aircraft formations, we envisioned a string of elements (two aircraft each) covering each other through time and distance and coded reporting points. We took this idea to Gabby and hashed it over and refined it over a couple of days. Finally Gabby was satisfied. "Let's try it," he said.

Colonel Mahurin was on temporary duty with the 51st then. Before coming over, he had stopped by North American Aviation and talked to test pilots George Welch and Bob Hoover. They gave him a new climb schedule for the F-86E that incorporated a faster climb speed to altitude. It fitted right in with our new tactics. As part of the program, I insisted on radio discipline so as not to make an unnecessary peep on the radio. I felt the Communists were monitoring our conversations and pinpointing our positions and intentions.

We started the new system and began shooting down a lot of MiGs. We got so far ahead of the other F-86 wing in total destructions for two months that the 5th Air Force sent people down to find out what we were doing. Gabby had what he had been striving for, a combat-oriented fighter wing from the ground support team, maintenance, armament, communication, supply, and food service to the airborne echelon of fighter pilots and aircraft.

We called the new formation the "Fluid Four," and before long it was the only one we used. It was this type of aggressive thinking that allowed the 51st to develop so quickly. I certainly didn't have all the answers, but I figured somewhere in the outfit we were likely to find ideas for handling any problem that came up. Our success was obvious when we tallied the score for January 1952. The wing had destroyed twenty-six MiGs. Our losses were just seven F-86s and pilots.

My contribution to the January score was one MiG destroyed on the eleventh while flying with the 16th Squadron. Thanks to our new tactics, we were able to catch the MiGs coming out of Antung before they got above us. The four of us in my flight took on fifteen MiGs, splitting them roughly in half.

I turned to chase a group that was trying to dive away from us. My wingman, Capt. Mose Gordon, and I were gaining slowly, and I lined up a shot on the tail-end charlie. I was about to fire when Gordon called a break because another gaggle of MiGs was coming down behind us. I gave a quick look over my shoulder and decided they were far enough back that I had time to get off a shot. Gordon broke, but I held my ground and opened fire on the MiG out front as he tried to turn toward the Yalu. I saw my API sparkle on the target, but he kept going.

The MiGs behind me didn't seem to be gaining, so I decided to give my target another burst. This time I pulled through his turn until I had one ring of lead in my gunsight, then let him have it. Flames belched from the MiG's tailpipe, and then part of his tail broke off. The plane went down in an uncontrolled spin. Now it was time for me to get out before I joined him in a death dive. I rolled the F-86 over and pulled the nose down in a high-speed split-S that left my pursuers far behind.

That was my fourth MiG victory. When I got back to base and we compared notes, I learned that Bill Whisner also had scored his fourth kill that day. Thus began the speculation about who would be the 51st's first MiG ace. It took more than a month to resolve the question.

On February 20, Whisner and I both led flights to the Yalu. He was some distance from me when my flight engaged a formation of MiGs. We chased them down through contrail level, and they headed in the general direction of Whisner's flight. Before long, his flight and mine converged behind the MiGs, but I still had the best shot.

I opened fire on one of the fleeing MiGs and saw hits on his fuselage. He began to smoke, but didn't seem to be slowing down as we approached the Yalu River. Then a piece of the MiG broke off and smacked my windshield, cracking it. Whisner called on the radio, urging me to continue chasing the guy until I got the kill. I thought better of crossing into Red China under those conditions and broke off the attack. Bill, however, stayed behind the MiG and followed him across the river.

I claimed a probable destruction of the MiG when I got back to K-13, but when Whisner returned later he filed a report confirming the victory for me. I knew that wasn't right, because the MiG hadn't been hurt that badly when I last saw him. I called Bill at his barracks and asked him if he had shot at the MiG after I left. He tried to talk his way around it, but finally after I pressed the issue he admitted hitting the MiG before it went down. However, he balked at my request that he change his report to give himself credit for the kill. That burned me up, and I slammed down the phone.

I thought about it for a while. I was as anxious as the next guy to shoot down MiGs and make ace, but I didn't want to get credit where it wasn't deserved. I felt sure that Bill felt the same way. So I decided that we would share credit for destroying the MiG. That would give each of us a score of four and a half, and save the ace race for another day.

As it turned out, Bill settled the issue three days later when he shot down a MiG off the tail of Maj. Don Adams to become the first ace of the 51st Fighter Wing.

Our social life at Suwon was pretty much confined to what enjoyment we pilots got out of being together. We did very little fraternizing with the local Koreans, though this didn't necessarily hold for the enlisted men. The pilots tended to congregate in operations, at their quarters, and at the makeshift officers' club on base. Of course, they also spent time with the individual ground crews who worked on their planes.

It was a pretty limited existence, so my ears perked up one day when I heard our wing chaplain, Father "Iron" Mike Finneran, talking about an orphanage he had run across in Suwon. The war had been especially tough on the children of this orphanage, because they had been caught right in the middle of it. The Buddhist priests who ran the orphanage needed help.

The chaplain and I went to visit the place a day or two later. It was located on the grounds of the Yongjoo Jahae Buddhist temple and monastery, which looked like something straight off a postcard. We entered a walled area through an ornate gate and were greeted by an elderly priest.

We got the picture quickly. These kids, who ranged in age downwards from about ten, were poorly clothed, sick, and hungry. Some showed signs of serious wounds suffered during the fighting. There appeared to be three hundred or more of them. The priests had no medicine or medical expertise, and precious little food. The sad faces of the children were enough to break my heart, and I readily agreed with Father Finneran that the 51st could help.

I went straight to the flight surgeon, Capt. Bernard Brungardt, when we got back to K-13. I described the scene to him and asked if he thought we could spare the time and supplies to help these orphans. In the best spirit of his profession, the doc said he would find a way. And of course he did.

The medical care was just the beginning. Our next thought was that we needed clothes and all sorts of other things that the youngsters could use aside from money. The 51st Fighter Wing took on the project of sponsoring the orphanage, and pretty soon we had everyone involved, airmen and officers alike. It became almost like a hobby for the men. They were glad to be able to help someone in distress. We sent truckloads of stuff to the orphans, including an organ the fellows had shipped in from Japan. We called the project "Operation Happiness."

Then I had another idea. I wrote a letter to the mayor of Oil City, Bill Morck, telling him of our project and asking him if the citizens of the town could do anything to help us. At that time I had pretty high visibility in Oil City because the U.S. Junior Chamber of Commerce had just named me their Military Man of the Year for 1951, based on my sponsorship by the Oil City Jaycees. The mayor took me up on the idea and made a real project of it.

The people of Oil City really responded. Clothing, medicine, food, school supplies, and even building materials poured in. In fact, they collected so much material that it got be more than they could send through the mail, and we didn't have a transport aircraft available that we could send to pick it up. Finally, the navy came to the rescue. Space was made available on a ship that was heading to Korea from San Francisco. The supplies were shipped to San Francisco, and the navy brought them the rest of the way.

It was a happy day for everyone when we showed up at the orphanage with this mountain of supplies. In gratitude, the priests and the children put on a big dinner for us, Korean style. A bunch of us who had been most deeply involved dressed up in our best uniforms for the occasion. When we sat down to eat, we faced heaping dishes of raw fish, squid, kim chee, and the works. It wasn't the kind of food we were accustomed to, to say the least. So there I was, trying to be polite with the priests and the children while I forced down some of this food, which wasn't exactly palatable as far as I was concerned. I ate a little bit, taking small bites and trying to get it down without making too many faces. I kept my composure, though it was the most torturous dinner I have ever consumed. But I would also have to say it was one dinner I'll never forget.

Operation Happiness was still going strong when I left Korea some months later.

The weather improved as spring arrived in late March. That meant the pace of our operations would pick up, too.

The mission of April 1, 1952, sounded routine during the briefing. As we had done so often before, we would be patrolling the Yalu east of Antung, running interference for the F-80 and F-84 fighter-bombers operating north of Pyongyang. I would lead a flight from the 25th Squadron, with Lt. Joe Cannon on my wing. The element leader was Capt. Ivan Kincheloe, and number four was Lt. Percy Saunders.

We started engines at 9:30 A.M., and by ten o'clock we were above contrail level at 38,000 feet over Sinuiju, turning northeast for a run up the Yalu. When we reached the end of our patrol area, I circled us back down the river. On our second run back up the river, I began to pick up contrails below us to the left. The MiGs were climbing up out of Antung in the relative safety of Chinese airspace—at least for the time being. Over the next few moments I counted upwards of thirty MiG contrails. It was time for action.

I was only too aware of our instructions not to cross the

river, but this was an opportunity I couldn't pass up. We were above contrail level and a small formation, so I was quite sure the MiGs hadn't seen us yet. I also knew they would soon be climbing above us into a position that would give them the advantage if their radar controllers decided to initiate an attack. Besides, I wanted that fifth kill.

I turned left across the river, with Cannon following. Kinch and Saunders made their own break in the same direction. Ahead of me climbed fourteen MiGs, just coming out of contrails. I had the sun behind me, so I was sure they hadn't seen me. I pushed over in a shallow dive and picked out a straggler from the formation. Closing in to about 400 yards, I opened fire. I probably hit him, but I couldn't see any damage. That wasn't unusual at this altitude, where the air was too thin to support a fire and our slugs, even API, would just punch holes in the MiGs.

My intended victim pulled into a climbing left turn as his partners scattered. Obviously he had radioed a warning to them. My dive had given me a speed advantage, so I had no trouble keeping up with my fleeing MiG. I pulled my nose through his turn, fired a burst, and watched as my API lit up his tail pipe. He kept on climbing, however, so I fired a third burst. That was enough for the MiG driver. He leveled out briefly, blew off his canopy, and punched out. The pilotless MiG nosed over and went down in a spin.

Cannon and I turned around and headed back out of China. On my radio I could hear Kincheloe bagging a MiG, and then I called him so we could re-form the flight and go home together. I had a good reason for doing this. I wanted to make sure I could talk to everyone in the flight as soon as we landed so we could coordinate our combat reports, blurring the fact that we had crossed the Yalu to attack the MiGs.

Almost before we landed the word got around K-13 that I had gotten a MiG. That gave me five and a half kills and made me the 51st's second ace. Someone showed up on the flight line with a bottle of champagne, and I got quite a shower in celebration.

I scored again on April 12 after I chased a MiG through his contrails for what seemed like hours, but now I had a problem. The 5th Air Force had a policy setting a maximum number of flights a pilot was supposed to fly during his one-year tour in Korea. I was rapidly approaching that number, but I still had two months to go on my tour, and I couldn't imagine commanding a wing from behind my desk. George Jones recalls my solution to the problem:

> In the 51st Operations Office a board was maintained on one wall containing the names of each pilot, flying time, number of combat missions, and number of MiG-15s destroyed. This board was often shown to higher headquarters personnel, the commander of the 5th Air Force, and others when they came for inspections or visits. The 5th Air Force policy was that once a pilot had 100 combat missions he was taken off of combat flying for that tour.
>
> Gabby and I arrived in Korea from Selfridge about the same time, and we flew with the 4th Fighter Wing before coming to the 51st. We had about the same number of missions when one day I noticed that I was pulling way ahead in missions, according to the board. Since Gabby was flying about as often as me, I went to my operations clerk and said, "You seem to be shorting Colonel Gabreski on his missions." He sort of laughed and said the colonel told him not to post any more of his missions on the board.
>
> Gabby was not one to let a 100-mission limit technicality keep him from hunting MiGs. After that we both stayed

neck-and-neck on the board, just short of the 100-mission limit.

George Jones was a real scrapper. He completed his tour slightly before I did, and Lt. Col. Bill Shelton took over as 51st Fighter Group commander. But George wasn't finished in Korea. He came back in 1953 to fly another tour with the 4th Fighter Wing, eventually running up a score of MiGs destroyed equal to mine.

My mission board charade lasted for only about another month. In mid-May I was grounded, and on June 4 I received orders sending me home. That was okay by me. I had put in a long year under frustrating circumstances, and I felt I had made the most of it. Under my leadership the 51st Wing had accomplished a complete change of mission and aircraft with astounding success. At the same time, I had added six and a half victories to my World War II score of twenty-eight. This made me the highest-scoring living American ace, an honor I proudly retain to this day. Just as important was the work we had done to help the kids in the orphanage.

Yes, I'd had enough. I missed Kay and the kids. I wanted to get on with my career. And I wasn't all that thrilled about the way the war in Korea was being handled. It was quite different from the war in Europe. We were in Korea to help someone out, not to save our own nation. Although I had a sympathetic feeling for the South Koreans and I opposed communism, it wasn't the same as the anti-Nazi sentiment of World War II. The threat wasn't the same. Here we had a little peninsula to worry about, and it was a very small effort on the part of the United States. Once we had run the Communist ground forces up to the 38th parallel and stabilized that line, the air effort was controllable. Our job wasn't to beat the enemy, but to hold him in check long enough to get the truce signed. At the time my Korea tour ended, I didn't know if that strategy was going to work or not. It was a frustrating way to leave a war.

I quickly put these feelings behind me when my flight from Korea touched down in San Francisco. There to greet me were Kay and our oldest daughter, Djoni. I didn't care about Korea or MiGs or even my next assignment. All I could think about was spending a thirty-day leave with my family.

It wasn't quite that simple. First was the matter of a ticker-tape parade though downtown San Francisco. As if that wasn't enough, I got word that my presence was required in Washington, D.C. It seemed that the president of the United States wanted to meet me.

So my combat career, which had begun more than ten years earlier on that fateful Sunday at Pearl Harbor, was capped off on June 24, 1952, when I was ushered into the Oval Office at the White House and accepted the personal thanks of President Harry S. Truman. It was quite a thrill for a Polish kid from Oil City who had almost flunked out of flight school.

KAY AND I get up early these days. We dress casually, then eat a healthy breakfast. We're pretty careful about our diets and exercise, especially since I had a stroke several years ago.

After breakfast we drive to St. Matthews Catholic Church, a six-minute drive from our home on Long Island, to attend 9 A.M. mass. It's a rare day when we miss this service, unless we're traveling. For us, worship is an essential part of life— just like eating and sleeping.

As I bow my head in prayer each morning, I remind myself that the Lord has been awfully kind to me. There's simply no other explanation for the fact that my life has contained so many blessings. I have a wonderful wife and nine children who make me very proud. In fact, two of my boys are Air Force Academy graduates and active duty pilots. My grand-children are a delight. Kay and I live in a comfortable home that has plenty of room for the kids to come and visit us.

I also think the Lord had something to do with my decision to make the air force a career. It afforded me no end of

challenge and excitement, all the while allowing me the pleasure of flying some of the highest-performance aircraft in the
world with some of the greatest pilots of the era. But considering that line of work, it's even a miracle that I've lived long
enough to tell my story from the perspective that seventy-
one years on this earth have given me.

I flew my last combat mission in mid-1952, but at that
point my air force career wasn't even half over yet. I spent
most of the next fifteen years continuing to fly fighter aircraft.
In some ways, the danger remained just as great for me as it
had been in the skies over occupied Europe and North Korea.
This was the early Jet Age, when engine reliability and aerodynamics were still being developed.

After Korea, my next assignment put me right into the
middle of jet aircraft development. I went to Norton Air Force
Base, just up the coast from Santa Barbara, California, to be
director of safety. My boss was Vic Bertrandias, who like me
had rejoined the air force after a stint with Douglas Aircraft.
We were part of the Inspector General's office, and I went all
over the country to investigate air accidents. We would com-
pile all the information we could at the site, then bring the
data back to Norton to be analyzed. This involved not just
the military but the aircraft industry as well. That's where
General Bertrandias was so strong, because he had been
involved in the industry.

This was a period of time when the air force inventory was
growing rapidly in the jet field. There was a whole lot to be
learned by the industry and also by the pilots themselves. In
Air Defense Command there was a buildup of specialized aircraft. These were jet fighters that could be controlled by radar
in all kinds of weather, day or night. In addition, the armament was changing from guns to rockets. It was a new era,
a new concept. First came the F-94B, which was like a T-33

with radar, rockets, and an afterburner on the engine. Then came the F-86D. It was a special version of the Sabrejet that supposedly was all-weather capable.

During that period I investigated one accident that struck me more than the others because it involved the death of a friend of mine, Maj. Don Adams. He was killed flying a low-level pass over Selfridge Air Force Base in an F-89 Scorpion fighter not long after I arrived at Norton. Don had been one of my squadron commanders with the 51st Fighter Wing in Korea and was an ace with six and a half MiGs destroyed.

I went out there to try to find a reason why such an experienced pilot would get himself into a position where his plane just disintegrated. We found out that the F-89 had limitations. If you got beyond a certain speed vibrations would set in, and eventually the wing would let go. Don had been moving pretty fast by the standards of the day. The F-89 wasn't like an F-86. It had straight wings with tanks built into the tips. These caused a certain amount of torsion, which was something we weren't too familiar with in those days. Eventually we figured out the maximum speed that the wings could withstand, and a directive went out to all the F-89 units warning their pilots not to exceed a certain mach.

That was a sad one to work on because my friend Don had been killed. Emotionally I was carried away by that. But it also brought home to me how important our work was.

An interesting temporary assignment came my way just about then. A pilot in the Polish air force, Frank Jarecki, had defected to the West in his MiG-15 fighter, and our air force needed someone to take him around the country. I got the call from the Pentagon because I could speak Polish and was pretty well known at that time.

The air force gave me a T-33, and I spent a couple of weeks flying Jarecki from city to city, introducing him to Polish-

American groups along the way. The Hollywood crowd really took to him when we got to Los Angeles. He was a well-educated man, and very clever. At one time he had been a staunch Communist, but then he had figured out that a better life awaited him in the United States. He was right. When last I heard, he was running a tool and die factory in Erie, Pennsylvania.

Later, I was called on to take a second defecting Polish fighter pilot on a similar tour. Jerry Jazwinski was more of a working-class guy like me, and he had a strong Catholic faith to hold onto. We got along very well. I understand he eventually settled in New Jersey.

After two years at Norton, it was time for me to go back to school. This time I would be heading back to Maxwell Air Force Base in Alabama, where I had won my wings thirteen years earlier, to attend the Air War College. This was a one-year course for field-grade officers to give them a better understanding of how the operational and the political aspects of the air force dovetailed. At the end, we were supposed to turn in a thesis paper that would lend itself to educating some of the other students. Mine was a very simple piece on leadership. Everybody laughed because it was so short and to the point. Basically, it said that you can't lead from the rear. You've got to get up front and have your team follow you. Those people behind you must have respect for your abilities, and you can't impose that on them. They have to see for themselves how good you really are, and when they find that out they'll follow you no end.

I think that thesis was right on the mark, but I didn't work on the backup material to that extent. I just gave my impressions based on my own experience in World War II. Today, time and conditions have changed. In retrospect, I can see they were beginning to change back then. Leaders are not born, they're made; and they are a different type of leader. Today's environment is so highly technical that to be a leader you have to understand your equipment and pull it all together to focus on the main objective, whatever that may be. Today's air force compared to what I was brought up in is a different animal.

In July 1955 I got back to work when I was named deputy chief of staff for operations of the 9th Air Force at Shaw Air Force Base, South Carolina. This was a staff job, which was foreign to me. I preferred to work closely with the airplanes, and I thought I was better suited to that kind of work. About a year later I had an opportunity to return to the cockpit. The air force was in the process of opening a new fighter base at Myrtle Beach, South Carolina, and I was offered command of the 342nd Tactical Fighter Wing. I jumped at it.

I found a brand new base at Myrtle Beach. It had a runway and a couple of hangars, plus a few buildings here and there. Not much else. I thought it would be an interesting challenge to build up an operational force and the installation at the same time. It certainly was that.

Col. Jim Hackler was assigned as my group commander, and the two of us started at square one. We had no men, no facilities, and even our unit designation changed from the 342nd to the 354th. I assumed command November 19, 1956. We built that place from scratch. For aircraft, we got North American F-100 Super Sabres, which at that time was the hottest fighter in the air force inventory. It also was the aircraft in which my old friend from Hawaii days, George Welch, was killed during a test flight in October 1954.

The F-100 was the first of what they call supersonic-capable American fighters. It could reach supersonic speeds in straight and level flight. But the F-100 was more than that. It was adaptable with the times. It could be modified to carry

251

two people, drop bombs, and refuel in the air from a tanker aircraft.

Air-to-air refueling was introduced about this time. It gave us tremendous deployment capability throughout the world. The thinking at higher headquarters was to have an organization based in the United States that could go quickly to a hot spot anywhere in the world. That was the theory, but reality was a little different in those days.

I believe I made five transatlantic crossings with air-to-air refueling. Some of the destinations were Turkey, Italy, Norway, and France. I had butterflies in my stomach for every one of them. We were still learning how to handle the crude refueling equipment. The tanker crews were inexperienced, and the equipment was not satisfactory.

The pilots were briefed on what to expect, and if everything went according to plan, refueling would have been a snap. But it never did. We had to improvise on the scene, and unfortunately the scene was usually out over open ocean somewhere.

The first obstacle to aerial refueling was the probe and drogue setup they developed. The tanker, which back then was a prop-driven KB-29 or KB-50, would trail a hose out behind it with a funnellike basket on the end. Our F-100s had a probe mounted on the leading edge of the right wing, and the pilot was supposed to poke it into the funnel to make the proper connection. This meant slowing a supersonic jet fighter down to the tanker's speed and descending to its best altitude, which usually put you in the most turbulent level of the sky.

Thunderstorms were catastrophic to us, because the turbulence would cause both the tankers and our fighters to bob up and down to such an extent that it was practically impossible to put that probe into the drogue. The drogue would start whipping around, so the fighter pilot had to keep one eye on it, another on the tanker, and another on his probe. Pretty soon he ran out of eyes. The best technique was to creep up behind the drogue and then punch the throttle just before you hit the drogue in order to make the connection with enough force to open the fuel valve. Then you had to get right back off the throttle; otherwise the hose would curl up on you. If that happened and the connection broke, the drogue could slam right into your canopy, probably breaking it and the F-100 pilot as well.

Refueling was definitely not an easy task, even for an experienced pilot like me. I'd have to say that every one of those missions I flew was a dramatically new experience. I would rather attack a squadron of Fw-190s alone in a P-47 than face one of those drogues again in an F-100. That was nightmare fodder.

The best example of the problems we had on those overseas deployments was Operation Double Trouble in 1958. I don't know what genius in the Pentagon thought up that name for the show, but it sure fit. Between inadequate planning and nasty weather, we had double trouble all the way.

Operation Double Trouble was supposed to deliver two squadrons of my F-100s to Adana, Turkey, as part of a peacekeeping force that was being built up in preparation for the crisis that was brewing in Lebanon at the time. I first heard about it in a phone call at about nine one morning, alerting us to shove off across the Atlantic at four o'clock the following morning. It was kind of a political deal within the air force. The Tactical Air Command, to which our unit was attached, had the responsibility for deploying air power to trouble spots like this one, but in reality we weren't ready to do the job. Gen. Curtis LeMay, who commanded the Strategic Air Command, threw down the gauntlet to Gen. O. P. Weyland, our boss at TAC, saying in effect that if Weyland's guys couldn't do the job, LeMay's could.

General Weyland called me to ask if we could do the job, since ours was the F-100 outfit closest to Turkey. I didn't even know where Adana, Turkey, was. And I didn't have much faith in the ability of the tankers or the likelihood of getting good weather. I told him something to the effect that if everything was in place, we'd do it. Of course, nothing was in place, but we got the job anyway.

I spent most of the day trying to create some kind of a plan. We had to get maps and flight plans together, then make preparations for an extended stay in Turkey. Looking back, the only good thing I can remember about Operation Double Trouble was that I didn't have to fly one of the F-100s. Col. Frank Fisher led one squadron and Lt. Col. "Rock" Brett led the other. I followed behind in a C-130 that was carrying some of our equipment and support personnel.

The whole thing was a fiasco. The route was supposed to take our twenty-four F-100s up the East Coast to Canada, across the Atlantic via the Azore Islands, on to French Riviera, and then into Adana. One of the pilots had to bail out over Labrador when he couldn't get into his alternate landing field. We lost a couple more planes before they even got out over water. Others kept dropping out at every point along the way. But the guys wouldn't quit. Four planes, including one two-seat F-100D, made it all the way, after twelve and a half hours of nonstop flight. That's no small trick in the cramped cockpit of an F-100, I'm here to tell you. Those pilots were Capt. George Branch and First Lieutenants Danny Walsh, Russell Youngblood, Craig Fink, and Jim Cartwright. Others straggled in over the next few days. The best thing I can say about the deployment is that we didn't lose any pilots.

We stayed at Adana for the duration of the crisis, which

was about a year. We flew missions offshore along Lebanon's coast to show that the task force was in place and ready to go if things heated up. It wasn't long before the planes started needing heavier maintenance than we could provide at Adana, so we established a rear echelon at Wheelus Air Force Base, Libya, which was a permanent station with the proper facilities to handle this type of work. Finally, the crisis passed and we were allowed to return to Myrtle Beach.

In July 1960 it was time to pack up Kay and the kids for another move. This time we were on the way to Kadena Air Base on the island of Okinawa, south of Japan. There I would command the 18th Tactical Fighter Wing, another F-100 outfit.

Despite the fact that we were flying the same type of aircraft that I'd had at Myrtle Beach, the duty on Okinawa was quite different. We were on more of a wartime footing there, compared to the States. We actually stood alert at Kadena—with tactical nuclear weapons loaded. Of course, at Myrtle Beach we had practiced all the mission profiles like strafing, air-to-air, and even the over-the-shoulder nuclear drops. But there was a much greater sense of urgency at Kadena, where our proximity to Korea made the Communist threat seem much more real.

We really enjoyed our stay at Kadena, even apart from my work. I felt I was doing something very constructive, and that would have been good enough. But much to my surprise, I also found a very comfortable base there. It was very well built up with good hangars and permanent buildings. The housing conditions were okay. Of course, I had practically the best housing on the base since I was the wing commander and one of the senior officers. Kay and the kids seemed to like Kadena as much as I did, but we couldn't really complain about our next assignment either.

In June of 1962 I got orders to the one place in the world that may be closer to my heart than Oil City. My new job was to be executive officer of the Pacific Air Forces at Hickam Air Force Base, Hawaii, under General O'Donnell. It was a nonflying job, but Kay and I couldn't have been more pleased nevertheless. I was able to keep up my air proficiency in Hawaii by flying with the Air National Guard unit at Hickam. They had F-102s, sluggish delta-winged interceptors, and also some T-33 trainers.

After about a year I was named inspector general of PACAF. My job was to inspect the tactical readiness of units throughout the Pacific, usually on unscheduled visits. I found it interesting to visit Korea during this period. It had changed a lot since I had been there in 1951–52. I could vividly recall seeing ladies washing clothes in the Han River back in those days, but it wasn't happening like that anymore. Chemical fertilizer had replaced human "night soil" in the fields, and the air bases had been cleaned up quite a bit, too.

I reached the crossroads in my air force career in 1964, when it came time to leave Hawaii. I had been wearing the eagle insignia of a colonel on my uniform since 1949, and I was hoping to get my star. General Moreman, vice commander of PACAF, asked me what I wanted to do next. I told him I'd like to get back into operations, and I'd like to stay in TAC. He told me there weren't any openings in TAC right then that fit my rank and experience, but the Air Defense Command had an opening for a fighter wing commander.

That presented me with a dilemma. On the one hand I wanted to go back to an operational job. On the other, I didn't want to leave TAC. I knew that when you change commands it's like starting over. There would be very little possibility for me to build up my reputation in ADC quickly enough to ever make general. I thought it over for a few days and discussed it with Kay. I knew it was a good job that I would enjoy. In the end I decided to take the ADC job and see what happened next.

In August 1964 I reported to the 52nd Fighter Wing at Suffolk County Air Force Base on Long Island, New York, as the new wing commander. Considering that I was coming back from four years in the Pacific, I found the base quite a shock. The equipment—the 52nd was flying F-101B Voodoos at the time—was great, the people were great, but the facilities were meager.

I soon found out that as an interceptor the F-101 was a super airplane, particularly when you kicked in the afterburner. It was capable of going Mach 1.7 without any trouble. It took a little while to get there, but it still was a more advanced airplane than I had been accustomed to flying, so it was a real joy.

Our mission was air defense, and the F-101 was excellent in that role. It would climb rapidly, and it was well armed with rockets and radar. We did a lot more all-weather flying, and that was a different challenge. As opposed to TAC, where most of the flying is close to the ground, here you were almost always in or above the clouds. A good portion of the work centered around instrument flying. About the only time we flew down low was for takeoffs and landings.

We were guided by ground radar for our interceptions, and that took some getting used to because I was accustomed to being my own boss in the cockpit. Here you had a controller on the ground radioing you instructions that would vector you onto your target. Normally we would fly practice missions with two planes, each taking turns as the target while the other one flew attack approaches. It was quite different from anything I had done in the past, and I enjoyed it very much.

It didn't take Kay and me long to realize that we had arrived in a very good place to raise our family. In the summer it was a tourist area, with lots of people coming to the beach. They all cleared out in the winter and we had the place pretty much to ourselves. It wasn't congested then like it is now; it was a place where people came to have a good time and relax.

In 1967 I got word about my next assignment. I was slotted to go out to Hamilton Air Force Base near San Francisco, California, and take over the Reserve program there. I knew what that meant: the end of the line. I could see that my making general wasn't really in the cards. Again, Kay and I sat down to talk it out. She liked the idea of moving out to sunny California, but she also felt very well established on Long Island. Then came the clincher. Lou Evans, president of Grumman Aerospace, offered me a job.

Grumman, located at Bethpage on Long Island, was well established as a builder of aircraft for the navy. During this period the company was trying to break in with the air force. (Bob Johnson, old eagle eyes from the 61st Fighter Squadron days, was doing some consulting work for Grumman at the time and suggested the company talk to me about coming on board.) Kay and I weighed the options and decided to get out of the service and accept the job with Grumman. I retired from the air force on October 31, 1967, and went to work at Grumman the very next day.

Trading in my blue suit for a business suit made for a pretty hectic couple of weeks. For one thing, we had to find a new place to live, since the family had been in base housing at Suffolk County. We found a development of new houses in a wooded setting that suited us just right, and we made a quick deal when someone backed out of his purchase at the last minute. That home continues to serve us well to this day.

I had a lot to learn about the airplane business. I started out in public relations at Grumman, getting exposure to all facets of the business—production, planning, testing, and so forth. Then I was assigned as assistant to the president. I would make trips throughout the plant with Lou, getting his views and ideas about the direction of the company and the people he was working with. He was teaching me to get into the heart of Grumman.

Again, fate took a hand. At that time Grumman was bidding on the space shuttle and we thought we were going to get it. But the bid went to North American Aviation instead. I don't know whether that news had a direct impact or not, but soon afterward Lou Evans had a heart attack and passed away. That left me without a sponsor at Grumman, so I went to work in the marketing end of it, where I could be of some use to the company.

Grumman was very strong on the electronics end of the business with the navy, and the company had a good track record. We were looking for some business with the air force in the area of electronic countermeasures. Our EA-6B aircraft wasn't suitable for the air force mission, so they finally settled on stuffing our electronics gear into the supersonic F-111, a Grumman aircraft they already had in the inventory, to create the EF-111. I'm proud to say those planes are still flying for the air force. We also tried to sell a version of the navy's A-6 Intruder bomber, but the air force want didn't a subsonic aircraft so that idea didn't go anywhere.

One of the great honors of my life came in July 1978, when I was inducted into the Aviation Hall of Fame in Dayton, Ohio. This event also led to my only excursion outside the business of flying and building airplanes. The previous winter, the Long Island Railroad had suffered terribly during a stretch of cold, snowy weather. The railroad, which is run by New York State's Metropolitan Transportation Authority, was out of commission for a couple of days because the electric motors in the trains couldn't generate power in all the moisture and snow. It was a condition beyond the control of the people who ran the railroad, but the public was howling. The politicians were looking for a scapegoat, and they had to put the finger on the president of the LIRR.

So the MTA needed a new president for the railroad, and that was just when I was getting publicity for the Aviation Hall of Fame induction. Governor Hugh Carey thought that made me an ideal person to run the railroad, so he contacted Grumman to ask if I could be made available for the job. I had to laugh when the president of Grumman called me in to ask me about it. I told him I didn't know anything about Lionel toy trains, let alone a real commuter line. At the end of the meeting, we agreed that I should talk to the governor about the job.

I went in to New York to talk to Governor Carey and the chairman of the MTA. They worked together on me, but at the end of the first meeting I had a feeling this wasn't something I wanted to get into, considering the political nature of the appointment. On the other hand, I understood it was something that Grumman wanted for public relations purposes. I decided to take the job on the condition that I could return to Grumman when it ended without losing my pay level or seniority toward retirement. The company accepted that, considering my time with the LIRR a leave of absence.

I took over as president of the Long Island Railroad in September 1978. I had to find out what this railroad was all about, so I traveled every inch of the line, inspecting the stations, the maintenance shops, and anything else I could find. I made friends with some of the people who I thought were very knowledgeable in their fields, and they were the ones who educated me. After about two months of this, it became clear to me that the LIRR had shortcomings in the areas of maintenance and supplies. It was so bad that we even needed replacement wheels and motors for the trains.

It didn't take long to figure out that the shortage of supplies was directly related to a shortage of funds from the MTA. I lobbied hard for the money I needed for the parts, and I set up a modification center for the generator motors to overcome the deficiencies that had caused the problems back in the winter of 1977.

We made a tremendous amount of progress in the first two years, but then the weather came into play again. It was a hot summer, not a cold winter, that cooked my political goose. We had a heat wave in the summer of 1980 when temperatures went into the upper nineties and stayed there. The air-conditioning systems in the newer cars did not operate properly under those extremes, and the windows weren't designed to open. The cars had a heat exchanger that would kick on the heater in winter and the air conditioner in summer. But the exchanger was mounted underneath the car, which meant it picked up all the oil, dust, and debris that was kicked up by the wheels. When the muck caked all the way through the core of the exchanger, it would heat up and trigger a circuit breaker that shut off the air conditioning.

The riders made a big fuss, and rightfully so. It took a little while to figure out the problem, and by the time we began to get a handle on it, the public outcry had overtaken us. The only way to fix the problem quickly was to soak the units in a very toxic cleaner and then wash them down with a high-pressure hose. That took care of most of the cars, but it took time. We didn't finish until after the hot spell was over.

Then it was my turn on the hot seat. The governor and the MTA board made it clear that they wanted to make another change, so I went back to Grumman where I belonged. I learned from experience that on the railroad you live from crisis to crisis. Certain things you have control over, and other things—probably the most important things—you have no control over.

I continued to work on air force projects with Grumman for six more years. By the time I retired in 1987 I was assistant to the vice president of marketing. Since then I've been enjoying the good life with Kay. We seem to be busy constantly, and I find myself wondering how I ever had time to hold down a job.

I don't spend much time dwelling on the past events of my life. I'm more interested in today and tomorrow. But when I think about what has driven me through the years, it comes down to three things: duty, faith, and responsibility.

When everything you do is contributing to the good of the nation, that's duty. Duty is your job, performance, and allegiance to your country—to your flag, and to your way of life. We're not on this earth to fight wars, but when it's necessary you do it for your country. Faith is another part of a person. You have to believe in your fellow man, and you have to believe in something over and above that fellow man. I don't mean to belabor religion; I've never felt it was right for me to impose my beliefs on other people. But you can't believe in nothing and still live a full life.

Responsibility completes the triangle. If you are put in a position of leadership, you have a responsibility to your people as well as a responsibility to complete the job at hand. It was the same for me whether I was leading a fighter outfit into combat, leading a company's effort in the business world, or running a railroad. I couldn't accomplish the tasks alone. I had to take my people into consideration before I made a decision to do something for myself.

This summer, Kay and I traveled out to Oil City for a community festival. The old town has changed a lot since my boyhood days. The oil companies all have moved out, and you aren't liable to hear people conversing in Polish on the street much anymore. But it's essentially the same typical American town that it always was. Young people still can grow up there and follow their dreams as far as their abilities will carry them. That's what happened to me, and I thank God for making it possible.

BIBLIOGRAPHY

Books

Andrade, John M. *U.S. Military Aircraft Designations and Serials since 1909.* Leicester: Midland Counties Publications, 1979.

Davis, Albert H, II; Coffin, Russell J.; Woodward, Robert B. *The 56th Fighter Group in World War II.* Washington, D.C.: Infantry Journal Press, 1948.

Davis, Larry. *MiG Alley.* Warren, Michigan: Squadron/Signal Publications, 1978.

————. *P-47 Thunderbolt in Action.* Carrollton, Texas: Squadron/Signal Publications, 1984.

Farnol, Lynn. *To the Limit of Their Endurance.* Manhattan, Kansas: Sunflower University Press, 1986.

Godfrey, John T. *The Look of Eagles.* New York: Random House, 1958.

Goodson, James A. *Tumult in the Clouds.* New York: St. Martin's Press, 1983.

Gurney, Gene. *Five Down & Glory.* New York: Ballantine Books, 1958.

Johnson, Robert S. and Caiden, Martin. *Thunderbolt!* New York: Rinehart & Co., 1958.

Morgan, Len. *The P-47 Thunderbolt.* Dallas, Texas: Morgan Aviation Books, 1963.

Morris, Danny. *Aces and Wingmen II*. Usk, Washington: Aviation Usk, 1989.

Rust, Kenn C. *Eighth Air Force Story*. Terre Haute, Indiana: Historical Aviation Album, 1978.

Scutts, Jerry. *Lion in the Sky*. Wellingborough, Northamptonshire: Patrick Stephens, 1987.

Sears, Stephen W. *Air War Against Hitler's Germany*. New York: Harper & Row, 1964.

Shores, Christopher. *Duel for the Sky*. Garden City, New York: Doubleday & Company, 1985.

Snyder, Louis L. *The War, A Concise History 1939–1945*. New York: Simon and Schuster, 1960.

Stafford, Gene B. and Hess, William N. *Aces of the Eighth*. Warren, Michigan: Squadron/Signal Publications, 1973.

Woolnough, John H. *The 8th Air Force Yearbook*. Hollywood, Florida: The 8th Air Force News, 1981.

Zemke, Hubert A. and Freeman, Roger A. *Zemke's Wolfpack*. New York: Orion Books, 1989.

Monographs

Bodie, Warren M. *Thunderbolt*. Granada Hills, California: Sentry Books, undated.

Freeman, Roger A. *Camouflage & Markings No. 15*. London: Ducimus Books Limited.

Freeman, Roger A. *U.S. Strategic Airpower Europe 1942–1945*. London: Arms and Armour Press, 1989.

Hess, William N. *P-47 Thunderbolt*. London: Arms and Armour Press, 1989.

Periodicals

Bodie, Warren M. "Whine of the Jug." *Airpower/Wings*, April, May, June, July 1974.

Foote, Tom and LePage, Fred. "Thoroughly Thunderbolt." *Echelon*, January–February 1980.

George, James A. "A Salute to America's Top Living Air Ace." *Aerospace Historian*, Spring 1968.

Kaufman, Mozart. "Colonel Spicer's Speech." *Eighth Air Force News*, January 1984.

Miller, Kent D. "Frank McCauley Thunderbolt Ace." *Fighter Pilots in Aerial Combat*, Spring 1983.

Seitz, E. A. "Flying Sword." *Wings*, October 1975.

Stafford, Gene B. "Zemke's Wolfpack." *The Squadron*, Winter 1972, Spring and Summer 1973.

———. "D-Day, A View from the Air with the 56th Fighter Group," *Air Classics*, January 1973.

Thompson, Warren. "The MiG Killers of Korea." *Air Enthusiast*, December 1981.

———. "King of MiG Alley." *Airpower*, September 1982.

Tregaskis, Richard. "Gabreski; Avenger of the Skies." *The Saturday Evening Post*, December 13, 1952.

Turley, Ed. "Mr. Inside and Mr. Outside." *AAHS Journal*, Winter 1980.

Unpublished U.S. Air Force Unit Histories

61st Fighter Squadron; 56th Fighter Group.

INDEX